POLICY, EXPERIENCE AND CHANGE: CROSS-CULTURAL
REFLECTIONS ON INCLUSIVE EDUCATION

Inclusive Education: Cross Cultural Perspectives

VOLUME 4

SCOPE OF THE SERIES

This series is concerned with exploring the meaning and function of inclusive education in a world characterised by rapid social, economic and political change. The question of inclusion and exclusion will be viewed as a human rights issue, in which concerns over issues of equity, social justice and participation will be of central significance. The series will provide an inter-disciplinary approach and draw on research and ideas that will contribute to an awareness and understanding of cross-cultural insights and questions. Dominant assumptions and practices will be critically analysed thereby encouraging debate and dialogue over such fundamentally important values and concerns.

For other titles published in this series, go to www.springer.com/series/6123

Policy, Experience and Change: Cross-Cultural Reflections on Inclusive Education

Edited by

L. BARTON
Institute of Education, University of London, UK

and

F. ARMSTRONG
Institute of Education, University of London, UK

 Springer

Editors
L. Barton
Institute of Education,
University of london,
UK

F. Armstrrong
Institute of Education,
University of London,
UK

ISBN: 978-1-4020-8731-8   e-ISBN: 978-1-4020-5119-7

Library of Congress Control Number: 2008931098

Printed on acid-free paper.

9 8 7 6 5 4 3 2 1

springer.com

CONTENTS

ACKNOWLEDGEMENTS

We are grateful to all the contributors for their continuing commitment to this project and for responding to our comments and requests.

Also our sincere thanks to Margaret for her excellent administrative/secretarial support that enabled us to complete the manuscript.

Thanks also to Zoe Armstrong of Writeup Solutions for her editorial advice.

CONTRIBUTORS

Mithu Alur founded the first Spastic Society of India in 1972, a model now replicated in 16 of the 31 States: educational reforms have been introduced on a macro level enabling children to move on to Higher Education. In 1989 Mithu obtained a PhD from the Institute of Education, University of London, entitled 'Invisible Children: A study of policy exclusion'. Mithu then returned to India and set up the National Resource Centre for Inclusion. Over 3,000 children have attended inclusive nurseries in the poorest sectors and, if upscaled, 4 to 5 million children's needs will be met.

Felicity Armstrong is a teacher and researcher in education, with a particular interest in and commitment to challenging inequalities in education and developing inclusive policies and practices. Her work focusses on cross-cultural and practitioner research. She is the author of 'Spaced Out: Policy, Difference and the Challenge of Inclusive Education' and of numerous articles and co-edited books. Felicity is the Course Leader of the internationally recognised MA in Inclusive Education at the Institute of Education, University of London.

Len Barton is Emeritus Professor of Inclusive Education at the Institute of Education, University of London. He teaches on an MA course in Inclusive Education and his research interests include exploring the nature and implementation of policy development; cross-cultural issues relating to Inclusive Education; the voices of excluded and marginalised groups including disabled people and qualitative research approaches to Inclusive Education.

Robert Chimedza works at the Zimbabwe Open University as the Pro-Vice-Chancellor for Academic Affairs. His training and working experience is mainly in Disability Studies and Special Needs Education. He worked as a teacher of deaf students for a long time before starting to train special education teachers at college and university levels. He also worked as an education officer responsible for policy in Special Education. In the process, he worked closely with people with disabilities in organisations of and for people with disabilities. He has published widely in the area.

Simona D'Alessio is a doctoral student at the Institute of Education, University of London. She is conducting research in the field of Inclusive Education and Disability Studies. She has been working as a research assistant and disability office tutor at the University of Rome (IUSM) and as a support teacher in state secondary schools in Italy. She is currently working part time for the European Agency for Development of Special Needs Education in Brussels.

Abdelbasit Gadour is Libyan and a member of academic staff at the faculty of Social Science, Al-Fateh University, Tripoli, Libya. He is currently coordinating a project in Netherthorpe, Upperthorpe and Langsett (SRB6 area) in Sheffield, which concerns children with specific cultural and learning needs. In addition he is Head of the Libyan school in Sheffield. He considers himself as an academic and an educator concerned with the well-being of children. His interest and expertise in the area of child and educational psychology has led him to carry out research both in Libya and the United Kingdom. This research has encompassed studies on pupils'/students' learning and behaviour, the assessment of teachers, school psychologists and social workers.

Jennifer Lavia is currently a lecturer at the University of Sheffield School of Education. She is Director of the School of Education's Caribbean Programme and joint coordinator of its Postcolonial Theory, Education and Development Discussion Group. Jennifer's main research and teaching areas include: globalisation and education policy; gender and education; teacher professionalism; critical pedagogies for social justice; narrative research; postcolonial theories and education; and educational leadership.

Tina Lowe returned to full time education in University College Dublin after losing her sight in 1993. She read for a BA (Hons) Degree in languages and Greek and Roman civilization. She then went on to complete a Master's Degree in Equality Studies. She now works for the Association for Higher Education Access and Disability (AHEAD) as Project Coordinator. Her particular research interests include disability awareness training and access to education and employment for people with disabilities.

Patrick McDonnell is a part-time lecturer in the Equality Studies Centre and in the Education Department at University College Dublin. He also lectures in the Centre for Deaf Studies at Trinity College Dublin. During his tenure as Newman Scholar at UCD in 2001–03 he carried out research on the ideological and historical dimensions of disability in Irish society. His other research interests include disability and education and the linguistics of sign language.

Angeles Parrilla is Professor of Special Needs Education at the University of Seville. Her research is linked to educational exclusion and inclusion processes, with a prefered focus on how schools, teacher education and classrooms can be made more inclusive. Collaboration between teachers, researchers and institutions is one of the most recurrent topics in her professional work.

Helen Phtiaka is an Assistant Professor of Sociology of Education and Inclusive Education at the University of Cyprus. She has published widely in Greek and international journals and books and is the author of two books published by the British Library and Falmer Press. She has recently edited a volume of the Mediterranean Journal of Educational Studies (MJES) on Special and Inclusive Education in the Mediterranean. She maintains a strong interest in educational policy and legislation in Cyprus and she is an active member of many international educational organisations and groups.

Eric Plaisance is Full Professor, University Paris 5 – René Descartes (Faculté des sciences humaines et sociales – Sorbonne; Départment des sciences de l'éducation). Research team: Research Center on Social Links (CERLIS, affiliated to the National Center for Scientific Research). Member of the Council for Studies and University Life (University Paris 5 – René Descartes).

Roger Slee is Dean of the Faculty of Education at McGill University in Montreal, Canada. Previously he has been a Dean and Professor of Education at the universities of London (Goldsmiths College) and Western Australia. He was the Deputy Director General of the Queensland Department of Education. Roger was the founding editor of the International Journal of Inclusive Education.

Vianne Timmons is the Vice President Academic Development, University of Prince Edward Island, Canada. She previously served as Dean of Education. Dr Timmons's research interests include inclusive practices, family literacy and knowledge translation. She has worked in the Aboriginal communities in Prince Edward Island researching children's perceptions of health. Dr. Timmons also works nationally and internationally, promoting best practices in Inclusive Education.

FOREWORD

One of the qualities of this book is the authors' engagement with personal experience. This is part of the contextualising of issues within particular cultural, historical and social contexts. I shall begin the Foreword in the same spirit by recounting an experience that is still a foundation for analysing and developing my own understanding. This happened some twenty-five years ago. I was going with Vic Finkelstein, a disabled academic and activist, to a seminar, on a hot summer's day, making our way across the Open University campus in Milton Keynes. The seminar was entitled 'The Problems of Integration'. Making conversation with Vic I suggested that the seminar sounded interesting. His response was immediate and direct: no it was not interesting – the problems for disabled people were the problems of segregation, not the problems of integration. As he did often for me, Vic turned understanding on its head and his seemingly simple observation carried ever-increasing ripples of critical questioning.

Reading of international developments and of the specifics of education policy, provision and practice across the widely differing circumstances found in different nation states, from the majority as well as the minority world, challenges, deepens and confirms understanding. There are, not surprisingly, considerable diversities and commonalities, and recurring themes that speak to both – and fire critical questioning.

The complexities pretty quickly give food for thought and ring bells of caution. The first for me is the lack of digestion – the impossibility of comprehensive knowledge. This is the peel of diversity that calls for continuous debate and re-examination of the given, the commonly understood. The second note of caution is for the dangers of transposing or importing ideas or, more apposite, the dangers of colonisation in the tidal wave of globalisation – westernisation. In general terms change is founded in people's actions in particular social, cultural and historic contexts, not off-the-shelf solutions. Furthermore, notions of progress beg critique, and for 'progress' read 'messy business'. But, a final note of caution that rang through my reading of this book was the imperative of maintaining, reaffirming, restating and holding on to ideals. However those ideals are framed – social justice, equality, celebration of diversity – they ring through these chapters and sing to commonality through diversity. Which takes me back to Vic's pronouncement against social injustice.

As mentioned above, the editors asked chapter authors to give a sense of how the changes they describe have affected them personally. Writing this Foreword I am particularly aware that I was educated in and speak from a UK perspective. Though I did not take the 11 Plus, I was educated in a Grammar School. It was in a deprived area of the city and for many of us who went there a means of social mobility, going on to university. Looking back I am now aware, though I was not then, that none of the pupils or the teachers were disabled (at least that I knew of). There was also a secondary modern school down the road, also totally non-disabled and in my time only one person transferred into the grammar sixth form from the secondary modern. I am a product of a segregated system. Underlining this thinking, as I was writing the Foreword, a document entitled 'League tables' drops through my door as a supplement to the daily paper. I do not usually look, but do this time as my thoughts are on this – I take a glance at the results for the city where I live. First obvious thing is that the 'complete secondary school performance tables' are incomplete. Segregated local authority and independent special schools are not listed. The most cursory glance reveals that there are six schools in the '% achieving A*-C at GCSE' column into the 90s, three of which have a 100%, and all the six schools have asterisks. No school with an asterisk has below 90%. Of the schools without asterisks the highest figure is 70%. Schools with an asterisk are 'independent/private' schools. The problem is segregation in the creation of privilege as well as oppression and social control. It is from this point that I select three recurring themes of this book that I can engage with and also Vic's challenge.

The first is that of language. Not surprisingly in an international text, the meaning of concepts is returned to again and again. Predominant is the shifts in policy, provision and practice encompassed in the shift from integration to inclusion. There are clear and also subtle differences of meaning within the use of, and between the use of the two terms, with inclusion taking the dominant position. This, however, needs turning. What is the obverse of each of these terms? The antonym of inclusion is most obviously exclusion, while for integration it is segregation. The notion of exclusion has some potential in that it broadens concerns to the experiences of some young disabled people in mainstream settings: integrated but excluded. Yet there is a danger in that it reconstructs debates. However it is practiced, manifested and rationalised, segregation remains the problem from the viewpoint of disabled people. It is the seat of injustice.

The term inclusion also comes under critical scrutiny. It could be that the 'problems of integration' are simply being recast as problems of inclusion', though there are significant shifts in thinking in at least two directions. The first is the refocusing from the needs of individual young people, the industry of special educational needs, to education systems, at national, local and school levels, be it structure, management, assessment or curricula: the system that grades, selects, sets child against child, school against school, and justifies social inequality and injustice. It is also about the processes of creating education that realises and teaches to the whole diversity of the population – class, gender, religion, disability and all the social divisions that characterise global societies. In doing so, the starting point is the experience, understanding and culture that each child brings to, and through which they engage with, education.

Inclusion is about all children and young people. This is the resonance of the term inclusion across the experiences within the countries represented in this book. It must be universal. Inclusion means inclusion – irrespective of all divisive social division. Yet here again I return to Vic. While the broad impetus for changing education can fuel inclusion, the problem for many disabled people, unlike many members of other minority groups, though there are commonalities of experiences as documented in these chapters, remains segregation.

The second recurring theme internationally is power relations. Language is crucial here too. Debates are controlled and given meaning by those in power. Vic's statement again has clear significance. Who controls the debate? Whose problems are being discussed? It is about educational change done to people, ostensibly on behave of, in the best interests of people. Though internationally the voices and views of disabled people remain marginalized, there seems to be a shift towards the voices of those directly involved. These are critical voices that recognise that inclusion is a process of changing a divisive system that sets child against child, group against group, and sorts, selects and certifies. Again dangers are recognised in the different contexts discussed in these chapters. Any claims to being inclusive, at whatever level, school, local or national, must always be greeted with scepticism. Equality, rights, participation and social justice are ideals to be worked towards, not products to be claimed. So too must be reactions against inclusion and claims, and 'proof', that 'inclusion does not work in practice'. This again returns to language. Much that is done in the name of 'inclusion', and deemed inclusive policy and practice, is in name only. The voices in this book maintain a critical eye and, I am pleased to say, will remain steadfast against the 'winds of change' and change promoted by those still formulating those 'problems of integration'.

The third theme I would pin-point is the positioning of inclusive education within a much broader picture of social change. Having worked in teacher education, I have felt for a long time that teachers looked no further than the playground wall and often no further than the blackboard (or maybe now the Smartboard!). This was certainly true of the perceived problems of integration. The ideals of inclusion, however, particularly when viewed through international glasses, are much broader – and there is a cacophony of questions. Is it possible to have inclusive education within a disablist society? And the reverse – what does inclusive education, or its creation, offer to the establishment of a less disablist society? Is it possible to include disabled children and young people without including pupils from ethnic minority communities? Is a non-disablist society possible in a society that is sexist, racist, homophobic and maintained and sustained through inequality? And finally, returning yet again to Vic, is it possible to claim the establishment of inclusive education while the social injustice of segregated education remains (as in UK policy)?

I am raising question after question – and for me this is the crucial quality of this book. I recommend Policy, Experience and Change to all who are interested in chiming the bells of critique and wielding the hammers of change against the social injustice of segregation.

Professor John Swain
University of Northumbria
England

INTRODUCTION

The purpose of this book is to explore some different perspectives and cross-cultural ideas on issues and questions relating to inclusive education. We hope that it will encourage discussion and further research in this important field of enquiry. Each contributor to the book has been asked to offer accounts of both a historical and contemporary analysis into the developments, barriers and future challenges that inclusive education raises for their own country as well as their professional and personal perspectives.

We have decided not to offer an overview of the contributions to this book. Whilst we have outlined what we asked the authors to provide in their accounts, the reasons for our choice of contributors and the ordering of the papers is multi-faceted. One major influence on our decisions, was the desire to provide some prominence and critical analysis of some countries that we felt have received limited attention in previous cross-cultural collections published in English.

One of the significant outcomes of working on the development of this collection of accounts, has been an increasing awareness of some of the exciting and complex issues that cross-cultural work on inclusive education involves. It raises conceptual, theoretical, empirical, pragmatic and policy-related concerns, ideas, insights and questions. The issues are complex and contentious, requiring a sensitivity to both contradictions and possibilities that emerge, for example, from a critical engagement with the different meanings and values underpinning the concept of inclusive education in different contexts.

THE CHALLENGE OF CROSS-CULTURAL UNDERSTANDING

We cannot underestimate the importance of recognising the particularities, as well as the commonalities, of some of the priorities, barriers and contradictions involved in trying to widen participation in education in different settings. It is very clear that we cannot just apply the language of 'inclusion' uncritically, assuming that meanings will be shared across cultures – or even within the same national context or education authority. Neither can we talk about 'inclusive education' as if it were an entity that can be clearly

1

L. Barton and F. Armstrong (eds.), Policy, Experience and Change, 1–4.
© 2008 Springer Science + Business Media B.V.

identified and defined, or free of historical context. And, to quote António Nóvoa (2001, p. 45) 'we know that we need to ask new questions, search from different meanings, imagine other histories'.

To talk about the 'history of inclusive education,' therefore, is misleading, as we are referring to a diverse international movement, which takes many forms and is rooted in very different social and historical processes and conditions. This 'movement' is overt and present in terms of, for example, international developments such as the Salamanca Statement (1994) and the UNESCO 'Education For All' programme, as well as by governments through legislation and documents. But it is a movement which is also occurring in some contexts at grassroot levels through the actions of local education authorities, schools and communities. This is not a 'movement' which rolls smoothly forward, unobstructed, for the effects of a global counter-current of 'raising standards' in educational performance, and competition between schools and countries as part of a wider global struggle for economic survival and dominance, present formidable obstacles to developing inclusive education.

Against this background, notions such as 'inclusion' and 'human rights' must be seen as contingent, geographically and temporally situated concepts, rather than representing universal, shared values. The ways in which 'inclusive education' has come to be used in different national and cultural contexts reflect different kinds of 'urgency'. The Education For All (EFA) (2000, 2002) (UNESCO) programme, for example, has free, mass, compulsory education for all primary school aged children as its principle goal. Like the Index for Inclusion (Booth and Ainscow, 2002), the question of the rights of disabled children is seen as part of a broader agenda relating to inclusive education. This is evident in some of the key Millennium Development Goals which were set out by the United General Assembly (Resolution A/56/326, 6 September 2001):

Goal 2. Achieve universal primary education

Target 3. Ensure that, by 2015, children everywhere, boys and girls alike, will be able to complete a full course of primary schooling.

Goal 3.

Target 4. Eliminate gender disparity in primary and secondary education, preferably by 2005, and to all levels of education no later than 2015.

A study of the work of different UNESCO initiatives, therefore, shows how the notions of 'inclusion' and 'inclusive education' are understood as connected to all kinds of marginalisations and exclusions in education, whatever form they may take.

In identifying and understanding the struggles for inclusive education cross-culturally, the extent of the work that still needs to be undertaken, if discriminatory and exclusionary barriers are to be interrogated and removed, remains a significant issue. One important aspect of this task concerns the urgency of creating inclusive research conditions and relations, generating adequate conceptual and theoretical frameworks to advance our knowledge and understanding and to raise the question of the purpose of research, its transformative nature and our responsibilities as researchers. Generating collegial, supportive and sustained comparative research networks is a perennial task which needs much more serious and focused effort. We have seen that one of the challenges that cross-cultural analysis raises, concerns the importance of foregrounding the issue of context concerning local and national factors in both their subtle and covert forms. This requires being sensitive to the social, cultural, political and economic conditions and relations of a society in order to begin to engage effectively with all the factors involved.

LANGUAGE AND THE EDITORIAL CHALLENGE

Another related issue which the accounts in this book raise concerns the question of language and the meaning and understanding of key concepts, ideas, interpretations and practices. The extent to which for example, 'inclusive education' is transferable in terms of its meaning and the assumptions informing it across different societies is a perennial challenge, especially in relation to encouraging meaningful discussions between participants from different societies. In editing this collection we have taken the decision not to interfere with the language and terminology used by different contributors. There was a temptation to 'correct' terminology used in the different chapters, in order to achieve some kind of 'consistency', and impose a particular order and set of values which we ourselves support. There was a further possible rationale for carrying out this kind of 'linguistic cleansing' in that many of the contributors are writing in a second language. In wielding the red pen, tidying up and sweeping away differences in the choice of phraseology, and thereby constructing a smooth and coherent text, we would, surely, have been doing no more than assuming ordinary editorial license? Such an approach, however, ignores the often subtle differences in meaning and perspective which are revealed by the words used by different writers. What is the interest in producing a homogenised, sanitised version of the original text? How can such an assumption of cultural hegemony be justified in a book which seeks to explore cultural differences, as well as possible similarities, in values and practices? We have seen how open the language of 'inclusion' is to being colonised by different groups and policy makers for all kinds of different purposes – many of them invested with values which, far from embracing principles of equity and participation, are concerned with narrow notions of achievement and success as measured by attainment targets and underpinned by competition and projects of selection (Fitz *et al.*, 2005). We want to distance ourselves, as far as possible, from such practices. A further reason for our decision not to tamper with the terminology used by contributors is a pragmatic one. By imposing particular semantic choices on the work of others, we would surely obscure meaning rather than enhance it. In addition, the suggestion that the terminology of 'inclusion', for example, could be imposed on other terminology which has – in the English context – slipped into disuse, if not become discredited as antiquated, disabling, politically 'incorrect' – implies a linear view of 'development' towards a common social world in which values and language will be shared. Of course, the way in which the concepts of equity, human rights and 'diversity' are expressed and enacted – to the extent that these concepts exist across all societies – will differ, often fundamentally, in different settings. We should not assume that the English use – and its multiple usages – of the term 'inclusion' implies more 'equity', more 'social justice' than, for example, the Italian term *integrazione*. Of course, we recognise that contributors themselves will have made selections from what is available to them in current English terminology. Sometimes the term 'special needs' has been used, or 'inclusive education' when these concepts do not exist in their home culture. Furthermore, there is a major difficulty which we have not explored, concerning the expression of ideas, values and social processes in a 'foreign' language. There is almost certainly just no way of expressing some concepts from different cultures in English – so contributors have, perhaps, had to borrow available terminology 'off the peg' – even if it is a distortion of what they wish to say. Finally, as editors, we have certainly done some 'interfering', in order to make the texts comprehensible, and this has probably involved some ironing our of subtle contours in thinking and the putting forward of arguments, although that has not been our intention. It is hoped that the reader will find the contributions in this book informative and thought-provoking, thereby contributing to the development of self-critical evaluation of their own presuppositions, priorities and practices and that active engagement with the reading of this text will involve a learning experience in which the question of change in its many different forms and degrees will be a perennial issue.

REFERENCES

Booth, T. and Ainscow, M. (2002) *Index for Inclusion: Developing Learning and Participation in Schools.* Bristol: CS1E (Revised Edition).

Fitz, J., Davies, B. and Evans, J. (2005) *Education Policy and Social Reproduction*, London: Routledge.

Nóvoa, A. (2001) 'Texts, Images and Memories: Writing new Histories of education' in S. Thomas Popkewitz, M. Barry Franklin, A. Miguel Pereyra, (eds) *Cultural History and Education: Critical Essays on Knowledge and Schooling*, London: Routledge Falmer.

UNESCO (2002) 'Education For All Global Monitoring Report, Education for All: Is the World On Track?' UNESCO Publishing, full report available at www.unesco.org/education/efa.

UNESCO (1994) *Salamanca Statement and Framework for Action on Special Needs Education*, Paris: UNESCO.

UNESCO (2000) Education for All: Meeting our Collective Commitments. Expanded Commentary on the Dakar Framework for Action, Para 33.

FELICITY ARMSTRONG AND LEN BARTON

1. POLICY, EXPERIENCE AND CHANGE AND THE CHALLENGE OF INCLUSIVE EDUCATION: THE CASE OF ENGLAND

INTRODUCTION

Looking back to England in the 1980s, it is evident that the initial hope of achieving participation by disabled children in non-segregated education announced by the 1981 Education Act, turned to disenchantment for many. It became clear that the new notions of 'special educational needs' and 'integration' ushered in by the Act and the Warnock Report (1978), rather than abolishing 'categories of handicap', introduced a new supercategory 'SEN', and 'integration' only concerned a limited number of children – those who could 'fit in' to existing structures.

The notion of inclusive education did not appear out of thin air. Its roots are deep and widely spread – reaching back into the aspirations and community values embodied in the ideal of comprehensive education in the UK – and to notions of civil rights and equity from the emancipatory struggles in many parts of the world during the 1960s. However, the idea which emerged in the 1990s came as a gust of fresh air, breathing life into tired debates and struggles. Inclusive education became – and remains – a flagship idea which has inspired many local education authorities, schools, teachers and communities to engage in projects to transform cultures and practices in schools in celebration of diversity. These achievements should not be underestimated. At the same time, the term 'inclusive education' has been colonised, hollowed out and transformed into an 'empty signifier' (Laclau, 1996), with powerful interest groups, including successive governments, committed to the continued role of special schools, struggling to invest and shape it with their own values and agendas.

The values we, as writers, bring to this debate are shaped by our own individual histories. Reflecting on the nature of our collaboration over a number of years, the small and not-so-small struggles it has involved, and the substantial differences in our life histories and perspectives, we are reminded of the constant flux and change we have experienced in our thinking. Writing together does not always mean agreement – rather, it is a process of turning over ideas, examining issues and arguments from different angles and reappraising sometimes deeply held positions. This is also what is so interesting and enriching about being involved in discussions with others from different settings and life experiences – in our teaching and in our work with colleagues from different cultures and disciplines.

5

L. Barton and F. Armstrong (eds.), Policy, Experience and Change, 5–18.
© 2008 Springer Science + Business Media B.V.

We are conscious that in carving out the personal in terms of our own values and interpretations, we are involved in a never-ending process. We recognise the importance of understanding factors in our personal and professional biographies that have shaped the way we think about the meaning of inclusive education. However, through a process of developing a strong working relationship and critical friendship, we have come to share some perspectives that now inform our teaching, research and this chapter. They include first, a deep interest in the question of change and its necessity. We recognise that the changes required in the pursuit of inclusive conditions, relations and values are systemic as well as attitudinal. Thus the barriers to change will not be removed quickly or easily. Second, in the present context, contradictions and compromises exist in which existing inequalities of opportunities and provision will be influential and understandable factors underpinning the support of some professionals and parents for segregated provision. Third, we are conscious of the demanding nature of the challenges that schools and teachers face and of the high quality of teaching and hard work that they are expected to provide. The question of the nature and extent of the support that teachers need to enable them to meet the inclusive agenda, is an urgent and perennial issue. Fourth, changes in policy need to be based on principles of equity, rather than on narrow conceptions of 'reasonableness' and economic rationality. In the current context, the possibility of creative and challenging relationships between ordinary and special schools is important but needs to be seen as transitional. Fifth, the complexity and stubbornness of the barriers to inclusion involve a recognition that schools and teachers on their own cannot effectively meet the challenges involved. It requires a multiagency, community-based partnership approach. Finally, the position and function of initial teacher education and professional development courses in relation to inclusive thinking and practice require urgent, critical attention and change.

Inclusive education, as understood in this approach, is not primarily about the position of particular groups of categorised pupils, but rather the well-being of all learners and their effective, sustained participation. For us, inclusive education is not an end in itself, but a means to an end. It is about contributing to the realisation of an inclusive society with the demand for a rights approach as a central component of policy making. Thus, the question of inclusion is fundamentally about issues of human rights, equity, social justice and the struggle for a non-discriminatory society. These principles are at the heart of inclusive educational policy and practice.

MEANINGS AND STRUGGLES

The concepts and ideas involved in debates concerning inclusive education are subject to struggles over their meaning and application. We need to emphasise that social, political and educational movements which support the struggle for equality and widening participation in community education, regardless of difference, have to contend with the might of other, dominant and deeply entrenched processes, ways of thinking and organisation which are based on a construction of the normal and normative ways of thinking about teaching and learning and desirable outcomes of education. These are frequently mono-cultural, not 'disabled', culturally mainstream and carefully tailored; they are profoundly exclusionary in their effects. Popekewitz (2001) explains:

> ... exclusions are produced through the systems of recognition, divisions, and distinctions that construct reason and 'the reasonable person'. The norms in the pedagogical discourses have no way of accounting for difference except in terms of deviation from certain universal standards. In this way, diverse groups are only seen from the perspective of a 'being' that is different from the norm. ... It is thus implied that the best thing that can happen to such a person is to become 'like the normal person' (p. 337).

This statement is particularly apposite when applied to education policy and practice in England and Wales over the past twenty-five years – a period in which the construction of what counts as 'reasonableness' in terms of curriculum, pedagogy and performance and the 'good pupil' has become increasingly coercive and restrictive. '*Reasonable* inclusion' is also used as a formula for criticism against those who would advocate '*full* inclusion' as if the latter were irresponsible wreckers or dreamers. The struggle for inclusive education in England could never be simple, because of deep-rooted conceptions about education which are based on measuring, sorting, selection and rejection. In England we have only to recall the regular public routing and shaming of 'failing schools' which do not fulfil the image and outcomes of a particular construction of 'the good school'.

The notion of 'the good school' as a hegemonic project is borne out by the government White Paper published in 2005 (DfES, 25/10/05) which supports greater 'independence' and 'choice' for schools funded by the state, under the banner of 'choice and personalisation' and 'real parent power'. In the guise of making 'choice' available to everybody, Ruth Kelly, the then secretary of state for Education, proposed the 'bussing' of children from their neighbourhoods so that they can gain access to a 'good school'. If the proposals become law, schools will be given far greater control over admissions than in the past.

It is not difficult to imagine which groups of children will be ferried out of their communities in the mornings to attend a 'popular school', nor is it difficult to work out which direction the busses will be going. In the morning, they will not, surely, be heading in the direction of schools located in estates where there are high levels of unemployment and economic deprivation. According to the proposals in the White Paper, state schools will become 'independent', with the schools themselves – and not local authorities – making the important decisions on selection, curriculum and pedagogy. Two groups of pupils will be given specialised classes – those deemed to be 'gifted and talented' (a discourse which is an affront to principles of inclusion in which children are valued equally and recognition given to the 'gifts', 'talents' and uniqueness of every child) and those who are 'struggling'. In our view, these proposals are likely to create deeper and more damaging and iniquitous divisions between children and communities than any legislation introduced over the past twenty-five years. Such proposals highlight the enormous chasm between the rhetoric of inclusion adopted by successive New Labour administrations since 1997, and the principles of inclusion which have been advanced by those committed to an open, equitable and democratic system of education.

So much for our immediate struggles. In the following sections, we link the notion of inclusive education to wider international developments and try to make some connections between policy developments in England with those in other places. We explore the relationship between inclusive education as a 'field' of study with other disciplines, and consider some of the uneven historical development of special education in England. The purpose of this is to highlight the complexities and contradiction in policy making in a highly contentious area – 'special educational needs'. In doing this, we do not seek to conflate the broad principles of inclusive education as being concerned with all learners and their communities with the very different notion of 'special educational needs'. However, historical developments in relation to education and the situation of disabled children and young people provides one entry point to many of the struggles against different levels and kinds of exclusion in education – struggles which are now joined for the first time by the principles of inclusive education and efforts to build an education which is truly inclusive of all learners. Towards the end of this analysis we will critically discuss the latest contribution that Warnock 2005 has made to the question of inclusive education.

HISTORICAL CONTEXT

The history of educational provision for disabled children in England is usually linked to the introduction of mass education through the education acts of 1870, 1876 and 1880 (Armytage, 1965; Armstrong, 2003). However, like the Workhouse and the Asylum, there are many examples of earlier projects, sometimes seen as 'experiments', of teaching or 'training' of children described today as 'having learning difficulties'. There were institutions for deaf and blind children where education, normalisation and Christianity were all regarded as important, and in the nineteenth century numerous asylums were established for children who, today, would be officially described as 'having learning difficulties'. The development of special education in the late nineteenth and early twentieth centuries was linked to the emergent professions of educationists, medics and psychologists as well as to the growth of official interest in the health of the general population and of school children in particular. Education was not routinely provided by special institutions which were more concerned with care and training, although there were certainly some notable exceptions to this. After the Second World War during which many disabled children attended ordinary schools as special schools were closed down or converted into hospitals for the wounded or barracks to house soldiers, attitudes began to shift.

The history of special education in England has centred on perceptions relating to sometimes contradictory concerns of identification and categorisation of impairments, and appropriate responses to the 'needs' of disabled children and young people within the structures, professional practices and values of the time (Riddell, 2002). For example, the 1944 Education Act (UK), while introducing eleven 'categories of handicap', also drew large numbers of disabled children into the education system for the first time, making Local Education Authorities responsible for their education. It was not until the implementation of the Education (Handicapped Children) Act 1970 that responsibility for provision for children categorised as 'mentally handicapped' was passed from the health authorities to local education authorities.

The Warnock Report (1978) marked an important change in perspective in challenging assumptions that the categorisation of impairment was a justification for 'special' provision.

> ... the idea is deeply engrained in educational thinking that there are two types of children, the handicapped and the non-handicapped. Traditionally the former have generally been thought to require special education, and the latter ordinary education. But the complexities of individual needs are far greater than this dichotomy implies. Moreover, to describe someone as handicapped conveys nothing of the type of educational help, and hence of provision that is required. We wish to see a more positive approach, and we have adopted the concept of SPECIAL EDUCATIONAL NEED, seen not in terms of a particular disability which a child might be judged to have, but in relation to everything about him, his abilities as well as his disabilities – indeed all the factors which have a bearing on his educational progress (The Warnock Report, 1978. 3.6, p. 37).

The 1981 Education Act provided a legislative framework for the concept of special educational needs (Armstrong, 2003) announcing the replacement of the categories of impairment encoded by the 1944 Education Act. Provision was made for the introduction of statutory assessment of learning difficulties to establish whether a child had special educational needs – ushering in the new label 'SEN' – and if so, what these needs were. 'Statements' of special educational needs, stipulating the nature of the 'needs', how they should be met, and the resources required, were issued for some children as an outcome of the assessment procedures. These procedures had important implications in terms of assessment, organisation of educational provision and resources, and the language used to refer to children who experienced difficulties and led to a massive rise in the number of professional assessments carried out. Paradoxically, although the term focused on educational needs rather than individual impairments, it also became a mega-category denoting difference or learning difficulty which co-existed with the established categories of impairment. Indeed, the history of the notion of 'special educational needs' is a fine example of the complexities and contradictions involved in imposing new discourses on deeply rooted traditions and practices.

More recently legislation such as the Special Educational Needs and Disability Act (2001) has adopted a change of emphasis in establishing a duty to educate children with special educational needs in mainstream schools, provided it is compatible with the wishes of the parent and the 'provision of efficient education for other children'. This Act has not made a clean break with earlier legislation in that the rights of disabled children remain contingent on the 'wishes' and judgements of the more powerful.

INCLUSIVE EDUCATION: THE EMERGENCE OF A CONCEPT

Although the term inclusion was not used widely before the 1990s, the principles of inclusive education were already emerging internationally. The UNESCO World Declaration on Education for All, adopted in Jomtien, 1990, called for 'a learning environment in which everyone would have the chance to acquire the basic elements which serve as a foundation for further learning and enable full participation in society' (http://www.unesco.org/education/efa). A number of countries had already introduced legislation in support of widening participation of disabled children in mainstream education, such as the Laws no. 118 (1971) and no. 517 (1977) in Italy, the Education of All Handicapped Children Act (1975) (reauthorized as the Individuals with Disabilities Act in 1997) in the United States, and the 1981 Education Act in the UK.

We recognise that contexts are complex and ever changing in ways which have a crucial bearing on the way concepts are understood and interpreted. We also recognise that concepts and terminology cannot be exported and imported across different settings and historical periods, as if they have a universal meaning and value. Neither should they be the subject of crude forms of 'cultural translation' (Burke, 2004), although inevitably processes of culturally mediated adaptation and translation of concepts and terminology take place at different levels across, and within, cultures.

Developments in social systems, concepts and language are historically situated and culturally specific. It is for this reason that we need to be critical of the unexamined adoption of terminology such as 'special educational needs', 'integration' and 'inclusive education', as if such terms had one fixed and universal interpretation, regardless of historical and social context. Anyone who has engaged in debates with colleagues from different countries, or even from different interest groups or local authorities within one country, will know that there is a real difficulty in establishing a shared understanding of terminology and a recognition of the different values, structures and practices which underpin language. The varied use of terminology, and the contrasts in focus and emphasis in the chapters which make up this book illustrate this point. It is for this reason that, from the outset, we need to be clear about how we are using some key terminology in the context of this chapter. We use the term 'integration' to refer to technical and administrative arrangements which are made in relation to an individual disabled child, or small group of children, to attend a mainstream school. Integration makes no requirement for the school to effect radical change in its culture and organisation because the expectation is that the child is accommodated to existing structures and practices or – at best, if organisational and pedagogical adjustments *are* implemented, they take place *around* the individual child or group of children identified as in need. Inclusive education, in contrast, is based on the belief that *all* children have the right to attend their local school, regardless of difference and that schools are part of communities. This will involve a cultural and educational transformation of the school so that all children in the community can be welcomed. Inclusive education is not concerned with one group – disabled children, or children who are identified as having learning difficulties – but with everybody. An inclusive school will seek to combat prejudice and marginalisation in whatever forms it takes. In this context, we share the interpretation of Plaisance and Gardou, (2001) when they observe that there is a strong opposition between *integration policy* which is situated within a continuity of the old structures (and we would add within a continuity in ways of thinking) of special education, and *inclusive policy* which implies a radical change in ordinary schools so that they are open to, and welcome, diversity in its widest sense (p. 11). In the context of England we can think of a number of groups – some of them very large – who are at risk of marginalisation in the educational system. Disabled students – of course – but also students from communities which experience social and economic hardship – and there are many in England: young asylum seekers, Travellers, gypsies, young people who are in prison, young people who are victimised on the grounds of their gender, sexuality, or race or cultural heritage.

Inclusive education is based on the belief in education as belonging to communities both in terms of what counts as knowledge and how educational processes are conceptualised and developed (Armstrong *et al.*, 2005). It is concerned with recognising what communities themselves share and bring to the curriculum and the experience of learning. That is why we support the idea of community-based schools 'without walls' in which the practice of education is based on principles of equality and participation and the opportunities it provides recognise the aspirations and diversity of their members. Rather than bussing people out of their communities, and returning them at the end of the day, we would advocate the generous resourcing of all schools, with the highest quality of teaching, opportunities and resources, because inclusive education is about providing the best possible education for all.

The concept of inclusive education is a terrain in which competing and sometimes contradictory values, policies and processes are involved. Legislation and policy statements concerning barriers to participation, which may, or may not, adopt the terminology of 'inclusive education', frequently focus on disabled students, rather than on *all* learners. The Special Educational Needs and Disability Act (SENDA, UK, 2001) is designed to remove physical, curricular and pedagogical barriers to participation in ordinary schools for disabled students in schools, colleges and Universities. While such legislation contributes to the development of inclusive education, it refers specifically to disability and learning difficulty. In contrast, the Irish Education Act (1998) sought to enact legislation to ensure that the education system is accountable to all for the education provided, and 'respects the diversity of values, beliefs, languages and traditions in Irish society and is conducted in a spirit of partnership ...' Similarly, The Irish Equal Status Act (2000) treats different forms of injustice and exclusion as part of one struggle to overcome inequality in society and in education, prohibiting discrimination on nine grounds, including gender, marital status, family status, sexual orientation, religion, age, disability, race and membership of the Traveller community. There is no reason, of course, to assume that policies which seek to widen participation and address inequalities in education should adopt the rhetoric of 'inclusion' or 'inclusive education'. Conversely, there should be no expectation that policies which call themselves 'inclusive' will necessarily deliver the goods, or that they are based on a commitment to ending selection and exclusive policies and practices in education.

What is the 'Field' of Inclusive Education?

There has been an increasing awareness of the emerging and complementary roles that different disciplines can play in developing understanding, as well as contributing to confusion, of issues from contrasting epistemologies, and their sometimes competing and contradictory claims to 'ownership' of the terrain. Traditional disciplines such as psychology, sociology, philosophy, history and medicine have all staked out their territories in research and debate on inclusive education. Other disciplines such as genetics, economics and politics are also tangentially linked, as are relatively new disciplines, which are making their entry in research and debates on education in general, and 'special education' is no exception. Disciplines such as linguistics and discourse analysis, social and cultural geography, and media studies – all of these fields provide fresh insights into issues relating to education systems and the way they respond to difference and diversity. We can learn a great deal from social geography and architecture about the way that identities are constructed through the use of space and the differentiation of sites and buildings for particular groups of people. Discourse analysis throws light on the power of labelling in assigning particular negative and dependent characteristics to whole groups of people on the basis of a category of impairment or 'difference' (Corker and French, 1999; Armstrong, F. 2003). Such discourses permeate and shape policies and attitudes. A study of the media has strengthened understanding about, for example, the creation of stereotypes in the moving image (Shakespeare, 1994, 1999).

It is useful to keep in mind that policy making and social relations in the field of education can be approached from multiple perspectives and forms of analysis. This can be enriching, but confusing at the same time. Disciplines do not share a common language or research traditions, and sometimes they are seen as being in competition with each other – such as the disciplines of sociology and psychology, for example. The claims of such a diverse range of disciplines to a connection with, or even ownership of, the field of inclusive education can be explained by the pervasive nature of the kind of social, organisational, economic, pedagogical, attitudinal and cultural dimensions and struggles which will be involved in developing inclusive schools and communities.

POLICY, CONFUSION AND REACTION

The OECD Programme *for International Student Assessment* (PISA) survey (2003) which focused on measuring performance in mathematics and student performance in problem solving in nearly 60 countries (OECD, 2003a, OECDb) is evidence of an increasing emphasis at the international level on student performance and measurement, and of an obsession with 'standards' that mirrors internal developments in many countries. The 'curriculum' has become increasingly controlled by the state in the interests of producing a labour force which will enhance productivity in the global market place. Narrowly prescriptive constructions of what counts as important knowledge in different subject areas are formalised as 'national' curricula such as the National Curriculum introduced in England and Wales under the Education Reform Act (1988). Similar processes, accompanied by a harmonised discourse linking efficiency, effectiveness and performativity have permeated education systems at all levels (Gewirtz, 2002).

In England, for over two decades, there has been a profound and far-reaching increase in government intervention at all levels of the educational system. This has influenced changes to the governance, funding, content and purpose of provision and practice. Education has increasingly been conceived as a positional good, one in which instrumental values are very significant. Competition and selection have intensified within the system as a whole, with performativity and government forms of inspection combining to relegate and control schools, teachers and teaching, through the introduction of targets and pre-specified outcomes. Supporting and legitimating these developments has been the introduction of extensive forms of new legislation.

The question of educational policy is a very significant issue, in terms of how it is created, defined, implemented, received and changed. This is a complex and problematic process, within which a linear and top down model of policy development can only provide a misleading and inadequate perspective. The policy context in England can best be described as providing a series of contradictory and competing policy directives. Some policies, therefore, are more significant than others in terms of government priorities and commitments. An example being the standards over the inclusion agenda. This has contributed to confusion, ambiguity and a lack of political will on the part of successive governments to offer the extent and forms of support, necessary for inclusive thinking and practice to be effectively realised.

Dyson (2005) explores the deeply complex situation which works against schools becoming inclusive, citing major barriers to change: The role of local education authorities in determining provision in their area; the continued existence of special schools; the existence of special units or resource bases attached to (or which are part of) mainstream schools; the growth of Pupil Referral Units (PRUs); the increase in selection and setting within schools according to perceived ability; the continued presence of fee-paying schools in the 'independent' sector; the social demarcation between different geographical areas particularly in urban areas; the effects of parental 'choice'; and the sharpness of competition between schools fuelled by the publication of league tables – are just some of the structural factors which present major obstacles to the development of inclusive education in England.

Debates concerning inclusive education in the UK have sharpened recently, and this was particularly evident during the 2005 general election campaign. There has been widespread concern about the general state of education, and, in particular, what might be described as a 'moral panic' concerning the education of some groups of children – particularly those who are considered disruptive to the smooth running of the school. In the election campaign, the conservatives promised the electorate that they would dismantle existing policies and reopen special schools – a policy, which they justify on the grounds of the rights of disabled children, or by evoking the difficulties such children present to teachers and in terms of the progress of other students in the ordinary class. Paradoxically, New Labour is also openly in favour of the continuation of segregated structures for the same reasons.

There has been a steady stream of policy documents and legislation introduced by successive governments since New Labour came to power in 1997 (Armstrong, D. 2005) which have placed increasing demands on schools and education authorities concerning the rights of disabled children to attend their local school. Athough there has been a definite shift in attitude in recent years in the general population, and a quite broad acceptance that children should not be segregated on the grounds of impairment, there is a counter-current moving against inclusive education which is gaining momentum.

There is evidence of this counter-current in recent statistics (OfSTED, 2004), which indicate that the percentage of pupils identified as having an impairment or difficulty of some kind, who attend a special school or unit, rose in 2004 when compared with the preceding years. The report found that while the government's revised inclusion frame-work had contributed to a growing awareness of the benefits of inclusion and response to it had led to some improvement in practice, there had been an 'increase in the numbers of pupils placed in pupil referral units and independent special schools'. Between 2002 and 2003, the percentage of pupils in all special schools including pupil referral units increased from 1.37 to 1.39. It will be interesting to see whether the Special Educational Needs and Disability Act has made any impact on these figures, now that the law is being enacted, although the most recent report on Segregation Trends published by CSIE (Rustemier and Vaughan, 2005) suggests that little progress was made between 2002 and 2004, with one-third of local education authorities having actu-ally *increased* segregation of disabled children over the three-year period.

The contentious nature of the question of inclusive education is reinforced by the pamphlet by Baroness Warnock (2005) in which the author provides a retrospective overview of particular aspects of the development of the Warnock Report (1978) and what she now believes are some of the damaging impacts of the outcome of the Report. This includes the position and function of statementing. A particular issue of consider-ation is the question of the position and future of special segregated provision. The title of the pamphlet claims that the content of the account is a 'new look'. Given the per-spective we have been developing in this chapter, we are critical of many of the assump-tions, interpretations and vision that this account supports.

It is now over 25 years since the publication of the Warnock Report and in this time an extensive amount of research, writing and developments have taken place with regard to the question of inclusive education in terms of its meaning, application and future challenges, both in relation to policy and practice. In a document that claims to be offer-ing a 'new look', one would expect some careful discussion of the ideas of those who represent an alternative perspective. Instead, we have no discussion of a serious nature with regard to such published material. This is particularly questionable when we recog-nise the central role that disabled people and their organisations have played in the strug-gle for inclusion. Not one serious reference is made to the extensive publications by disabled people supporting inclusive education such as, The Campaign To End Segregated Education by the year 2020, Alliance For Inclusive Education (2004) and the clear demands that disabled people have outlined with regard to their approach. Such voices are excluded from consideration. This does raise the question of whose voice is seen as significant and on what grounds.

On what grounds does Warnock support her criticisms? What constitutes the evidence to legitimate the demands 'for a radical view'? (p. 12). We are offered several unsubstan-tiated claims and assertions including 'There is increasing evidence that the ideal of inclusion … is not working' (p. 35). That inclusion 'can be carried too far' and it involves 'a simplistic ideal' (p. 14). Particular support is derived from Warnock's experience of the work of a school for 'pupils with moderate learning difficulties' about which she asserts,

'This successful special school seems to be a model that could be followed by other ...' (p. 48). What is important from our perspective is that no single experience or example should be used to justify a general comprehensive theory or approach.

Whilst we agree with Warnock that education also includes being 'directed towards the future, towards life after school' (p. 41) we would clearly disagree over the place in which this is to be taught and experienced and the role of education in the development of that future, especially if it must be inclusive and non-discriminatory. Our fundamental disagreement is best illustrated in her demand '... that governments must come to recognise that even if inclusion is an ideal for society in general, it may not always be an ideal for school' (p. 43). This form of thinking if realised in practice will contribute to the building up of serious individual and socially divisive problems for the future. It fails to recognise that schools are a fundamental part of, and contribute to, 'society in general' and are not something apart from, or in the margins of, society. If we accept that schools play an important productive and reproductive role in shaping society, then the idea that inclusion might be 'an ideal for society' but 'not always' for schools is a contradiction.

One of the features of an inclusive approach is to question existing categories and language including, the validity of the discourse of 'special needs' and 'special educational needs' which the authors of the *Index For Inclusion* (2002), for example, endeavour to do. Part of the reasoning for such a critical approach is that this language contains the unacceptable assumptions that legitimate and maintain existing exclusionary, discriminatory policies and practices. While we agree with Warnock's statement that there is a need for 'rethinking the concept of special educational needs' (p. 28), we note that the pamphlet contains the non-problematical use of such language.

Many encouraging and effective developments have taken place with regard to inclusive policy and practice. However, Warnock seems to exaggerate the extent of these achievements in order to support her general argument. Advocates of inclusion are very aware of the contradictory and competing policy context in which inclusion is located. This has led to the lack of political will on the part of government to unreservedly support inclusion and as Rustemier and Vaughan (2005) maintain, in England there are:

> ... wide variations in practice in spite of all LEAs responding to the same legislation covering the education and placement of disabled pupils (summary).

The barriers to inclusion are stubborn and multi-varied and it is important to recognise the distinction between laudable rhetoric and actual practice. Exaggeration and unqualified assertions are a style of presentation that encourages moral panic.

One of the most problematic statements that Warnock makes concerns her claim that 'the most disastrous legacy of the 1978 report, (was) the concept of inclusion (formally known as integration)' (p. 22). The lack of recognition of the significant differences in the antecedents and meaning of these concepts arises from the confusion that inclusion is about specifically categorised individuals or special needs. Inclusion, as Frederick (2005) argues, '... also means tackling racism, homophobia and bullying. It's a whole school issue ...' (p. 19) and as such, is concerned with challenging all forms of discrimination and exclusion.

From our perspective much more thought and resources must be given to providing mainstream schools with the necessary support to enable them to begin, or continue with the work of, developing inclusive cultures and practices and meeting the entitlements of *all* learners. Given the demands of this challenge, the development of more multi-agency engagements and a widening of community involvement are called for.

CONCLUSION

In this chapter we have argued that identifying, understanding and explaining the position and function of education in relation to the development of inclusive conditions and relations, necessitates a broad historical, social, cultural and political perspective. We have drawn on the English context as a framework for our discussion. This approach is necessary because of the multi-dimensional, complex and inter-related nature of the issues involved. These include policy, conceptual, theoretical and practical dimensions. Understanding and exploring these issues and questions is a difficult and challenging task and the concept of 'struggle' assumes such a demanding process and engagement.

We have also maintained, that the struggle for inclusion involves a critical analysis of discrimination and exclusion, and that this entails a developing appreciation of the multi-layered, contradictory, deeply-rooted nature of these barriers to inclusion. Investigating and understanding these factors contextually is essential in the pursuit of change. It entails a serious and continual process of examination and re-examination. This critical engagement includes interrogating the question of 'inclusive education' itself. With regard to our society this is particularly important, given what we believe is a misplaced assumption, that our educational system and society is at an advanced stage of inclusive development and a model for other countries to emulate.

In producing this chapter and editing this book, we have been forcefully reminded how little we know and understand and how much there is still to be examined and changed. This has several important consequences. For example, it foregrounds the significance of humility and encourages a recognition that we are always *learners* in this ongoing process. Also, it reinforces the centrality of critical friendships and the establishment and maintenance of a collegial culture of support and collective endeavours in a world that is excessively individualistic and self-centred. Finally, it encourages an alertness to the serious and urgent task of challenging empty rhetoric and seductive platitudes, which lack effective significance in the daily experiences that we encounter and participate in.

From our perspective it is important to recognise that in England the struggle for inclusive conditions, values and practises has, and continues to take place, within a policy context that is contradictory and competitive. Thus, the extent to which there is the political will to support the development of effective policies, their implementation and the appropriate legislation to support them, remains a serious problematic issue. We contend that this unacceptable situation has contributed to the frustration, uncertainty, disappointment that, for example, many schools, teachers, parents, experience in their daily endeavours to be more inclusive. It is also against this background that the very real achievements and inclusive developments that are a testimony to the determination, creative energies and alternative conceptions need to be understood and built on. The importance of networking is particularly essential in the process of creating and sustaining support.

We are conscious of the serious and perennial task of critically engaging with key concepts including 'inclusion', 'special educational needs', 'choice' and 'standards'. In England the emphasis given to a market-led discourse in which competition and selection have increasing prominence, remains a fundamental challenge for those of us engaged in the pursuit of inclusive values, relations and practises. Also, the introduction of a category of 'gifted and talented' (Miliband, 2002) with its elitist and exclusionary assumptions and applications demonstrates the extent of the barriers that need to be challenged and changed. It also reminds us of the varied ways in which discrimination and exclusion can be expressed.

REFERENCES

Alliance For Inclusive Education (2004) *2020 The Campaign to End Segregated Education*. London: Alliance For Inclusive Education.

Armstrong, F. (2002) The historical development of special education: humanitarian rationality or 'wild profusion of entangled events'? *History of Education*, 31, 5, 437–456.

Armstrong, F. (2003) *Spaced Out: Policy, Difference and the Challenge of Inclusive Education*, London and Dordrecht: Kluwer.

Armstrong, D. (2003) *Experiences of Special Education: Re-evaluating, Policy and Practice through Life Stories*, London: Routledge Falmer.

Armstrong, D. (2005) 'Reinventing "inclusion": New Labour and the cultural politics of special education', *Oxford Review of Education*. 31, 1, 119–134.

Armstrong, F., Russell, O. and Schimanski, E. (2005) Action Research for Inclusive Education: Innovations in Teaching and Learning in *Education in the North* (in press).

Armytage, W.H.G. (1965) *Four Hundred Years of English Education*, Cambridge: Cambridge University Press.

Booth, T. and Ainscow, M. (2002) *Index For Inclusion: Developing Learning and Participation in School*, Bristol: Centre for Studies in Inclusive Education.

Burke, P. (2004) *What is Cultural History?*, Cambridge: Polity Press.

Corker, M. and French, S. (eds) (1999) *Disability Discourse*, Buckingham: Open University Press.

DfES (2005) Education White paper: Higher Standards: Better Schools for All.

Dyson, A. (2005) 'Philosophy, politics and economics? The story of Inclusive Education in England' in Mitchell, D. (ed.) *Contextualising Inclusive Education: Evaluating Old and New Perspectives*, London: Routledge/Taylor and Francis.

Education Act, 1944 (UK).

Education (Handicapped Children) Act (England and Wales) 1970.

Education Act 1981 (England and Wales).

Education of All Handicapped Children Act (1975) (USA).

Education Reform Act (England and Wales) 1988.

Elementary Education Act 1870.

Elementary Education Act 1876.

Elementary Education Act 1880.

Frederick, K. (2005) 'Let's take the special out of special needs', in *Times Educational Supplement*. July 15, 19.

Gewirtz, S. (2002) *The Managerial School: Post-Welfarism and Social Justice in Education*, London: Routledge.

Individuals with Disabilities Act 1997 (USA).

Irish Education Act 1998.

Irish Equal Status Act 2000.

Laclau, E. (1996) *Emancipation(s)*, London: Verso.

Law no. 118 (1975) (Italy).

Law no. 517 (1977) (Italy).

Miliband, D. (2002) Speech given at the National Gifted and Talented Education Conference in Birmingham http://education.guardian.co.uk/schools/story/0,,838608,00.html (last accessed on 18-11-05).

OECD (2003a) Learning for Tomorrow's World – First results from PISA 2003, Paris.

OECD (2003b) Problem Solving for Tomorrow's World – First Measures of Cross-Curricular Competencies from PISA 2003, Paris.

OfSTED (2004) Special Educational Needs and Disability Towards Inclusive Schools.

Popkewitz, Thomas S. (2001) 'Dewey and Vygotsky: Ideas in historical spaces', in Popkewitz, Thomas S., Franklin, Barry M. Pereyra, Miguel A. (eds) *Cultural History and Education: Critical Essays on Knowledge and Schooling*, London: Routledge Falmer.

Plaisance, E. and Gardou, C. (eds) (2001) Situations de handicap et institution scolaire, *Revue française de pédagogie*, n°134 (dossier spécial).

Ridell, S. (2002) *Policy and Practice in Education*, Edinburgh: Dunedin Academic Press.

Rustemier, S. and Vaughan, M. (2005) *Segregation Trends – LEAs in England 2002–2004*. Bristol: Centre For Studies on Inclusive Education.

Shakespeare, T. (1994) 'Cultural representations of disabled people: dustbins of disavowal?' *Disability and Society*, 8, 3, 249–263.

Shakespeare, T. (1999) 'Art and Lies? Representations of disability on film', in Corker, M. and French, S. (eds) *Disability Discourse*, Buckingham: Open University Press.

Special Educational Needs and Disabilities Act 2001, UK.

Warnock Committee (1978) *Special Educational Needs: The Warnock Report*. London: D.E.S.

Warnock, M. (2005) *Special Educational Needs: A New Look. London*: Philosophy of Education Society of Great Britain. http://www.unesco.org/education/efa

ÁNGELES PARRILLA

2. INCLUSIVE EDUCATION IN SPAIN: A VIEW FROM INSIDE

INTRODUCTION

I see this chapter as an opportunity to explain my own perspective on the reasons, circumstances and social, legal and professional events that have shaped the current situation regarding Inclusive Education in Spain. It is not my intention, therefore, to describe that situation in an impartial way. What I recount here reflects my convictions and experiences, the evolution of my thought and professional activity, inseparable from my own participation in social and educational development in my country. Another person would surely analyse and explain the past and present of Inclusive Education in Spain differently. Consequently this chapter is an account of my unique experience, closely linked to the people, institutions, ideologies, policies and contexts that have surrounded my career and personal evolution.

Looking back I perceive my professional trajectory as a gradual development that has led inexorably to a commitment to constructing a more inclusive society. I firmly believe that Inclusive Education can only be reached by advancing in the direction of democratic educational communities. However, the profile of Inclusive Education has become blurred on the hazy horizon of Spanish educational policy today. Laws and regulations modifying the educational system at all levels speed up the tendency to veer further and further away from the idea of an education based on equality. The Educational Quality Act, passed three years ago (*Ley Orgánica de Calidad en la Educación, 2002*[1]) seeks to guarantee quality in education by establishing educational itineraries and different paths for certain groups of students. This implies setting up selection and competition structures that constitute a clear cutback in the right to a quality education for all students.[2]

This chapter traces developments leading up to the present day. The early days of School Integration in Spain coincided with my own early days as a professional in the world of education. Reflecting on my own professional development, therefore, I discuss the evolution of positions and practices in relation to integration and inclusion in Spain from the early 1980s to the present day.

19

L. Barton and F. Armstrong (eds.), Policy, Experience and Change, 19–36.

FIRST STEPS TOWARDS SCHOOL INTEGRATION

Spain underwent a period of major reconstruction following the death of General Franco in the late 1970s. Among other important political and social changes introduced at the beginning of the 1980s,[3] the educational policies of the day aimed to transform an educational system – until then selective and dual with its corresponding general and special institutions, curricula and legislation – into an integrative, comprehensive educational system.

Two key regulations served as guidelines for moves towards Integration: the 1982 *Ley de Integración Social del Minusválido* and the 1985 *Real Decreto de Ordenación de la Educación Especial*.[4] Both laws were fundamental landmarks in the search for educational solutions for students labelled at the time as 'special education' pupils. The so-called process of school integration in Spain had its origin in these measures as well as in the educational decentralisation[5] under way at the time.

My experience and professional development are closely linked to those early days of Integration. After getting a degree in Pedagogy, my first professional experience was in Galicia as part of an External Support Team (also known as a Multi-Professional Team). Eleven External Support Teams were created in 1980 (all experimental) and distributed throughout the country as part of a support infrastructure designed to anticipate and aid the implementation of laws and regulations on Integration. These teams were made up of professionals in the fields of medicine, psychology, pedagogy and social work. They spread throughout Spain in 1982 following the passing of the Social Integration Act for the Handicapped. The principal mission assigned to these teams was to promote the incorporation of students from the special education system into mainstream tracks and, once there, to support their integration in regular classrooms. This was by no means an easy task. At this time in Spain there was a *de facto* double education system: *General* Education and *Special* Education. Although all schools (both *special* and *general*) have theoretically always been under the jurisdiction of the Department of Education, in practice it was the National Institute of Special Education, a separate organization under the aegis of the Department of Education, that regulated and normalized all issues related to special education. All those students labelled as 'deficient' attended *Special Education Schools*. Only a small minority attended special education classrooms full time, starting in the late 1970s with a handful of mainstream *general education* schools.[6]

Working with the External Support Team was, in and of itself, an opportunity to confront and question my recently acquired university education, which had promoted a deficit-centred, individualised approach to the needs of students assuming they would be segregated in terms of educational mechanism and presented a view of professionals as technical experts. My experience with the Team served also to channel and develop some of the ideas and projects forged with Professor Zabalza in the university that had shaped my thinking: the French May of 1968 or the Italian anti-psychiatry movements and their emphasis on recognising rights common to all people, criticising totalitarian institutions and rejecting views based on technical and scientific answers to human problems. Today, I recognise those ideas as being key in the evolution of my understanding of Integration and the conditions required for its development.

However, the educational reality in schools had little or nothing to do with the ideas that I had been coming to terms with. In-service teacher education was practically non-existent, technical and individualistic work patterns were the norm, classrooms were overcrowded (around 40 students per class in Primary Education), and public schools were virtually incapable of developing and managing their own ideology and values systems. For example, the curriculum used in schools at this time (developed in the Seventies during the Franco dictatorship), was a tightly controlled, pre-set curriculum that left a very small margin for action by schools and teachers themselves, who all too often acted as mere executioners of external guidelines. Schools were therefore quite homogeneous, organised around the principle until then unquestioned of dividing and grouping students according to learning capacity and speed. I clearly remember the debate and constant dialogue with schools and teachers, with whom we 'negotiated' the incorporation, almost always partial, of certain students into mainstream schooling. Back then integration was based on a child by child and teacher by teacher approach. I believe I'm right in saying that in those days, all over the country, those of us committed to promoting the Integration process were focused on guaranteeing the right of those children classified as 'special education pupils' to receive schooling in mainstream schools. Special education students in mainstream classrooms were quite ostracised in those early years and the dilemma of how to incorporate them into established school cultures was a major concern. The response to diversity in the classroom, the question of homogeneity and the celebration of diversity would not be a focus of concern until the late 1980s, following the launch of the National Plan for School Integration in 1985 and the advent of the documents and ideas clearly promoted from the National Centre for Special Education Resources.

Other students belonging to a variety of different fringe groups were experiencing very similar situations of inequality. Gypsy children, the largest ethnic minority in Spanish schools in the 1980s, were placed in separate *schooling groups* (always under the auspices of the Department of Education). Economically underprivileged students were generally channelled (by way of different control mechanisms, including exclusive entrance exams for the different education phases) towards compensatory education and devalued professional education tracks. By today's standards these education models were discriminatory and perpetuated segregation and inequality among students.

My thinking during this period was, without a doubt, influenced by all these circumstances I have mentioned. Yet much more influential was the intensity of the personal and professional relationship that, as a member of the External Support Team, I shared with the schools and teachers who on a daily basis faced the challenge of admitting disabled students to their classrooms. Efforts to get these students to participate came later, as has already been pointed out. The single most fruitful source of learning for me was listening to teachers talk about challenges, fears and hurdles they faced; trying to understand the situation from their point of view, discussing and participating in new initiatives and taking steps to deal with the new reality in the classroom.

Soon the solid practical focus of my career found an interesting counterpart in a fledgling research experience on the Integration process in the mid to late 1980s, first at the University of Santiago de Compostela and later as a Lecturer at the University of

Seville. In the first case, research was carried out in Galicia as part of a study on teachers' views on Integration in its first year of development (Parrilla, 1986). The second research project consisted in a unique case study of diversity in one school in Seville over the course of three years (Parrilla, 1990). Most remarkable in both studies today is the clear break with more traditional models of education research in a decade dominated by positivist analysis and study models for special education research. Both studies reflect the increasingly open-minded approach to *research into teaching and learning* characteristic of the 1980s in Spain, with a clear shift towards ecological and interpretative models of research. Secondly, these research projects owe their relevance to the fact that, focusing on the process of Integration, they examine special education from the standpoint of General Education and mainstream teaching approaches, thus distancing themselves from the medical and psychological models that had dominated the field of special education until then.

My research activity embraced international policies and the writings and reflections on Integration of a wide range of authors from different cultures, setting the stage for conceptual, methodological and comparative analyses of the ideas born of practical experience. From then on I was convinced of the need for collaboration (both between professionals and agencies, and between those working in practical and more theoretical settings) in the creation of a knowledge base capable of supporting steps towards an educational response to diversity. The following key points serve as the canvas for a rough sketch of my thoughts on education at that time:

- The degree to which a 'culture of equity' was deep-rooted in my thought: though my first professional point of reference was an individual and technological response model to student needs, the ideological and political character of any response to such needs is clear from this first phase of professional development. During this phase I came to consider Integration an inalienable right. This stand involved setting aside classic misgivings about Special Education versus Integration in terms of efficiency, and instead, setting out to meet the challenge of how to facilitate and improve the Integration of all students.
- Integration in schools as a new educational model: at the close of this phase I undoubtedly identified, to some extent, with a number of the most radical positions of the 1980s, criticising proposals for Integration that encouraged a view of mainstream schools as 'special' and advocating the merging and restructuring of 'special' and 'general' education (Stainback and Stainback, 1984). I considered that Integration, in this context, would boost participation among all students in the community as Booth and Potts pointed out in 1983 in a book which served as an important theoretical milestone for me in the early steps along my path towards formulating and consolidating my concept of Integration.
- The primacy afforded teachers in the Integration process: the orientation I received in schools, along with my own research, helped me come to understand teachers as reflexive professionals, actors and 'thinkers' within their profession, fully equipped to make decisions, design and create contexts for learning specifically tailored to the unique characteristics of each school and group of students. I must point out here

that all these events took place at a time when teaching research was opening up to new models. Those models referred to as *Ecological teaching and learning analyses*, especially, as well as such new approaches as the *Teacher Thinking Paradigm* were adopted and put into practice by a considerable number of colleagues and universities.

- The institutional character of the Integration process: If teachers do indeed enjoy a privileged position within the process of integration, it is the direct result of efforts made on the part of the school as a whole rather than by the isolated efforts of individual teachers. My interest in linking integration in schools to more far-reaching institutional and organisational development, especially to those frameworks that encourage and support approaching Integration processes from a position of co-operation, is also defined in this stage of my professional development.

- The rejection of professional assessment and support models dependent on the intervention of experts, with special aversion towards psychological and clinical models: during my years with the External Support Team, the systemic reasoning of the Italian scholar Mara Selvini Palazzoli, who I had discovered in my final year at university, became the point of reference for a new way of relating among professionals as well as for analysing problematic situations. This new model linked up nicely with proposals suggested by the recent Warnock Report (1978) for analysing and comprehending Special Educational Needs (SEN) in the United Kingdom.

- The potential for collaboration among professionals, the stimulus for what would become one of the most recurring concerns of my career: in these early years the importance of teamwork, of working through and across disciplinary and professional borders in order to collaboratively respond to the complex situations inherent to educating students in mainstream contexts, became all too evident.

- The new-found importance of qualitative education research due to a deeper understanding of the possibilities research offers for improving educational practices, enhancing professional growth among teachers participating in the research, and building bridges linking education theory and practice.

A New Culture in a New Educational and Social Setting

Change, that emblematic concept by which the Socialist Party had come to power in 1982, served as a backdrop for a variety of initiatives that gradually transformed conditions and lifestyles across Spain. In 1990, the General Education System Layout Law (LOGSE)[7] marks the end of special education as an independent educational system, merging special education and mainstream education in a single educational system under a Common Curriculum (*Diseño Curricular Base*). This same law regulates the transformation of all stages and levels of the Spanish education system, extending compulsory schooling from 14 to 16 years of age and calling for a comprehensive educational system.[8]

The LOGSE represents a broader framework from which to approach the issue of diversity. In fact the law really goes out of its way to set up and defend comprehensive education in compulsory Secondary Education (12–16 years old) as well as to pave the way for an acceptance of Integration as intrinsic to the education system, at least during compulsory schooling stages. To this end the LOGSE employs a series of specific measures aimed at paying attention to diversity, including Curricular Adaptations or adjustments to fine-tune the Curriculum to student needs. The Law itself coins expressions like 'educational attention to diversity' which gain popularity in Spain and are used in reference to heterogeneity and difference among students not only due to Special Educational Needs but due as well to socio-economic, cultural, gender or other factors, for which schools must be prepared.

Needless to say, with such a hefty mandate, the beginning of the decade was rather stimulating. In vast sectors of the education community, the atmosphere was ripe for changes backed by the LOGSE's strong theoretical and ideological base. It was not easy to foresee at the time, however, the difficulties involved in getting such changes off the ground. Early barriers included, among others, a lack of support for teachers and schools in terms of training, guidance, resources, improved working conditions, funding and feedback opportunities.

What stands out, looking back at this period in my own career is steady academic progress immersed in the fluctuating tides of change swaying society and the Spanish education system of the day. The issue of change in schools is precisely one of the main research areas I had taken up in my professional field as well as in collaboration with a research group[9] I was in at the University of Seville. Our line of research and the development of our research group directed by Professor Marcelo, renowned for his noteworthy contributions to qualitative research methodology unquestionably provided an ideal context for learning, research and professional interaction of great importance in my first years at the University.

CURRICULUM AND INDIVIDUAL STUDENTS: FOCAL POINTS FOR GLOBAL CHANGE

During this period schools worked to replace rigid academic practices left over from the prior pedagogic model with fresh ideas such as Constructivism, autonomous learning on the part of students and interactive teaching methods and procedures. The LOGSE-based curricular model places clear emphasis on teacher participation in planning and designing adaptations to the Common Curriculum according to the particular context and needs of the school, classroom and individual students in question. This idea is especially pertinent when responding to diversity, where it is necessary to think of the regular teachers as people committed to participating in the adaptation of teaching approaches to the individual needs of students and classrooms. The challenge teachers face is a tough one: there is neither a consolidated tradition to fall back on, nor adequate training and feedback to look forward to on their quest to bring about this transformation.

Perhaps the greatest challenge of the decade involved precisely that: transforming the curriculum. The question of how to make Individual Curricular Adaptations (ICA) for students spearheaded response to diversity throughout this period. Despite the support of schools and teachers for the process of tailoring the curriculum, making ICA remained a highly bureaucratic administrative activity. Though aided by the use of documents and forms filled out by teachers, making ICA is considered a perfunctory chore, far from requiring detailed feedback. The ICA-making process has become symbolic of the overall response to diversity in schools. The more adaptations a school makes, the more it is regarded as responding to diversity. Reflection on the Common Curriculum (rather than individual adaptations), or on the institutional, ideological, professional or methodological changes needed in order to articulate an institutional response to diversity is all too often put on the back burner. In the end, the paradox is always fulfilled: Curricular Adaptations designed to facilitate an even-handed response to diversity end up blocking such response, becoming goals for the future rather than the everyday tools they were originally intended to be.

Therefore, only insignificant alterations to life in the classroom occur as student diversity increases. I am convinced that progressive adaptation of the Common Curriculum is being attempted at the school level by way of Curriculum projects unique to each school, though some studies (e.g. Arnaiz, 2003) argue such adaptation is characteristically very bureaucratic. Be that as it may, adaptation measures at the school level undoubtedly tend to atrophy as we move towards individualised response mechanisms in the classroom. Though the number of students per classroom has decreased (in the 1990s down to an average of 25 students per classroom) and resistance to the presence of children, labelled throughout the decade as 'Integration students', has faded considerably, their participation tends to be limited to individualised assignments versus working in groups with others. Such students are rarely included in the general dynamic of the mainstream classroom, which, as a rule, only partially adapts to meet situations of diversity.

Around this point in my career, I participated directly in several interesting projects that addressed some of these issues. In one case, a 15-person team (Support Teachers, External Support Team members, etc.) made up a task group which I co-ordinated. For 2 years, on a bimonthly basis, we discussed the question of a Common Curriculum and how to adapt it to diverse student groups. We followed action research methodology: a cycle of reflection, discussion and analysis within the task group followed by onsite fine-tuning in the participating teachers' places of work, in turn analysed and evaluated by the group.

In the first place, this activity lead us to consider the importance of questioning and analysing our own practices, ideology and methods (in Support services and schools alike) as well as analysing the curricular framework itself as a first step in adapting the curriculum to situations of diversity. Second, the collaborative support we were able to offer one another throughout this process of mutual self-analysis and feedback proved to be a decisive factor when facing the inherent uncertainty of searching for and trying out new ways of working together and redefining professional roles. Third, the unequivocal endorsement of an institutional support model translated as a clear message to the education community that the task group rejected the deficit-based expert dependent model, prevalent in schools up till then. Finally, work carried out within the group itself prompted us to propose, design and develop an ecological analysis model for the classroom, providing a deeper understanding of the needs of students and teachers in situations of diversity.[10]

Throughout the 1990s this was a hot topic in academic circles involved in developing a Common Curriculum. A review of publications in the last 10 years proves this beyond any shadow of a doubt. A case in point is the fact that a significant number of talks presented at national conferences on University and Special Education have focused on the topic of Curricular Adaptation processes. As in the practice, however, attention within universities has backslid towards individual rather than global approaches to diversity due to a tendency to focus excessively on the *process* of adaptation itself, rather than in-depth reflection on, and discussion of, the Common Curriculum.

INCLUSIVE EDUCATION ON THE HORIZON

Yet another indication of the changes taking place in the 1990s is the incorporation of the term *Inclusion* to university research agendas and lists of topics for discussion by professionals of what had till then been referred to as *Special Education*. As could be expected, however, this change was neither immediate nor applied across the board. Influential special education circles approach inclusive education with caution and scepticism.[11] To some degree the Inclusive Education model, well known in Spain following the 1994 UNESCO Conference in Salamanca and the international AEDES (Special Education Association of Spain) conferences held in Murcia in 1995 and Madrid four years later, met with resistance reminiscent of the opposition the concept of Integration had received back in its day. All three conferences were key milestones in the diffusion of the concept of inclusive education and were attended by a large number of professionals representative of different views on social and educational inclusion in a variety of countries. In Spain, however, still largely immersed in debate over the pros and cons of integration, this line of work is still poorly developed.

In my case, these new ideas supporting inclusion found fertile ground in what would be a constant throughout my evolution as a professional: an open-minded approach to other academic forums where reflection, research and debate on the exciting possibilities offered by inclusive education were taking place. In addition to the habitual opportunities the University offered for international exchange, especially germane in the progression of my thought during this period are my travels and academic stays in places such as the Open University (UK), as well as universities in Bologna (Italy) and South America. The milestone for me in terms of exposure to the key concepts of the moment such as Social and Educational Inclusion, and their evolution both at home and abroad, was my stay at Open University in 1994 alongside Patricia Potts. Access to a variety of collaborative support models (in line with results we had obtained and needs we were facing in our own research) originated in my efforts to discover and document alternative ways of thinking about, planning and organising education and support structures in schools, taking all students into account. In fact projects creating and developing Teacher Support Teams (TST) in Seville area schools[12] are just one example of an ongoing collaboration with Professor Harry Daniels (at the University of London at the time) and proof of the possibilities for collaboration among different teachers, institutions and even countries to come up with flexible, centralised approaches for the demands of diversity.

Mid-way through the 1990s it started becoming more and more evident that the Government's undernourished finance and support structure was falling short of its goal to promote transformation in schools. The enormous effort invested in designing and setting up the reform was not backed up sufficiently during the implementation phase. Some voices from academic circles warned of an overemphasis in the LOGSE on the psychological dimension at the expense of a sociological dimension (Varela, 1999). Others highlighted the importance of understanding schools as educational communities and approaching Inclusion at the school, rather than solely at the curricular level.[13]

Inclusive education research in Spain was limited at this time to a handful of universities and research groups. Noteworthy research aimed at promoting Inclusive Education includes collective contributions from task groups at several Spanish universities, in addition to a number of individual contributions. Arnaiz's research at the University of Murcia, where she has supervised studies for years, has centred on the process of Inclusion specially, but not only, in the case of groups discriminated against or segregated for ethnic or cultural reasons (Arnaiz, 2003; Arnaiz y De Haro, 2003). The Universidad Autónoma de Madrid has made some important contributions including a Spanish translation of the British Index of Inclusion and a series of studies shedding light on student and teacher perceptions of building schools for all (See: Echeita, 1994; Echeita and Sandoval, 2002 among others). López Melero at the University of Málaga proposes a line of research centred on the introduction of research projects in schools in order to facilitate building an exclusion-free school (López Melero, 2004). The University of Cantabria has been the stage for a controversial debate led by Susinos and Rojas (2004) questioning the role of Support services in the University. Susinos co-directs, with the University of Seville (Parrilla and Susinos, 2003) a biographical study of social exclusion processes in young people. Very well known and noteworthy, as well, is the ongoing research in Catalonia and the Basque Country within the framework of the 'Comunidades de Aprendizaje' (Learning Communities) Project, which for over 10 years now has managed to take root in an ever-growing number of Primary and Secondary schools. The goal of this innovative project is, through the creation of school networks, to transform traditional schools into *Education Communities* for all (Elborj *et al.*, 2001). Our task group at the University of Seville (with the special collaboration of Carmen Gallego) is also committed to this line of thought, as evidenced by the variety of different studies referred to in this chapter.

Despite these isolated efforts, the overall situation at this time was anything but optimistic. When the Partido Popular came to power in 1996, a change of course was felt in the air. The second half of the decade has been characterised by backslides in opinion that aggravate and intensify the difficulties schools face dealing with diversity, and to a certain extent question and discredit the professional mandate of schools and teachers to respond to diversity. There was talk of the need to return to technical models of professional development, traditional values, and specialised organisation in education.

Nevertheless, the work of those above mentioned groups and individuals that consider inclusive education an inalienable right, not subject to the ups and downs of political fluctuations, persisted in a context in which confusion tainted every step taken and objective met, and uncertainty clouded the horizon. In my case, in the second half of the 1990s I led a series of local research and teacher education projects, which had a clear focus on the practical experiences of Greater Seville schools and which aimed at encouraging and participating in non-exclusive educational processes.[14] Though they differed in scope and duration, the common thread linking these projects is the search for ways to empower inclusive practices in schools. In one case we worked closely with Support professionals from all over the Province of Seville over the course of one school year; in another (from 1996 to the present), our focus was on small groups of teachers in the process of developing a collaborative support network within the school (Teacher Support Teams); a third project brought us into contact over a 3-year period with a vast number of experiences resulting from attempts at both Primary and Secondary stages to approach situations of diversity from the standpoint of Inclusion. All three projects meet at least two conditions I consider basic to facing and dealing with the challenges of inclusive education: (1) collaboration among professionals and (2) networking or co-operation among educational services and institutions. Hence the fact that in the three projects mentioned there is clear collaboration on the part of the university, schools, teacher centres and peripheral educational services.

While working on these projects we've run into hurdles and learned how to work around them, and along the way we've unearthed some of the keys that open the door to an education for all. Among the hurdles are the difficulties involved in transforming classrooms and whole schools away from individualised models exclusively centred in a curriculum for response to diversity; the need to approach diversity on the classroom and school level rather than groping for individual student-based solutions; the urgency of resolving student needs from a social and not merely from an individual perspective. Second, working on these projects has allowed us to verify first hand the inherent intricacy of any attempt to transform traditional models of therapeutic support into non-exclusive educational support models. Even in cases where the general atmosphere was favourable towards such a change we didn't have the faintest idea how or where to begin. Here the role of the TSTs in the school was a decidedly favourable factor. Finally, participation in the projects brought to light the always complex nature of professional relationships among members of different educational services as a potential stumbling block to Inclusion in schools. Equitable relationships among peers seems to be a prerequisite that professionals must learn (it is not just a simple question of the right attitude), and is an issue that can meet with much resistance, given the prevailingly exclusive, expert-based system characterising the world of education (especially in this case among External Support Team members and teachers, but likewise among Support teachers and Regular teachers, between the university and schools, etc.).

As a result of working on these projects we were also able to draw the following ideas:

- Transformation projects are more adaptable and viable when linked to specific situations and in direct response to real needs, resulting in steady progress in the form of 'baby steps' that, in the long run, tend to reshape reality itself.
- The institutional characteristics of teacher education projects must be retained and we should necessarily approach training for change from within the school. We should make sure to invite all education professionals, cordially and unconditionally,

to participate, in the hopes of facilitating integrated collaborative work and co-operation among teachers.

- Broadening our understanding of diversity to include students with a wide range of characteristics, not only students labelled as having SEN, and working towards understanding them more fully in terms of the social framework where they grow and develop, is an enrichment.
- It is crucial to acknowledge the practical knowledge that schools represent as well as to recognise the possibility of knowledge generating structures arising from professional collaboration among peers. Work done by Teacher Support Teams confirms and strengthens the latest research that understands schools as both learning and support communities.
- We have the obligation to delve into, and advance our understanding, of the different types of collaboration already in full swing in some schools, including *inter-institutional* (collaboration among schools), *inter-professional* (between education professionals), *inter-agency* (between the school and peripheral educational and social services), *inter-student* (collaboration among students in the classroom, during the learning process or in the social dimension), *inter-community* (between the school and members of the family or community).
- Theory and practice, research and action must go hand in hand if headway is to be made in the construction of a knowledge base capable of freeing schools and teachers from depending on external sources of support and aiding in their autonomy.
- The imperative to make the voices and actions of those groups and individuals that are potential victims of exclusion, the key ingredients of any and all processes that strive to be inclusive. An analysis of our own work at this time makes all too evident the grave error inherent in not putting the participation of those experiencing exclusion at the forefront of any attempt to approach and initiate the inclusion process. This idea, linked to the social interpretation of inclusion, is central in our present approach to understanding and implementing principles and processes of inclusion.

On the whole, for the academic community, education services, professionals and teachers, the 1990s represented a phase full of transformations and successive changes in processes which were often still just getting off the ground. I participated both on the personal and professional level, consolidating and expanding my initial commitment to the concept of integration to eventually adopt the precepts of Inclusive Education. Belonging to a stable research group dedicated to exploring responses to diversity, a period of international open-mindedness to discussing and developing models for inclusive education, and a strong anchor in local educational development projects were key pillars in my professional evolution. The expression 'think global, act local', in a nutshell, reflects my own view of the direction I was moving during this period. For me, 'think global, act local' is an attempt to express how to think and build an inclusive education knowledge base together. I consider access to other socio-political and educational approaches, other experiences and views of Inclusion in alternative contexts and realities to be undoubtedly enriching when the knowledge acquired serves as a catalyst for self scrutiny, contrast and constructive criticism of ones own concepts, values and positions. Knowledge thus acquired is powerfully effective when responding to our most immediate local reality, avoiding problematic excess, localism, and neutralizing colonial attitudes derived from uncritical application of notions about others. Perhaps most importantly, contrastive knowledge building allows and facilitates participation in projects which have practical, concrete repercussions in local social reality.

All of these factors resulted in my distancing myself ideologically at the end of the decade from the increasingly conservative positions of the Education Administration, even in my own Autonomous Community where the Socialist Party is still in power, as it progressively dismantled the weak structure supporting transformations made by the LOGSE. Teachers' Centres, crucial to these transformations, suffer the damaging effects of severe cutbacks in staff, teacher education policies backslide into traditional models of in-service training, External Support Teams lose their role in promoting change (some Autonomous Communities actually eliminate them completely), the new university curriculum maintains highly segregated teacher education models for would be special education specialists, etc. The mass media, without appropriate external evaluation, paint an exaggerated picture of defeat for the LOGSE reforms. It is my impression that, at the close of the decade, all efforts and advances, some of which have been very important, are shadowed and at times hidden completely due to the influence of political, social and educational pressure groups that make up Spanish society in the twenty first Century.

FACING THE FUTURE: THE PRESENT CHALLENGES

As we have seen thus far, education in Spain today is immersed in a fluctuating transformation process and the reforms taking place can be described, for the most part, as regressive. All this at a time when Spanish society is itself going through important changes on its path towards becoming a more plural society. The profile of a new social structure where diversity is more and more visible is beginning to emerge, exemplified by a notable increase in the presence of citizens from other minority cultures. Other factors include the reduction and diversification of the traditional family, advances in Women's Rights and basic changes in the very way we live. Today more than ever we tend to cluster around large urban centres.

The ideological conservatism of ideas and provisions for educational responses to diversity built into the 2002 Educational Quality Act[15] is irrefutable. It is also true, however, that the law has not yet triggered any real changes in school practices (not enough time has gone by for things to evolve out of the legislative stage). Nevertheless, a regressive tendency is evident in efforts to guarantee quality in education by establishing educational itineraries and differential tracks for certain groups of students. Also, the language being used is a throwback to classificatory, labelling terminology and there are unquestionable cutbacks in the autonomy schools have reached in recent years. Professional specialisation is promoted as the best way to respond to diversity, while the definition of inclusive education is restricted and simplified to the point of reducing it to 'the right to schooling in a mainstream school'. There is then, in this new law, an important dissociation between educational policies and society, and certainly between the recent past and the path the law is taking.

Academic and practical spaces, among others, are feeling the tensions and facing the difficulties of the current situation. I am not so sure the concept of inclusive education is going anywhere at all on academic and professional fronts. Despite possible increases in the number of people using Inclusive Education-type language in the workplace, authentic advances are generally speaking almost undetectable (repetitious, stereotype-riddled discourses are repeated over and over, never forging new paths or routes leading away from empty rhetoric). A considerable number of gaps in the literature on inclusive education are brought to light in the recent review of publications on the topic in Spain (Susinos, 2002). Talking about inclusive education – often put down as overly theoretical or utopian (in the sense of unreachable or impractical) – is more and more going against the grain (there is less resistance to Social Inclusion discourse). In its place, limited one-track thinking is legitimised and installs itself and education (special) as 'the only "natural" way of going about things'.

My impression is that *Inclusion*, as a concept, has become an over generalised catchphrase (used to refer to all people, all professionals, all layers of society, all types of education, all walks of life …), interpreted and understood differently and often contradictorily, depending on the group or institution in question. In my opinion, some of the most common misconceptions regarding Inclusion in Spain today are as follows:

- Linking Inclusion to certain groups or collectives. To speak of *Inclusion* in education all too often means centring discourse on one given group of people or another rather than on the more universal process intrinsically implied by this term. I'm afraid we are in danger in our country of associating Inclusion with the named SEN collective due to the use – and abuse – of the term among 'Special Education professionals'. Paradoxically, by the same token, other education professionals don't take students identified as having special educational needs into account when they refer to groups at risk of exclusion. So, the terms *inclusion* and *exclusion* are used inappropriately to the extent that we forget or ignore that both processes imply and affect all individuals and all groups rather than one section or part of them.
- Second, I believe that among academics the use of the term *community*, so crucial to a working understanding of *inclusion*, stems from *exclusive* thinking, in the sense that a very traditional view of community persists, maintaining – implicitly or explicitly – that both the school and surrounding local community are patrimony of the dominant group. Hence the tendency to speak of 'including others', 'taking in others', 'welcoming them', etc. in the existing community rather than collectively and collaboratively building and shaping a new unique community for and by all. We speak of *inclusion* without a clear recognition of the fact that all people belong to the community of origin, which they form a part of. As a result, all too frequently social and educational inequality is perpetrated through situations and practices of domination in the name of *inclusion*.
- Third, I believe that in many studies and legislative propositions, the concept of *participation* is watered down to mere 'activism'. According to this line of thought,

simply guaranteeing a role to those who access a given community is sufficient. This means keeping people busy, ignoring or avoiding analysis of exclusion risk factors inherent in certain proposals (frequently changes to the Curriculum, individualised programmes or certain education tracks and options fulfil this function). Thus we fail to guarantee equal participation on a common project designed to come up with answers to people's needs. Needless to say, we tend to altogether forget the reciprocity that should be the cornerstone of all inclusive relationships.

- As in academic circles, in school communities with notable exceptions there is no shortage of hurdles to making progress towards Inclusion. In schools there is gravitation towards so-called 'safe ideas'. A large sector of education professionals (especially in high schools) seems to celebrate the advent of the Educational Quality Act as a triumph for Inclusive Education inasmuch as it organises and classifies diversity. Along these lines, we detect a certain relapse to practical approaches and disdain for ideological questions, showing a lack of critical thought. On the other hand a great number of professionals are disappointed and disenchanted with the way changes have been occurring and the direction things are going. Not even the statistical surveys (Moriña, 2002) offer clear results on which students and how many of them are receiving attention, support or special aid. Though such surveys do confirm a spectacular increase in students in mainstream schools, services and other regular spaces throughout the 1990s, they do not shed enough light on current trends. Some Autonomous Communities are considering the possibility of reopening Special Schools closed in past decades, and there is some talk of new categories of 'integration' or, more precisely, new forms of segregation.

- The advent of this new culture, which questions the achievements and values of the previous stage and promotes a set of educational values that are very closely linked to market ideologies, competition between schools and even among students, calls for further critical reflection and the development of new approaches to diversity and equity in education. Still fully immersed in the uncertainty of the moment and therefore in a risky position to speculate about the future, I close this chapter by outlining some challenges I believe must be addressed in my country and which, in many ways, reflect my most recent concerns.[16]

- Broaden the scope and meaning of Inclusion. The aims of Inclusive Education cannot be met if all planning and content issues are left up to the existing educational system. Links between social, political and education communities must be reviewed, set up and maintained. It seems to me that a good way of doing so is to conceive inclusive education within the broader framework of each community where it is developed, understanding and fully employing its educating capacity.[17] Inclusive education undoubtedly calls for new social and political pacts based on the coordinated efforts of all those involved, moving above and beyond the dissociated spheres which have served as a fragmented framework for action thus far.

- Denounce exclusion. Perhaps the discourse of inclusion – politically correct, but inefficient in Spain to date – should give way to the analysis of exclusion as a mechanism for change. A good way to modify the non-critical or ingenuous evolution of the concept and application of *inclusion* could be in-depth analysis of the internal sources and processes of exclusion in both individual schools and the educational system as a whole. In doing so we would pave the way for much needed analysis of implications and consequences hidden in the mire of certain educational practices and models; practices such as different education tracks or eliminatory exams, etc., described as 'inclusive', yet which do little more than validate the status quo within the system and perpetuate segregation and situations of inequality among students.

- Studies on inclusion should not be designed nor carried out under the sole influence of self-interested research or academic trends, divorced from practice. Rather, such studies should be undertaken out of a deep respect for the needs and interests of schools and teachers, assuming a solid commitment to contributing to improving Inclusion processes. This should lead us to approach our research from a standpoint which recognises the need to study and deal with inclusion processes from an angle where the real protagonists teachers, students, members of the education community are in the foreground. This outlook must be maintained throughout the entire research period, embracing the possibility of mutual learning and enrichment, and thus inverting the vertical or hierarchical relationships that typically dominate in research processes.

- Reaching an understanding of inclusion and exclusion in the terms I have set forth above implies acknowledging the need to analyse not only processes of construction but the personal, subjective dimension as well. This means we must analyse the very experience of exclusion itself, the way exclusion is interpreted by those being excluded, the opinions and perspectives these people – immersed in processes of exclusion for belonging to marginalized groups – have of their situation. Most definitely we must free ourselves of the unfortunate habit of observing inclusion issues through the prism of dominant professional and theoretical (politicians, doctors, psychologists, teachers, caretakers, social workers, etc.) models alone, and work towards adopting more democratic, participative attitudes. This will allow us to come to the realisation that the voices of the excluded should not only be heard when analysing inclusion processes, but those excluded themselves should actively participate in the broader processes of decision making.

- Collaborate to generate knowledge about inclusion. The inherent obstacles and complexity of inclusive education lead me to persist in that conceptualisation of knowledge-building that emphasises its critical and dialogical character, underlining its foundation in 'conversation' and debate between theory and practice, as well as its support for the shared construction of both discourses and professionals. This implies advancing past simplistic renderings of collaboration (as mere teamwork) or misunderstood developments (that tend to lead to overlapping tasks), to forge ahead towards collaboration among diverse professionals and agencies, teaming up services with different professional status and disciplinary affiliation.

- Actively resist the forces behind exclusion. We have the obligation to defend the position that inclusive education is not a technical education model which can be displaced by other models of response to diversity as formal and authorised (even legally) as they may be that present themselves as more efficient or ideologically neutral. On these terms, we will have an opportunity to learn to be citizens in a society that recognises and includes differences while excluding inequality. *Inclusion*, as some authors have pointed out, is a way of life, a way of building and being in society.

- The last challenge on my list has to do with the need to rebuild a workable inclusive education knowledge bank. The first step requires opening our work up to related ideological and practical movements in other countries and regions. This means that those engaged in inclusive education need to enter an international debate to share in more global perspectives on common issues and mutual problems (with other professionals, politicians or excluded collectives) as well as to find new approaches and, most importantly, to have access to much needed tools for self-criticism and analysing one's own theories and thinking. In order to achieve this we must create and seize opportunities for discussing, contrasting and collaborating with international research teams and different people with different identities and cultures engaged in the pursuit of an inclusive society. Obviously this is opposite to one-way relationships. I do not mean that a sort of unique thinking should develop, just the contrary. This kind of international interaction will be fertile soil for deeper, richer, more varied thinking. Neither do I wish to imply that everybody should behave as clones of each other, nor simply imitate what is being done in other countries. The enhanced knowledge derived from international debate and inquisitiveness can do nothing but boost our capacity de act and adjust to local realities.

NOTES

[1] Educational Quality Act, 2002.

[2] At the time of this chapter's revision (May 2004), the Spanish Socialist Party had just won the Presidential Elections in Spain. Among other campaign promises the winning candidate pledged to reverse the Quality Education Act passed by the then governing *Partido Popular* during an absolute majority Administration. However, the unexpected suddenness of the political turnover has clearly put a damper on specific steps towards changes in education legislation. Furthermore it has proven very difficult to freeze existing legislation as long as replacement laws still haven't got past the drawing boards. In any case, the Socialist Party has persistently denounced the unequal and discriminatory nature of the Quality Education Act as well as promising to block the implementation this coming school year of the most conflictual and excluding measures endorsed by the Act.

[3] An internationally recognised transition towards democracy took place in the 1980s. Some of the most important milestones and social policies of this period include: political decentralisation in the 17 autonomous communities that make up the Spanish geopolitical map, the advent of the Socialist Party in the Government and the extension of free nation-wide social services.

[4] The 1982 Social Integration Act for Handicapped and the 1985 Royal Ordinance on Special Education.

[5] Gradually the Ministries of Education of the different Autonomous Communities became more and more responsible for their own educational policy. In practice, this entailed decentralisation and diversification when it came to launching the general measures adopted.

[6] Available data from this period, though scarce, reveals over 100,000 students enrolled in Special Education schools and classrooms.

[7] Ley de Ordenación General del Sistema Educativo.

[8] The Spanish education system is divided into four levels: *Educación infantil*, equivalent to Preschool and Kindergarten, is the education phase for very young children between the ages of 0 and 6; *Educación primaria obligatoria*, Primary or Elementary school, is designed for students between 6 and 12 years of age; *Educación secundaria obligatoria*, equivalent to Middle School and the first two years of High School or Secondary school, is for students between the ages of 12 and 16. 16- to 18-year-olds attend *Bachiller*, equivalent to the final two years of Secondary school, prior to college.

⁹ Please visit our website at http//:prometeo.us.es/idea for further information.

¹⁰ As a result of this project a book was published (Parrilla, A: ed., 1996) *El apoyo a la escuela como proceso de colaboración*. Bilbao: Mensajero) representing a final opportunity for joint reflection on the ideas we had been kicking back and forth as a task team over the two years prior to publication.

¹¹ With the logical exceptions, rejection or indifference towards the Inclusive Education model was quite common during this period, both among those educators working predominantly with so-called *individual* and *deficit*-based model and those coming from psychology backgrounds who approached from an individual and clinical concept of human differences.

¹² From 1996 to the present we have carried out a total of four 2-year TST setting up and development projects. These projects were funded by the Ministry of Education (*MEC*) and provincial Teacher's Centres. A book has been published about this experience (Parrilla and Daniels, (1998) (eds): *Creación y desarrollo de Grupos de Apoyo Entre Profesores*. Bilbao: Mensajero).

¹³ Along these lines see the example set forth in: Arnaiz, 1996; García Pastor, 1993; Illán, 1996; León, 1994; Orcasitas, 1997 y Parrilla, 1992.

¹⁴ Three of these projects deserve special mention: Inter-professional Support Groups, 1996; Training and Developing Teacher Support Teams (DGES, 1998); Analysis and Educational Innovations as a Response to Diversity in Greater Seville Area Schools (MEC – CIDE, 1996).

¹⁵ *Ley Orgánica de Calidad en Educación* passed in 2002.

¹⁶ I am currently participating in two projects centred in these issues. One is a joint research project (Parrilla and Susinos) carried out and co-ordinated by the University of Seville and the University of Cantabria. It is narrative-biographical study called, '*The construction of the social exclusion process in young people belonging to groups in conditions of inequality: Indicators of social and educational exclusion and an e-learning teacher education programme'*. The other project aims to spread and use Collaboration as a learning strategy and encourage communication between agencies and education professionals (municipal services, health services, social and schooling services, etc.) in a city in the Seville Province. This project is being carried out within the framework of the international proposal to create and develop *Educating Cities*.

¹⁷ See also Potts, P. (ed.) (2003) *Inclusion in the city*. London, Routledge

REFERENCES

Arnaiz, P. (2003) *Educación Inclusiva en una escuela para todos*. Málaga: Aljibe.

Arnaiz, P. and López de Haro, R. (2003) Alumnos magrebíes en las aulas: analizar y comprender el presente para transformar y mejorar el futuro. *Educación, Desarrollo y Diversidad*, 6, 63–82.

Booth, T. and Potts, P. (eds) (1983) *Integrating Special Education*. Oxford: B. Blackwell.

Echeita, G. (1994) A favor de una educación de calidad para todos. *Cuadernos de Pedagogía*, 228, 66–67.

Echeita, G. and Sandoval, M. (2002) Educación Inclusiva o educación sin exclusiones. *Revista de Educación*, 327, 31–48.

Elborj, C. *et al.* (2001) *Comunidades de aprendizaje: transformar la educación*. Graó.

García Pastor, C. (1993) *Una escuela común para niños diferentes: la integración escolar*. Barcelona: PPU.

Illán, N. (1996) *Didáctica y organización en educación especial*. Málaga: Aljibe.

León, M.J. (1994) *El profesor tutor ante la integración escolar*. Granada: Adhara/FORCE.

Ley de Integración Social del Minusválido, 1982. Madrid. MEC.

Ley Orgánica de Calidad en la Educación, 2002. Madrid. MEC.

Ley Orgánica de Ordenación del Sistema Educativo, 1990. Madrid: MEC.

López Melero, M. (2004) *Una escuela sin exclusiones*. Málaga: Aljibe.

Marchesi, A. (1999) Del lenguaje de la diferencia a las escuelas inclusivas. In J. Palacios and A. Marchesi (eds). *Desarrollo Psicológico y Educación*. Madrid: Alianza.

Moriña, A. (2002) El camino hacia la inclusión en España. Una revisión de las estadísticas de Educación Especial. *Revista de Educación*, 327, 395–413.

Orcasitas, J.R. (1997) La detección de necesidades y la intervención educativa. Educar, 21, 67–84.

Palazzoli, M. (1985) El *mago sin magia*. Buenos Aires: Paidós.

Parrilla, A. (1986) El pensamiento educativo-didáctico del profesor sobre la integración: una investigación cualitativa. Universidad de Santiago: Facultad de Filosofía y Ciencias de la Educación. Tesis de Licenciatura.

Parrilla, A. (1990) La integración escolar como experiencia institucional: Estudio de caso del C.P. Reina Sofía de Morón de la Frontera. Universidad de Sevilla: Tesis doctoral.

Parrilla, A. (1992) *La integración escolar como experiencia institucional*. Sevilla: GID.

Parrilla, A. (2002) *Acerca del origen y sentido de la Educación inclusiva*. Revista de Educación, 327, 11–30.

Parrilla, A. and Susinos, T. (2003) La construcción del proceso de exclusión social en jóvenes pertenecientesa grupos en condiciones de desigualdad: indicadores de exclusión social y educativa. Investigación en desarrollo. Departament of Trabajo y Asuntos Sociales.

Real Decreto 2639/1982, de 15 de Octubre, de Ordenación de la Educación Especial, BOE, 29-10-82.

Stainback, S. and Stainback, W. (1984) A rationale for the merger of special and regular education. *Exceptional Children*, 51, 102–111.

Susinos, T. (2002) Un recorrido por la inclusión educativa española. Investigaciones y experiencias más recientes. Revista de Educación, 327, 49–68.

Susinos, T. and Rojas, S. (2004) 'Notas para un debate sobre los servicios de apoyo en la Universidad Española', Revista de Educación, 334, 56–66.

Varela, J. (1999) Una reforma educativa para las nuevas clases medias. In M. Fernández Enguita (ed.) Sociología de la Educación. *Ariel*, 739–746.

ERIC PLAISANCE

3. THE INTEGRATION OF 'DISABLED' CHILDREN IN ORDINARY SCHOOLS IN FRANCE: A NEW CHALLENGE[1]

The Salamanca Statement of 1994 set out the aims and programme of action for the transformation of a system of education, traditionally referred to as 'special' and specifically designated for children deemed 'deficient'. It adopted the notion of 'inclusive education' as its fundamental principle, rather than embracing the dominant discourse of 'special educational needs'. Similarly, the Luxembourg Declaration (1996) proclaimed the principle of 'schools for all and every one', in order to ensure access for all to education. Other European declarations have stressed the more general principle of non-discrimination. These declarations demand that we critically challenge dominant representations of some groups of children and the way they are referred to, as well as addressing educational and institutional issues.

In this chapter, I shall argue that 'inclusion' is not straightforward but represents a new challenge and the forging of new ways forward to transform schools and perceptions of difference. In other words, inclusion is a process of *construction*, and not something which can be simply 'delivered' or brought about.

The analysis in this chapter is concerned with the French context. I shall try to draw out the contradictions between a commitment to *integration*, which has been officially recognized since the beginning of the 1980s, and the realities experienced by many parents, including the obstacles they come up against. I shall also attempt to present the main arguments put forward in the current debates surrounding the 2005 Law concerning disabled people. Finally I shall suggest some ways forward in support of the changes which are necessary in the present situation.

THE POLICY GOVERNING THE INTEGRATION OF 'DISABLED' CHILDREN IN ORDINARY SCHOOLS: OFFICIAL GOALS AND REAL BARRIERS

The question of special education has a long history in France: 'special' classes or institutions for children presenting various 'problems' (the 1975 and 2005 laws refer to 'disabilities', but the term 'special educational needs' is beginning to be used) are long-established structures gradually set up on the traditional model of what is considered

37

L. Barton and F. Armstrong (eds.), Policy, Experience and Change, 37–52.

'special', that is, on the basis of a perceived 'difference' from ordinary educational establishments (Chauvière and Plaisance, 2000, 2003).

The first departure from this traditional approach was made towards the end of the 1960s and early 1970s. At that time, the critical analysis of a whole range of social institutions (the school in general, but also psychiatric hospitals, the legal system, etc.) also focused on the functioning of institutions designed for children hitherto termed as 'maladjusted'. The question raised was the following: How can we justify an unlimited increase in the number of special classes and institutions, along with an increase in the numbers of specialized personnel, at a time when academic failure and educational difficulties confront a large number of children and, therefore, call into question the performance of the ordinary educational sector? Why continue to imagine an extension of 'special' institutions to try to solve problems that are in fact related to what is 'normal'?

In the 1970s, new frameworks were formulated first in the name of the 'prevention of maladjustments' and then in the name of 'integration'.[2]

The so-called law 'of orientation in favour of disabled persons' dated June 30, 1975 called for actions concerning children, adolescents and adults, with the purpose of providing them with access to ordinary institutions, open to the population as a whole. This position suggested forms of integration in school and society at large, but the same law also decreed an 'educational obligation' towards disabled children that could be addressed by ordinary or by special schooling.

In fact, it was only in the 1980s that the goals and resources related to the integration of disabled children and adolescents in ordinary schools were given more explicit expression in official documents jointly drafted by the Ministry of Education and the Ministry of Social Affairs (circulars published in 1982 and 1983). The principal characteristics are as follows:

- The early integration of a disabled child in an ordinary school environment favours his or her social integration.
- The different institutions – both ordinary schools and specialized institutions ('specialized institutions in the area of prevention, assistance in educational psychology or of a psychological or medical nature') – must evolve in such a way as to favour the decompartmentalization of institutions, to avoid 'phenomena of exclusion and segregation'.
- The integration of disabled children in ordinary schools can take on a variety of different forms: so-called 'individual' integration (presence of a disabled child in an ordinary class); so-called 'collective' integration (presence of a disabled child in a special class existing in an ordinary school); part-time integration in either of these structures.
- A written 'integration project' is drawn up for each child. This project must cover the three aspects of school, education and therapy.
- The different categories of professionals are invited to assume their responsibilities in this transformation process, in collaboration with the parents.
- The specialized healthcare and support services can lend their assistance to the ordinary structures through the adoption of related agreements.

It is clear, however, that 'French-style'*integration*, while appearing well-defined at a formal level, nevertheless suffers from ambiguity because it leads to the coexistence of a wide range of possible structures: integration in the full sense of the word, – that is, in an ordinary class – but also special schooling either in a special class or in a special institution. This ambiguity is all the more apparent when compared with the situation existing outside France, in Italy for example, where integration is a radical, if not revolutionary, measure necessarily implying the presence of disabled children in ordinary classes (with 'support' teachers) and where there exist neither special classes nor special institutions. Unlike this model, the French approach is a 'reformist' model, based on gradual reform, adding the principle of integration to the earlier system of special schooling.

Severe criticism has been levelled at this complex system, which tends to leave the parents of disabled children confused and disoriented. Criticism has chiefly pointed to the fact that official policies which appear to support the integration of disabled children in ordinary schools has led to little concrete application. At the end of the 1990s, an official report (published by the *Inspection générale de l'Education nationale* and the *Inspection générale des Affaires sociales*, the supervisory bodies responsible for monitoring the state education system and social affairs) considers that the integration policy is exposed to a great many obstacles, with the effect that only very few disabled children are included in ordinary classes (no more than 25 per cent of all disabled children of school age, and some of them on half time). This report notes the cases of denied access and exclusion of disabled children outside the ordinary education system, and concludes that 'integration is a delicate process, constantly liable to being called into question'.

It is this situation which led to the development of a plan designed to 'revive' the school integration policy and which was adopted in 1999. This action plan – entitled 'Handiscool' states that disabled children must enjoy the same 'right to school education' as all other young people. On this basis, priority should be given to individual integration in ordinary classes. More precisely, a new official text specified in 1999 that:

- Schooling is a right.
- Acceptance is a duty.[3]

In practical terms, this means:

- That parents are entitled to demand schooling for their child, and that they are entitled to do so as early as the nursery school, which is not a part of compulsory education.
- That schools cannot, in theory, refuse to accept a disabled child. They can only do so when this is justified by specific reasons related to the difficulties presented by the situation. 'Each nursery, elementary and secondary school that does not welcome a disabled child must realize that it is not completely fulfilling its role and must identify the means to do so' [the official text of 2001].

NEW STRUGGLES FOR RIGHTS

Testimonies

A large body of evidence concerning concrete situations shows that earlier official positions, in spite of their declared 'good intentions', have not been entirely successful in terms of their realization. There are multiple cases in which government and local governmental organizations receive numerous demands from parents of disabled children who protest against situations which they find unacceptable. Unfortunately, there are no figures nationally concerning the number and type of these demands from parents. However, the different associations take on board parental demands and raise these regularly and publicly in the hope of exerting pressure on policy makers and those responsible for public services, to work towards finding solutions (Plaisance and Lesain-Delabarre, 2003).

One example of this occurred in Paris in 2002 when a small group of parents demanded the integration of their children *under the right conditions* – including the presence of learning support staff. These were parents of children described as having learning difficulty (although a more exact translation of the term used is 'mental handicap') or who identified as having conditions such as Down Syndrome or autism. These parents were members of a newly formed association – 'Disability – Right to school and social integration' or 'Handicap – Droit à l'école et à l'intégration sociale (HANDEIS)'. This small organization was set up independently from the large associations of parents of disabled children. It was supported by different unions and local organization of parents' organizations and attracted attention in the national media.

In reality, in the face of the failure of negotiations with the education department of Paris the president of the organization was placed in a such position where she saw a hunger strike as the only option left open to her.

A draft agreement was eventually signed with the education department, through the intervention of the Deputy Mayor for Paris, witnessed by representatives of the Ministry of Education, and the Minister representing the Family, Childhood and Disabled People (La Ministre déléguée à la Famille, à l'Enfance et aux Personnes Handicapées).

A further example can be found concerning the national body which groups together local organizations in support of people with Down syndrome. During 2003, a parent who belonged to one of these, gave me a personal account of the difficult situation created by bureaucratic procedures. Her daughter had been accepted for an individual integration placement at a nursery school, but when it came to moving on to the elementary school, the departmental special education commission (the 'commissions' are the local and regional bodies responsible for the arrangements made for children who have special educational needs) designated a special institution, rather than integration in an ordinary school. The parents refused this placement and demanded continuity and integration for their daughter. Pending an outcome of this situation, they kept her at home – a situation which led to the parents being involved in a judicial procedure, because the departmental special education commission reported the case to the public prosecutor on the grounds that they were flouting the law by not sending their child to school. I am not aware of the outcome of this case, but this example testifies to the barriers experienced by parents who seek continued integration in education for their child.

Members of the Association of Disabled People (within the Ministry of Finance) have experienced similar situations. Here again, the testimony of a father illustrates the struggles undertaken for the right to continuity in integration in ordinary education rather than being placed outside the education system, in a medically orientated institution (Institut medico-éducatif). These include formal appeal through the courts for a legal settlement, protests against the measures proposed unilaterally (without consultation) by the authorities, meetings with the educational hierarchy, a seeking after temporary solutions in the private sector. ... What emerges quite clearly is that the channelling of children towards the specialized sector is presented by the administration as being guided by the 'well-being of the child' accompanied by a discourse of parental 'choice', whereas in reality only one 'choice' is available to parents – or rather, a pre-programmed direction which parents are expected to passively accept. The administrative management is thus more powerful than the consideration of the needs of children or the opinions of parents. The fact is that parents who protest are those who are able to protest – those from the middle or upper classes who, thanks to their social capital, do not hesitate to take on the administration. It is no surprise, then, that in these conditions, specialist establishments receive a proportionally higher number of working class children, even taking into account the statistical differences in the number of disabled children in different social classes (Mormiche and Boissonnat, 2003).

The Right to Go to School

In spite of all these difficulties, since the year 2000, there has been a rise in the level of demands for the right to regular schooling. The discussions concerning the revision of the Law of the 30 June 1975 'in favour of disabled people' are indicative of these developments because they reflect a transformation in the social representation of impairment and difference. The 1975 law, Article 4, stated that children and young people are the subject of an 'educational obligation'. This seemingly ordinary – even anodyne – statement opened up extremely important debates at the time when the law was being prepared. Some members of parliament were in favour of a *right to schooling* ('obligation scolaire') rather than a *right to education* ('obligation educative'). Indeed, a number of exchanges had taken place concerning this issue between the Chambre de Députés and the Sénat during the elaboration of various projects in 1974–1975. However, Parliament finally chose the term 'right to education'. In doing so, it embraced the principle that all children are 'educable', regardless of impairment, thus marking a major change and the end of a relatively recent period which lasted until at least the end of the 1960s, in which subtle but nonetheless stigmatising distinctions were made between children who were deemed 'educable', 'semi-educable' and 'ineducable'. The last group of children – those described as 'ineducable' – were the sole responsibility of the Ministry of Health, not Education.

How has the situation evolved in the domain of social representations relating to the education ('scolarisation') of disabled children since 1975? I will now attempt to evaluate the current situation through the perspectives of different social actors (representing unions, associations and administration) which were gathered during meetings of a working party which I chaired between 2001 and 2002 at the ministry responsible for the Family, Childhood and Disabled people (see Assante, 2002). The notion of the right to schooling (i.e. to attend school), in contrast to the right to education (not necessarily in a 'school' at all) was unanimously accepted by all those consulted – a position which is based on a recognition of the fundamental principle of the right of all children to go to school. However, some differences in position emerged among the different delegates. For some parent representatives the right to go to school was interpreted as meaning integration in ordinary schools, indeed even into an ordinary class. For others, the kind of schooling provided could vary, according to the choices of parents or legal guardian, depending upon their perceptions concerning the educational needs of the child concerned. It could even include the possibility of 'schooling' taking place in a specialist setting such as a 'médico-éducatif' establishment, rather than a school. The powerful association of parents – the Union Nationale des Associations de Parents et Amis de Personnes Handicapées Mentales – (UNAPEI), which was established in 1960 and which is roughly translatable as the 'National Union of Associations of Parents and Friends of People with Learning Difficulties' – affirmed 'the right of every child from the earliest age, to education *and* schooling in their own neighbourhood, adapted to meet their potential, with the necessary support to ensure its realization'. However, the same organization added: 'A diverse range of forms of schooling and support must be provided in a rational and coherent system across the country, in order to respond top the specific needs of every child as well as to the expectations of families [working document, November 2001]'.

The organization APAJH (Association pour Adultes et Jeunes Handicapées – the Association for disabled adults and young people), created in 1962, has expressed concern that school integration was presented in official texts as a 'preference' (the 1975, translatable as Act) or as a measure which should be 'favoured' (the 1989 Act), rather than as an 'obligation' (or requirement). For this organization questions relating to disability should be posed not in terms of 'integration' which positions disabled people as outsiders, or as coming in from the outside, but to situate the debate within a critical engagement with the question on non-exclusion. The consequences of such a position in the school context would be to support the right of all children to go to school. This would, of necessity, involve putting into practice in concrete terms the fundamental principle of equality for all (equalization), through support and the adaptation of the environment (see *La revue*, no. 74, June 2002).

A New Law Relating to Disabled People

The socialist government lost the election of 2002 and was not able to bring in a new Bill ('projet de loi') in the parliament proceedings. Under the new rightist government, the process of revision finally entered its parliamentary phase in 2004. At the beginning of 2005, a new Law was passed: 'For equality of rights and opportunity, participation and citizenship for disabled people' (Law no. 2005-102, 11 February 2005). Schooling is treated as part of the broader theme of accessibility for all. In other words, if the law supports across-the-board accessibility for all, it must first establish a school for all. Such an approach is in keeping with international declarations such as the Salamanca Statement referred to above. According to the Law, public education assumes the role of ensuring that disabled children, and those who have medical conditions, have access to 'schooling, vocational training and higher education' (Article 19). They should be enrolled in their local mainstream school nearest to their home, but some children, depending on their 'special needs', could receive their schooling at other establishments, that is, medical-pedagogical establishments, or other services. Furthermore, one of the innovatory aspects of the Law is the reference to the role of higher education which was absent from the 1975 legislation. Higher education establishments must accommodate and teach disabled students, and those who have health problems, through the provision of the necessary support and adjustments.

It is not possible to have a full picture of the ways in which this new law is currently being applied, but it is now possible to state that a disabled child is not only considered to be 'educable' in line with the 1975 Act, but that they are also '*scolarisable*' – that is, *schooling* is appropriate for them. This, of course, raises a new question – that of the *types* of schooling which will need to be diverse, in order to respond to individual differences. As we have seen, the Law maintained the option of schooling taking place in a medical-pedagogical establishment, while at the same time respecting the requirement that children and young people would be enrolled in an ordinary setting: what would be the nature of the relationship between the ordinary establishment and the medical-pedagogical? There are already some examples of collaborative practices, but they are now to become a legal obligation. In fact, the proposal makes no reference to education in terms of 'special' and seems to support the development of services and the provision of specialized support in ordinary social spaces.

Critique of the 2005 Law

The Law contains other aspects which have provoked some serious criticisms. On the one hand, a number of organizations are demanding a clear financial commitment on the part of the State in support of widening participation in the life of the community, and are wary of statements of principle on the part of government which do not lead to sufficient funding. On the other hand, the way in which those people most concerned by the legislation are defined poses a fundamental problem. The 1975 Act was cautious, providing no clear definition of what constituted a disability ('*handicap*') or of the criteria to be used in describing someone as a 'disabled person' (*personne handicapée*); the task of interpretation was left to the specialist teams (*commissions spécialisées*). On the contrary, the 2005 Law puts forward a definition which is very 'traditional' and narrow, focusing entirely on the individual person and their deficits:

> A handicap is present when a person is permanently limited in his/her activities
> or in terms of his/her participation in social life because of an impairment in one
> or more areas – physical, sensory, intellectual or psychological, polyhandicap or
> medical conditions.[4]

International debates and, especially the work of the World Health Organization, have led to a radical reassessment of the concept of 'handicap'. The International Classification of Functioning (Organisation Mondiale de la Santé, 2001) has put forward a scale spreading across three levels: 'organic' functioning (including the bodily anatomy), activity and social participation. The overall functioning of the individual is considered in relation to contextual, environmental and personal factors. The question of impairment is placed within a global framework which relates to the complete range of health issues which concern everybody.

Other models have been suggested, for example, ones which focus on the 'production of disability' (*production du handicap*) and 'risk factors' (*facteurs de risque*) such as that put forward by Pierre Fougeyrollas of Quebec (Fougeyrollas, 1998). In general, however, the evolution of international classification demonstrates broader conceptualizations of the notion of 'handicap' through the importance placed on the environment and contextual factors.

It is in this new context that several French commentators seek to break the mould of traditional conceptualizations of the meaning of 'handicap'. This has led to the introduction of the term 'in position of handicap' in the place of the term 'handicap'. Vincent Assante, representing the Economic and Social Council (Assante, 2000) supports the social model of disability. He argues that the term (*'situation de handicap'*) incorporates the consequences of the environment with an acknowledgement of the capacities for autonomy of a disabled person (*personne handicapée*) and maintains that the 'position of handicap', (*'situation de handicap'*) is always the product of two factors. One of these is the individual impairment, the other arises out of the environmental, cultural, social and statutory barriers which are presented and which the person cannot overcome because of their particular circumstances. In this situation a person experiences discrimination when the necessary adaptations to the environment, such as the presence of a ramp to facilitate the use of wheelchairs, are not in place.

This 'situational' perspective (*perspective 'situationnelle'*) is shared by Henri-Jacques Stiker (in Assante, 2002). He observes that this position:

> in requiring that everybody, from the wider society to the most highly specialized institutions, pay attention to social and environmental factors, [it] supports the cause of (disabled) people and strengthens the exercise of their rights. (p. 62)

Therefore, the notion of Situation of Handicap (*'situation de handicap'*) '... forces society and policy makers to change the environment, and therefore to integrate, rather than focusing on categorization and merely helping individuals.'[5] (p. 65). This conception, open and non-discriminatory, is supported by the National Council 'Handicap: raise awareness, inform, and train'[6] (Kristeva, 2003; Gardou, 2005) of which I am a member. The principal aim of this council is to 'de-insularise' disability and to place the question of disabled people at the heart of debates on citizenship. This involves changing perceptions about disabled people and breaking with the devaluing stigmatization, which they frequently experience. It is for this reason that the Council regards the proposed legislation with some skepticism on the grounds that it is very limited in terms of achieving a transformation in the environment and challenging dominant representations of disabled people.

A resolution of these conceptual issues constitutes the precondition for any discussion concerning institutions, technical measures and financial arrangements. In this respect, it is significant that a group of associations and unions have publicly established the relationship between the term 'situation of handicap' (*'situation de handicap'*) and demands for the right to attend school. In their *Manifesto in support of the right to education of all disabled children and young people*, the group writes:

> We believe that all children and young people have the right to a place in school, including those who are disabled. It is therefore the duty of institutions to create and develop the necessary adaptations, and individual adjustments. ... Together, we demand that recognition of the right to go to School. ... The State is the only possible guarantor for ensuring respect for this right at a national level.[7]

A BETTER ACCEPTANCE OF DIFFERENCES AT THE EARLY CHILDHOOD LEVEL?

The question of the integration of disabled children in schools begins at the nursery school level. It should first be remembered that attendance at this level in France concerns all the 3, 4 and 5-year age groups. In other words, 100 per cent of children aged 3, 4 and 5 are involved in so-called 'pre-elementary' schooling although the parents are not legally obliged to do so. In fact, nursery schools generally command considerable respect from the parents who want their children to benefit from these classes either to round off their socialization skills or to prepare them for subsequent academic study. Nursery schools also boast a long tradition of welcoming a wide variety of children, and it is recognized that the integration of disabled children is easier at this level.

What can we learn from research focusing on the integration of disabled children in nursery schools? We shall restrict ourselves to a few brief comments, without going into elaborate detail:

> Disabled children are more easily accepted in a nursery school class if the teachers have general attitudes of 'teaching tolerance' making it easier for them to accept differences. We can then define a 'child-centred' educational model, focused on the children as individuals, unlike the 'normative' model focused on the learning of rules. What is more, these attitudes are related to more general social attitudes such as the welcome given to foreigners, rejection of the death penalty, etc. (Thouroude, 1997).

Another survey analyses, in cases of integration, the collaborative relationships between the teachers and specialized personnel (present in the school or not) such as teachers of children with special needs, psychologists, doctors, speech therapists, etc. The greater the number of exchanges between specialists and teachers on the question of integration, the more these exchanges focus on the question of classroom practices such as, for example, their transformation to cater for the presence of a disabled child. Teachers in nursery schools state that the fact of including a disabled child has led them to change their behaviour towards, and for the greater benefit of, the other children. This integration has led the teachers to think differently about their practices and, indeed, to modify their classroom practices: for example, the motor difficulties of a disabled child lead them to think about all aspects of motor learning. The presence of the disability then becomes a stimulus for reflection about educational matters that benefit the other children (Belmont and Vérillon, 1997). However, these integration measures should, surely, begin even before nursery school – in the crèches, kindergarten and other child-care settings? What kind of welcome, what level of acceptance, is there in these pre-school settings which, are often referred to as 'welcoming institutions for very young children (i.e. children aged from 0 to 3 years)'? A government decree (1 August 2000) stated: 'The establishments and services for very young children are concerned with the health, their safety and well-being of the children with whom they are entrusted, as well as with their development. They are working towards the social integration of disabled children and those who have a chronic illness ...' Thus, the authorities encourage the accommodation of young disabled children, without making this an obligation. In fact, these measures, on the one hand legitimate certain existing practices in relation to the arrangements made for enrolling children in crèches or kindergartens, on the other hand they reflect the demands of parents who insist that their child should be integrated into an ordinary setting.

In the fieldwork we carried out in 2003, we observed that in relation to very young children there were a number of different forms of integration of children in ordinary settings. We found, for example, arrangements for provision which were put in place very rapidly or, in contrast, provision which had been developed as a global teaching and learning project that included wider issues relating to diversity and impairment; we came across examples in which a group of disabled children were integrated in an ordinary setting, and others which involved a single disabled child (Plaisance, 2005). We also gathered the opinions of some of the most experienced professionals concerning integration practices. For them, integration is fundamentally the outcome of teamwork in liaison with the parents concerned. As Aubert and Morel (1993, p. 188) observe,

> The main thing is that from the start the practice of integrating disabled children in ordinary settings should not be considered self evident but, on the contrary, as involving structural creativity and adaptation in response to the specific difficulties experienced by the child.

This position is radically different from one which adopts what is often a rather moralising discourse of 'integration for the good of everyone', which does not clearly recognise difficulties which may arise, or the means for overcoming them. It is this very insistence on the inventiveness necessary which dominates the analysis of 'collective integration of young disabled children' by Cécile Herrou and Simone Korff Sausse (1999). These authors write about their experiences in a day nursery (*halte garderie*) in Paris, the 'maison Dagobert', where one-third of the total number of children present are disabled – a choice made by the team of people who work there. The authors describe the day nursery as 'a place for the asylum seekers (*les sans papiers*) of the early years'[8] – in other words, it is a place for children who are not accepted elsewhere. These authors demand an end to exclusion, rather than calling for 'integration' which is considered to be a more ambiguous concept for it presupposes that the individual is situated *outside* the ordinary setting.

ANALYSIS OF BARRIERS TO INTEGRATION AND
SUGGESTED IMPROVEMENTS

We have seen that the integration of disabled children raises new problems for ordinary schools or ordinary services and that it encounters a large number of difficulties. What is particularly striking is the contrast between, first, the official position adopted by the State, supported in this by the parents' associations, to impel changes in integration practices in schools and, second, the slow progress made at the level of transformations, and the poor application of the concrete measures related to integration.

Let us sum up these difficulties by offering, for each type of difficulty, a framework for theoretical analysis and prospects for improvements in existing policies and practices.

First Type of Difficulty: The Fear of What is Different

We know that this type of fear of an individual perceived as being different lies at the root of all distancing practices and of exclusion itself. This theme was given a conceptual framework by the American sociologist Erving Goffman (1975) who termed it 'stigmatisation'. In this, he means that in everyday interactions, certain individuals are 'stigmatised' by the others because of their characteristics (race, disability, behaviour, etc.), that is, they are the victims of discredit and disfavour. In the cases where a school refuses to accept a disabled child, the underlying causes are frequently mechanisms of a similar nature: negative perception of the child in question, reduction of his overall identity to the observed disability, without taking account of his potential.

To overcome these fears, we could imagine general awareness-building campaigns having a wider scope than the school, in the mass media, for example. It is just this kind of action which is being undertaken by the National Council 'Handicap: raise awareness, inform, and train'. We could also suggest parents' meetings organized in an attempt to dispel their prejudices (such as the belief that the disabled child will act as a brake on the academic progress of the other children) and to stimulate tolerance for the different 'other' (Herrou and Korf-Sausse, 1999).

Second Type of Difficulty: Institutional Resistance

The aim is not to draw up a list of obstacles created by institutions. The 'sociology of organizations' (e.g. through the work of Michel Crozier, 1963) has made it possible to analyse the barriers to innovation in bureaucratic organizations. In centralized systems having a strict hierarchical structure – which also provide a framework for power struggles – routine becomes dominant and the acceptance of change and innovation becomes difficult. French institutions are still deeply marked by these traditions and by the frequently separate, if not competing, management structures of the public services (e.g. education and health, education and justice, etc.). What is more, French schools remain deeply marked by 'republican' elitism aimed at promoting the 'best' pupils, which inevitably produces a gradual elimination of pupils encountering difficulties as they move through the educational system (Lesain-Delabarre, 2000).

The ability to overcome these practices implies promoting decentralized decisions, local initiatives as well as support for innovation. In the case of the integration of disabled children in ordinary schools, this means a number of things (Mège-Courteix, 1999):

- The direct responsibility of local agents in the definition of how the child will be welcomed and educated. In this respect, the official guidelines published by the central authorities are merely incentives and specify that 'integration projects' should, in each individual case, be defined by local actors (who are also responsible for implementing the project).
- Cooperation between the various local actors, something that is now known as 'partnership'. The question frequently raised is that of support available to help teachers in their everyday classroom activities. Integration implies the adoption of solutions that do not leave teachers isolated in their work. A number of examples can be given: first, the teaching assistants and integration helpers who accompany the disabled pupils in the classroom (in this case, they can directly assist the class teacher) or outside the classroom, in public transport, for example and, second, the special education and healthcare services (SESSAD) which are multidisciplinary services, with several categories of professional (physiotherapists, speech therapists, psychomotility specialists, etc. as well as specialized 'Peripatetic' teachers) specifically responsible for special support for children in the ordinary situations of everyday life and education. Such services can be specialized in a given type of disability (hearing, sight, etc.) and be provided within or outside the school in question.

Third Type of Difficulty: Contradictions Between Professional Cultures

The question raised here reverts back in part to the previous question of the partnership between the different professionals. However, it can be given a stronger conceptual basis in terms of 'professional cultures'. The sociology of professional occupations (Dubar, Tripier, 1998) has focused on the constitution of professions, that is, their definition at a given historical moment, implying training, systems of practices and perceptions, official recognition or even different forms of trade union corporatism. However, the professional framework is also a way for individuals to define themselves, the assertion of their identity.

In these conditions, it is easy to see that the integration of disabled children in an ordinary school environment comes up against differences, indeed contradictions, between different professional cultures. Thus, a 'psycho motor' specialist, a psychotherapist and a teacher do not all perceive the same disabled child in the same way.

Practically, the aim is not to eliminate the professional particularities based on different bodies of recognized knowledge, but to encourage these professionals to work together, to exchange their points of view and expertise. The principal goal is the coordination of various actions. As expressed by Professor Canevaro, an Italian specialist in the integration of disabled children in ordinary schools working at the University of

Bologna, the integration of these children is first of all a question of the integration of the expertise of the adults. From this viewpoint, the training of professionals – either in their initial or subsequent continuing training – should include elements that guide them towards the question of collaboration, towards what certain French psychoanalysts refer to as 'practice involving the several'. Training in partnerships represents a vast programme of work that, generally speaking, has not yet been approached, irrespective of the professional framework.

If we think above all of the way French teachers are trained in the teachers' training colleges, it should be emphasized that what is frequently missing from their courses is their training in disability-related issues and the integration of disabled children. In other words, above and beyond the training of specialized teachers (which has a long history in France and was developed further from in the 1960s) the training of all teachers in this area to make them appreciate that at a given moment in their professional careers, they will undoubtedly have to welcome a disabled child in their class.

CONCLUSION: BEYOND ABSTRACT MORALISM, FOR AN ETHICAL REALITY

By making these suggestions for improving the existing system, I am advocating no miracle solutions, but rather a few concrete ways to make progress on this question of such great importance to our modern societies, namely, the acceptance of differences between individuals.

I want to emphasise the importance of going beyond what I call the 'abstract moralism' concerning the question of disabled children. By this I mean that inclusion in ordinary settings (educational or other) is sometimes treated in a kind of sentimental or abstract way – appealing to an ideal of everybody being together, without giving attention to the possible ways in which this might come about in practice. Some invoke a 'love of children', or the 'duty' or 'vocation' of the teacher. Such abstract slogans and high-minded discourses, which adopt the moral high ground, can become self-defeating, given the practical difficulties experienced by teachers. *From utopia to reality*, the danger is not only that disillusionment will arise but also that a paradoxal situation will emerge in which some forms of exclusion will be reinforced and, in particular, exclusion from the inside (*exclusions de l'intérieur*), in which disabled children are physically present in ordinary schools, but are not participant members of the school community.

The first priority, therefore, is the adoption of an ethical position from which concrete practices can be developed – a position which might be described as an 'ethical reality'. Of course, the notion of an 'ethics' is based on fundamental values such as those of non-discrimination. It is defined in the context of this chapter in terms of the right to go to school. However, beyond the formal affirmation of a right, which is clearly crucial, it is important to be clear about concrete measures and approaches which must be developed in order for this right to become firmly rooted in practice. In this sense, inclusive education has to be given concrete expression in order to respond to the challenge of diversity and answer the many counter-arguments to inclusive education which are still widespread. In this article I have tried to show through examples taken from 'the field', inclusion is a struggle for the effective application of rights. It is also a continuous process, which requires permanent creativity in terms of developing innovative practice in daily social life.

NOTES

[1] Paper revisited, previously submitted to the International Symposium on Pre-school Education, University of Rethymnon, Crete (Greece), October 18, 2001.

[2] 'In France and in the UK the term "integration" is used loosely to refer to arrangements which increase participation or contact between a disabled pupil or pupils enrolled in some form of segregated provision and those in mainstream educational settings. While the term "exclusion" is widely used and understood in France to refer to political and social processes which discriminate or exclude groups in the context of work, social, economic, cultural and education opportunities and participation (…) the term *inclusion* has hardly been used in this context (…). The term *integration* is sometimes used in French in ways which are similar to the wider use of the term *inclusion* in England in relation to social policy'. (Armstrong, F., Belmont, B. and Vérillon, A. in Armstrong, F., Armstrong, D. and Barton, L. (eds) (2000).

[3] Circular 19 November 1999 states, 'Every school, every college, every lycée, without discrimination, has a duty to provide for disabled children and young people whose families seek integration. This general rule will apply, unless, after a detailed study of the situation, important difficulties make integration objectively impossible or too demanding for the pupil concerned'. This statement is repeated in its entirely in the more recent Circular 30 April 2002.

[4] 'Constitue un handicap (…) toute limitation d'activité ou restriction de participation à la vie en société subie dans son environnement par une personne en raison de l'altération substantielle, durable ou définitive d'une ou plusieurs fonctions physiques, sensorielles, mentales, cognitives ou psychiques, d'un polyhandicap ou d'un trouble de santé invalidant [2005 Law, Article 2]'.

[5] 'In forcing everybody, starting with the global society and finishing with the most highly specialised institutions, to take into account environmental and social factors, it is possible to support the cause of people and the exercise of their rights. The notions of "situation of handicap" ("*situation de handicap*") forces society and the public administration to change situations, and to integrate instead of simply categorising and helping people' (Stiker in Assante, 2002, p. 62).

[6] Handicap: sensibiliser, informer, former.

[7] The 'manifesto' was published in *La revue* de l'association APAJH, no. 83, September 2004, pp. 3–4. It can also be noted that the official texts of 5 January 2004 of the Ministry for Education on the training of teachers uses the term 'pupils in a situation of impairment' (élèves en situation de handicap).

[8] 'un lieu pour les sans-papiers de la petite enfance'.

REFERENCES

Armstrong F., Armstrong D. and Barton L. (eds) (2000) *Inclusive Education. Policy, Contexts and Comparative Perspectives*, London, David Fulton.

Armstrong F., Belmont B. and Vérillon A. (2000) 'Exploring context, policy and change in special education in France: developing cross-cultural collaboration'. in, F. Armstrong, D. Armstrong, L. Barton (eds) (2000), *Inclusive education. Policy, contexts and comparative perspectives*, London, David Fulton.

Assante V. (2000) *Situations de handicap et cadre de vie*, Paris, éditions des Journaux officiels, (Avis et rapports du conseil économique et social). Site internet: www.vincent-assante.net

Assante V. (2002) avec le concours de Stiker H.-J., Plaisance E., Sanchez J., *Mission d'étude en vue de la révision de la loi d'orientation du 30 juin 1975 en faveur des personnes handicapées*. Rapport remis à Ségolène Royal, Ministre déléguée à la Famille, à l'Enfance et aux Personnes Handicapées, 2002.

Aubert G. and Morel J. (1993) Des enfants handicapés accueillis en crèche collective: une action de prévention? *Journal de pédiatrie et de puériculture*, 3, 184–190.

Belmont B. and Vérillon A. (1997) Intégration scolaire d'enfants handicapés à l'école maternelle: partenariat entre enseignants de l'école ordinaire et professionnels spécialisés, *Revue française de pédagogie*, 119, 15–26.

Chauvière M. and Plaisance E. (2000) *L'école face aux handicaps. Education spéciale ou éducation intégrative?*, Paris, Presses Universitaires de France.

Chauvière M. and Plaisance E. (2003) L'éducation spécialisée contre l'éducation scolaire? Entre dynamiques formelles et enjeux cognitifs, in: Chatelanat G., Pelgrims G., *Education et enseignements spécialisés: ruptures et intégrations*, Bruxelles, De Boeck, 29–55.

Crozier M. (1963) *Le phénomène bureaucratique*, Paris, Seuil.

Déclaration de Salamanque sur les principes, les politiques et les pratiques en matière d'éducation et de besoins éducatifs spéciaux, juin 1994, Site internet: http://www.unesco.ch/pdf/salamanca

Dubar C. and Tripier P. (1998) *Sociologie des professions*, Paris, Armand Colin.

Fougeyrollas P. (1998) La classification québécoise du processus de production du handicap et la révision de la CIDIH, *Handicaps et inadaptations, Les Cahiers du CTNERHI*, 79–80, 85–103.

Gardou C. (2005) *Fragments sur le handicap et la vulnérabilité. Pour une révolution de la pensée et de l'action*, Ramonville Saint Agne, Erès.

Gottman E. (1975) *Stigmate. Les usages sociaux des handicaps*, Paris, Editions de Minuit 1st edn in English, 1963.

Herrou C. and Korff-Sausse S. (1999) *Intégration collective des jeunes enfants handicapés. Semblables et différents*, Ramonville Saint-Agne, Erès.

Kristeva J. (2003) *Lettre au président de la République sur les citoyens en situation de handicap, à l'usage de ceux qui le sont et de ceux qui ne le sont pas*, Paris, Fayard.

Lesain-Delabarre J. M. (2000) *L'adaptation et l'intégration scolaires. Innovations et résistances institutionnelles*, Paris: ESF.

Mège-Courteix M. C. (1999) *Les aides spécialisées au bénéfice des élèves. Une mission de service public*, Paris, ESF.

Mormiche P. and Boissonnat V. (2003) Handicaps et inégalités sociales: premiers apports de l'enquête «handicaps, incapacités, dépendance», *Revue française des affaires sociales*, 2, 267–285.

Organisation Mondiale de la Santé (2001) *Classification du fonctionnement, du handicap et de la santé* Site internet: http://www.who.int/classification/icf

Plaisance E. (2005) (avec la collaboration de Catherine Bouve, Marie-France Grospiron, Cornelia Schneider), *Petite enfance et handicap. La prise en charge des enfants handicapés dans les équipements collectifs de la petite enfance*. Rapport pour la Caisse Nationale des Allocations Familiales. Dossier d'études, 66. Site Internet: http://www.cnaf.fr

Plaisance E. and Lesain-Delabarre J. M. (2003) Le rapport aux institutions des parents d'enfants en situation de handicap. Sous l'angle sociologique, *Informations sociales*, 112 (spécial Handicaps et Familles), 96–106.

Thouroude L. (1997) La tolérance pédagogique à l'école maternelle, *Revue française de pédagogie*, 119, 39–46.

SIMONA D'ALESSIO

4.   'MADE IN ITALY': *INTEGRAZIONE SCOLASTICA* AND THE NEW VISION OF INCLUSIVE EDUCATION

INTRODUCTION

Comparative research is often characterised by the predominance of official governmental statistics intended to provide evidence of the efficiency of 'one's own' education system. Although such data may be helpful to understand the general trends in relation to meaningful educational issues, from my experiences in attending international conferences and seminars, it seems that this type of data are often presented to appear to excel in comparison with other countries, rather than to learn from the comparison with other countries. In contrast, through the introduction of 'life stories', autobiographical insights can be transformed into meaningful historical data promoting a deeper understanding of what is happening in a given context.

With this in mind, I decided to approach the issue of inclusive education in my own country, with the idea of going beyond official descriptions. I have tried to understand the role of experience in shaping perspectives, the contingency of one's values and individual approaches to analysing situations and the need to critically examine contexts and ideologies as a means of challenging dominant assumptions which are treated as 'natural' (Armstrong and Barton, 2001).

As a doctoral student from Italy with experience in school teaching and in disability studies, currently living and studying abroad, I have had the opportunity of coming into contact with two different national contexts, the English and the Italian, and of trying to engage critically with different values, cultures and assumptions. As a consequence of this dual engagement, there has emerged a complex feeling of being a stranger in my own country, of belonging to both countries emotionally and critically and, at the same time, of not belonging to either. I believe this feeling of uncertainty allowed me to look with different eyes at the different national contexts and to understand that, as a researcher, it is essential to come to grips with uncertainty and complexity (Morin, 2000), that is, the forces driving one's 'sociological imagination' (Mills, 1959; Hart, 1998). Drawing on Ainscow and Booth (1998) I also learnt that this is the standpoint condition that can lead the process of 'making the familiar strange and the strange familiar' (Ainscow and Booth, 1998) necessary to promote understanding and an 'open' approach to research.

L. Barton and F. Armstrong (eds.), Policy, Experience and Change, 53–72.

Departing from some reflections on the current changes occurring in Italy, with particular reference to the education of disabled students, my goal is to demonstrate that *integrazione scolastica*, based on 'progressive' social legislation, is not enough to realise a more inclusive society. Although I acknowledge the manifold struggles that have been fought, and the educational breakthroughs that have been achieved in the name of *integrazione scolastica*, I also believe that the development of a more inclusive way of thinking requires a wider cultural transformation and the investigation of sociopolitical policies both at macro and micro levels.

Considering the centrality of the issue of language in my research, a first section of the present chapter will focus on the complexity of the linguistic issues concerning the interpretation of the terms integration and inclusion. A second section will instead be concerned with the barriers I was confronted with as an insider which can be defined as 'internal barriers' to the development of more inclusive thinking. To allow an understanding of these issues, I will draw from a series of significant experiences that I have encountered as a school support teacher and specialised university tutor, with particular reference to the actors I came into contact with, and the relationships I established with them. The considerations and thoughts that I present in this section represent my understanding of, and views about, '*integrazione scolastica*' and do not represent the dominant views of the Italian educational community. A third section will deal with the implications of recent educational changes that are challenging the implementation of a more inclusive education system, and the extent to which these changes represent 'external barriers' to the development of inclusive education. This third section will also analyse current globalising trends and the complexity of the policy making process. Finally, I will discuss a series of core suggestions concerning the development of more inclusive thinking.

THE LINGUISTIC SCENARIO

During my first years as a research collaborator at the University of Rome (2001), I was appointed as the English/Italian translator and interpreter of my research team in international settings. The task of translating from one language into the other, in particular translating words such as inclusion and integration, became increasingly more difficult. I came to learn that this was due to the fact that the comparison between the two terms represents a traditional contested terrain of confrontation that goes beyond the semantic problem of translation to encompass ideological and political issues. The same linguistic problem was raised while I was working as a documentalist for the European Agency for Development in Special Needs Education (2002), a European partner of the European Commission and the Italian Ministry of Education, where the two terms, along with special education, appeared to be often used interchangeably.

While working in this international setting I came to the conclusion that each term acquires a different meaning, in relation to the context in which it is used, and that the two terms under examination (i.e. inclusion and integration), had different meanings. Furthermore, current literature discussing the issues of inclusive education in Italy is very limited and, as a consequence, the two terms have often been used as synonyms.

I needed, therefore, to further investigate the linguistic scenario and the discourses being deployed by means of spoken and written language, and I found out that the term inclusion was deliberately not being used in the Italian setting as argued by Canevaro (in Nocera, 2001):

> We prefer to use the term *integrazione*, because in our language, it acquires a positive meaning when compared with the broader terminology provided by pressing international organisations. The latter insist that the term should be substituted for inclusion, that, in our language, evokes something which is not natural but forced. Although we are aware of the willingness to provide a new linguistic term to describe the new current situation, we acknowledge that, probably, it is not possible to provide a comprehensive, literary, English translation of *integrazione*. Consequently, we would like to maintain the term *integrazione* that means not being outside the social context in order to be included in it afterwards, but already belonging to it (p. 214).

In this paragraph, Canevaro seems to put the emphasis on a long established tradition of strongly committed struggle for the civil rights of disabled people that are, in Italian, embedded in the word *integrazione* and that would disappear if the word inclusion were to be used instead. At the same time, however, he does not consider *inclusion* from a wider perspective, beyond that of international agencies. Drawing on Morin (2000), for example, I argue that the principle of inclusion is fundamental, as is the adoption of the word, since it allows the encounter with the other, promoting a falling away of the separation between 'you' and 'me', not in terms of assimilation, but rather in terms of communication.

Currently, in Italy, there seems to exist a general trend to adopt new terminologies also in relation to the term 'disability', drawing on the terminology used in international contexts where historical and cultural changes have taken place. I recognise that this endeavour is not only linguistic, but it expresses the need to challenge cultural and attitudinal assumptions embedded in the terms 'handicap' and 'disability'. For example, at the end of the 1990s, in the academic setting, the definition *persona handicappata* was replaced by *persona in situazione di handicap* (de Anna, 1998; Canevaro, 1999), following the International Classification of Disability, Impairment and Handicap (1980). Recently, with the opening of the European Year of People with Disabilities, 2003, the term *diversamente abile* (Canevaro and Ianes, 2003) was introduced as a possible substitute for the term 'disabled':

> *Diversamente abile* has a positive connotation; it embodies positive expectations in relation to the person's competencies (even if outside the standardised 'norm'), as well as trust in the development, growth, and realisation of one's own potentials. This trust is very often a self-fulfilling prophecy producing growth and new abilities (p. 217).

Although Barton's words criticising the use of 'special needs' as a euphemism for school failure (Barton and Slee, 1999) immediately resonated in my mind, I believe that the Italian scholars' paramount intent, which I share, was to challenge the concept of normalisation through the use of *diversamente abile* terminology. However, there is the risk of creating a new label for old prejudices, rather than creating a plural society where diversity is the norm and a resource. It is necessary to envisage a wider cultural change in society, otherwise we risk becoming more discriminatory, despite attempts to move in the opposite direction.

Borrowing from the tradition of the Warnock Report (1978), the definition of *bisogni educativi speciali* has been recently introduced in Italy (de Anna, 1998; Ianes, 2005) to refer to those students who do not possess a statement (corresponding to the Italian certificate of handicap issued by a medical and legal board at the local health authority or AUSL) but who experience difficulties in learning and who require individualised intervention (Ianes and Cramerotti, 2003). Significantly, in England, the Warnock Report and the following Education Act (1981) challenged the dominant mentality and managed to focus attention on the context. However, it was also strongly dominated by the vested interests of professional groups, that is, of experts. It required some effort on my part to understand that in the Italian context the definition of 'special needs' was not interpreted as a label, but that, on the contrary, its purpose was rather to oppose the process of labelling students. Ianes and Cramerotti (2003) attempted to create a less labelling language by articulating the concept that all students experience difficulties in their school career, and that the school is the main arena in which to provide for the adequate provision for each student depending on their particular interests and requirements. Thus, considering the Italian historical context, it is necessary to remember that as a result of 30 years of *integrazione scolastica* disabled students represent an integral part of the school population in ordinary classes. With this in mind, Canevaro (1999) argues that the word 'special' is to be interpreted as a synonym of 'speciality', rather than as a medical discursive practice of segregation and categorisation (Canevaro, 1999, 2004). Supporting the use of 'special' is a way to underline the diversity of students whose manifold needs must be provided with 'special' responses. He also states that it is necessary to depart from the diversity of the needs rather than to flatten it under the pressure of an egalitarian spur. In addition, he suggests that in order to remove all disabling barriers, different needs must be articulated and provided with 'special' responses in terms of professional expertise and integrated competences. I certainly agree that to deny the 'specificity' of the need would deny the fact that difference exists and that this difference requires different responses according to different settings and people. I also believe that this interpretation of 'special' is very central in order to understand how the language is used depending on different cultural contexts, and how as a researcher it is possible to engage with it in the process of mapping all possible inclusive features of the Italian education system. Considering current developments at the time in which I am writing, a 'special' response identifies an action which is 'not common' but necessary in order to promote the participation of all students facing difficulties at school. At the same time, however, such action must be soon transformed into something ordinary, an integral part of the educational response to all students (Canevaro, 2004).

Nevertheless, I am trying to understand how teachers and in particular support teachers make sense of the language of 'special' in the attempt to unmask all possible discourses that may hinder the full participation of disabled students in the process of learning. I wonder if the use of the 'special needs' language reinforces a medical approach to disability, with the introduction of a further defining category which underlines the separation of 'special' and disabled students and consequently, contributes to the dichotomy between 'normal' and 'not normal' students.

INTEGRAZIONE SCOLASTICA: A STEP TOWARDS INCLUSIVE EDUCATION?

The literature on *integrazione scolastica* in Italy is very much characterised by a shared belief that the integration of disabled students is a 'special normality' (sic) (Aprea, 2003; Ianes, 2003), that is, a common feature of the Italian education system where special schools have almost completely disappeared and students who are experiencing learning difficulties, have been placed in the mainstream for more than 30 years. In fact, Italy boasts one of the most progressive body of social legislation regulating *integrazione scolastica* and the provision of social services. The national Constitution contains two Acts (3, 34) that safeguard the right to education and employment to the whole population regardless of differences. The long tradition of educating disabled students in ordinary classes in compulsory education (primary and lower secondary schools) began in 1971 with the Law no. 118 and it was subsequently implemented in 1977 with the Law no. 517, following a short period of experimentation under the Falcucci's Government in 1975–1976.

This pioneering phase was informed by values of equal opportunities and social justice. It was a spontaneous movement from the bottom, directed by local municipalities, trade unions and associations of disabled people that led to the placement and assistance of disabled students in mainstream settings as a rights issue (Nocera, 2001). Although I was not there to witness how integration took its first steps, I have met some of the scholars and activists such as Canevaro, de Anna, Iosa and Nocera, who strongly influenced my thinking and who contributed to the struggle for the rights to education of disabled people. Their personal and professional commitment made integration a reality, despite the inevitable difficulties, the differences between Northern, Southern and Central regions and the struggles that took place daily, in the different settings, and at different levels of society.

The milestone of social and *integrazione scolastica* is the Law no. 104, enacted in 1992, known as the Framework Law on Handicap (sic). This regulation draws together, in one act, all the major anti-discriminatory legislative measures enacted between the 1970s and the 1990s. It paved the way to the second phase of *integrazione scolastica*, that considers diversity as a resource and aims at matching the pupil's need with the right provision. Following the Salamanca Statement (1994), the term inclusion began to appear in the Italian setting, although the word integration was still used in all official documents and regulations.

Inclusive education and *integrazione scolastica* present many similarities as they are both dynamic processes contributing to the realisation of a more democratic society. Integration, however, is usually used to refer to the education of disabled students while inclusive education is concerned with all pupils. Despite the scarce literature about inclusive education in Italy, inclusion seems to be intended as a more radical and socio-political project that engages society as a whole and considers integration as just part of its project (Barberio, 2002). Nevertheless, previous Italian literature often seems to mistake inclusive education as a synonym of integration. Canevaro (2002) for example, in one of his critiques of the Moratti school reform, reports:

> ... little is said about disabled people, perhaps after thirty years, it means that possibly, we do not need to corroborate the reasons and the issues that drove us to adopt a certain model – that is, *the inclusive model or the integration model* – and that we do not need further explanation (p. 229).

Moreover, in comparison to the American system, the Italian school is often described as inclusive because special schools have disappeared (Faloppa, 2003), and thus mistaking inclusion as something related to the issues of placement of disabled students in the mainstream system only.

My frequent travels to England and the opportunities to confront scholars from the field of Inclusive Education, exposed me to spurring reflections that contributed to my critical and political understanding of inclusive education and *integrazione scolastica*. On the one hand inclusive education appears to be a broad theme that goes beyond the educational domain to encompass political, societal, ethical and economic values and actions. On the other hand, my understanding of integration is that it consists of a series of structural, organisational and curricular responses to meet diversity in regular schools related to the educational domain and, for the most part, in relation to disabled students. Canevaro and Ianes (2001) argue that there is an attempt to look at the wider cultural dimension of integration to encapsulate the societal and political dimensions, but despite these attempts, the integration movement is still strongly rooted in the welfare and disability domains.

Perhaps we should welcome a new 'adult' phase of *integrazione scolastica* (Pavone, 2003), one which sets long term objectives aiming at encompassing the necessary changes at a cultural and social level, following the examples of the systematic dimensions of Bronfenbrenner and fostering the cooperation among different actors.

Significantly, sociological analyses often raised key challenging issues about the real purposes of schooling and the reasons that guided educational reforms (Arnot and Barton, 1992). I envisage therefore, that a wider interpretation of the concept of integration, leading to more inclusive thinking, should depart from the incorporation of other disciplines, in particular the political, historical and sociological ones. It should also support a change in the language, since the definition of integration has become too narrow to encompass all key issues emerging from current national and international changes. I prefer, therefore, to use 'Inclusive Education', not as a substitute for integration, from which it differs in many aspects, but to trigger off a chain of reactions and reflections leading to the creation of a more just society.

Fortunately, words and their meanings change, shift and evolve. It is emblematic that significant studies have recently raised a number of issues in the attempt to engage more critically with the meaning of inclusive education in relation to the Italian context, and as a result of this, the term inclusion, has been introduced (Canevaro, 2004). Canevaro's suggestion is that it is necessary to look at '*integrazione scolastica*' from an 'inclusive perspective'. In seeking to address this new perspective, I have identified three main trends: the first one is to move '*integrazione*' beyond the condition of 'emergency' and to operate changes at structural and contextual levels. The second trend is that an inclusive perspective of '*integrazione scolastica*' does not deny 'special' responses but it suggests that they should be integrated in ordinary teaching. Finally, a third trend is that an inclusive perspective envisages a change that does not only concern schooling but that includes society as a whole.

AN INSIDER'S PERSPECTIVE: INTERNAL BARRIERS TO INCLUSIVE THINKING

As a school teacher my thinking was strongly influenced by a traditional idea of policy and policy making as top-down processes. I thus interpreted the flaws of *integrazione scolastica* as deriving from the lack of policy application. This was the reason why well-designed legislative measures failed to achieve their goals. I am grateful to the readings of policy analysts like Ball (1993), Fulcher (1999) and Armstrong F. (2003) who investigated the issues of policy making, both at a macro and micro levels and that helped me to challenge the traditional knowledge of policy as a straightforward top-down action. These authors favoured a notion of policy and policy making that arises from the struggles and the discourses being deployed at different levels and for different purposes (Fulcher, 1999) in a range of settings.

With this in mind I realised that I was not teaching in a vacuum, and felt influenced by a series of forces that impinged on me. These forces transformed the teaching location into an arena where different actors, including me, with different purposes, were making policies through their own practices.

Looking back at my experience as a newly qualified support teacher, a series of struggles and dilemmas began to challenge my naïve interpretation of policy in new ways. In conformity with the Law 104/92, the support teacher is in charge of the whole class, gives advice to the curricular teachers in relation to the best modalities of teaching, and learning and designs local projects and specialised individualised interventions. The current legislation (Law 449/97) envisages the ratio of one support teacher for every 138 enrolled students (disabled and non disabled), but the school principal can appoint more support teachers to face school needs (Ministerial Circular 27/2003).

In my experience as a support teacher appointed by the school principal, I came to discover that the 'emergency need' was represented by a disabled pupil. On the one hand, with my appointment, the school was provided with an additional professional resource, in the form of a new teacher that, was sometimes used illegally to replace colleagues who did not turn up for work for some reason. On the other hand, my colleagues tended to derogate the education of the disabled student to me, in spite of the fact that, according to the law, we were all responsible for working with the student (Law 970/1975, Law 199/1979, Law 104/1992). The reasons conveyed by the teachers were manifold including, lack of training, organisation and personal fears in interacting with disabled pupils. In other words, I provided relief for my colleagues so that they could teach the rest of the class without any disruption. Sometimes, the parents of the disabled students were the only actors who promoted and responded to the call for collaboration among school personnel, local health practitioners, local units professionals and family, envisaged by the law relating to the formulation of the Individual Education Plan. To overcome the difficulties concerning the collaboration among the different actors, a Presidential Decree was enacted in 1994, to support the framework law 104/92. This decree represented the technical documentation to build up an alternative route, educational, rehabilitative and vocational, for the disabled pupil. The meetings required by the decree, usually scheduled twice a year, envisaged the participation of different actors (e.g. teachers, parents and local health units experts, NGO members etc.). Significantly, the disabled student never appeared among the members allowed to participate at the meetings to discuss the Individualised Educational Plan. Furthermore, the head teacher's attitude towards integration was often influenced by budgetary considerations and policies and the level of commitment varied according to the amount of economic resources provided to the school. Finally, the local health practitioners were very important actors in the process of integration. The eligibility for statementing is provided by the medical personnel who writes the clinical diagnosis of the student under parental permission (Law 104/92). Without statementing no action is taken to 'assist' the student. My contacts and relationships with the local health practitioners, in particular with the psychologist, were very limited and the consultation process was often ruined by an unequal rapport with the 'expert' who hardly knew the student and contested educational intervention with medical intervention.

In contrast, the relationships with the students indicated a possible way to remove a series of barriers, both at a school and at a university level. The students, in fact, represented the most important actors for the implementation of more inclusive thinking, and their role was central to my professional and personal growth. I started working with disabled students as a specialised tutor in order to facilitate their access to higher education (Law 17/99). Although access to university has been safeguarded since 1992, some universities, in particular those with a sports orientation, registered a very limited number of disabled students. Those were the years of the struggles, successfully fought by Lucia de Anna, leading to the enrolment of disabled students in sport focussed universities with the collaboration of associations of disabled people.

At school level, disabled students and their peers represented one of the most important resources in the integration process. Consequently, those were the years when new teaching approaches were promoted, in particular cooperative learning, considered as one of the most effective methodologies to improve teaching and learning in a mixed ability classroom and as a means of responding to diversity (D'Alessio, 2001). In both educational contexts, school and university, the students were the main actors who helped me to understand where the real barriers were set and to challenge the deeply rooted assumptions about what students could do or could not do, because of their 'impairments' and that the real limitations were situated in the contexts rather than in the person.

EXTERNAL BARRIERS TO *INTEGRAZIONE SCOLASTICA* AND INCLUSIVE THINKING

In March 2003, the current Italian government passed a decree regulating the reform of the current education system. After a short trial period in seven schools, the Moratti

Reform (Law 53/2003) was implemented in September 2004[1]. The reform has the principle stated purpose of raising the overall quality of education and primarily consists in the division of the school system into two main cycles, the primary (4 years of elementary school, plus 3 years of lower secondary school) and the secondary cycle. The latter envisages the early separation between those students who, at the age of 13, will have to choose between vocational training (4 years plus one to access University) and grammar schooling (5 years plus university courses). The key elements of such reform, that is, flexibility, choice, differentiation and efficiency, aim at creating an autonomous and decentralised state school focused on the needs of the students and on parental choice, so that the national curriculum can be subjected to local variations and private funding. Paradoxically, at the same time the private sector will receive state financing. Much in agreement with many Italian scholars (Canevaro, 2002; de Anna, 2002; Ianes, 2002; Iosa, 2002) I think that such reform may jeopardise both the long established tradition of *integrazione scolastica* as well as state education. Hardly any consideration is given to the issues of disabled students. The document merely states:

> The right of *integrazione scolastica* is guaranteed, by means of adequate inter-
> ventions, for those students in a condition of handicap, in conformity with the
> framework Law 104/92 (Section 2.C).

There may be many reasons why the reform dismisses the issues of *integrazione scolas-tica* in one paragraph, and led me to some serious reflections:

- To improve the level of efficiency, schooling will be tailored according to the needs of each student, whose special requirements will be met also by the appointment of private external personnel. Part of the school time will become optional, and differentiated according to the attitudinal skills and performance of each pupil, the so called 'natural talent' of the student (Barton and Slee, 1999). Consequently, it is probable that disabled and disadvantaged students will attend workshops, separated from the rest of the class. There is in fact a great difference between an individual and individualised educational path. Canevaro (2002) argues that '*individuale*' (i.e. individual), carries with it a fragmentation of the school system into differentiated paths according to personal attainments while '*individualizzato*' (i.e. individualised) requires the school community to struggle for the implementation of integration by means of mutual adjustments and structural changes.
- Although there is an opportunity to move from one type of secondary schooling to the other by means of examination, the early separation between vocational training and the '*liceo*' (corresponding to the English grammar school) is a threat to the education of disabled students. Currently, the majority of disabled students attend professional and technical schools, in particular agricultural ones (M.I.U.R., 2003). Thus the early school separation introduced by the reform will presumably encourage the existing trend rather than correcting it. In contrast, the 'best' students will probably attend the 'liceo' controlled by the national education system, where the future ruling class will be educated.
- Parental choice is not always the best basis on which to plan a child's education. Such a policy is based on the assumption that all parents share the following

two criteria: that they are really advocating the rights of their children, and that they have been advised by the same people, who, in turn, are actually advocating the rights of the children. Conversely, depending on their different cultural, economic and psychological backgrounds, parents often prefer to commit to something which is more feasible, such as getting a job after school. I share with Iosa the resentment towards the 'compassionate conservatism' (Iosa, 2002) embedded in the new education system that substitutes hope with pragmatism, 'utopian' beliefs in human potentialities, with profits. In other words, parental choice allows for the exacerbation of already existing family differences, and the reproduction of social injustice, 'a celebration of difference' based upon social, racial and possibly, gender inequalities (Arnot and Barton, 1992).

• Another possible consideration is that the Moratti's Reform dismisses the education of disabled students in one paragraph since, it argues, they are already part of the student population. However, considering that the main purpose of the reform is to improve standardised performances and increase market driven achievements, there is very little evidence that the Moratti's definition of 'all' students includes disabled students as well.

The new reform also envisages the creation of a national system of evaluation, known as INVALSI or pilot project no. 3, approved in 2004, based on students' performance as possible indicators of the quality of the school. The modalities in which science, maths and Italian tests were administered during the pilot phase of the INVALSI reform revealed a strongly exclusive mentality. Disabled students were literally excluded from the assessment procedure, because of concerns that their attainments might lower the level of school performance relative to set standards imposed by the national evaluation office. During the pilot stage of this project in my school, a student bearing the label of Down syndrome was allowed to participate in the tests along with his classmates. However, once the test was finished, his paper was carefully labelled with a code number and excluded from the final evaluation process. I felt all the deep hypocrisy of the system that does not attempt to create tests that could 'evaluate' the progress of all students including the progress made by those students whose level of performance does not comply with 'accepted' statistical standards. It was deemed that only the students without statements, therefore, could contribute to the success of the school! Moreover, in the INVALSI guidelines there is no mention of those indicators which can be used to evaluate schools whose intake consists of students coming from peripheral housing projects or disadvantaged areas (Nocera, 2001). This latter type of school has often undergone structural and procedural modifications designed to welcome the whole diversity of students and could, possibly, lead to very good examples of inclusive education in the coming years. Indeed, these schools' endeavours to implement integration are ignored. Serious questions should be asked concerning what is socially considered a success and whatever and how we can monitor it.

GLOBALISATION AND EDUCATION: SOME CURRENT ISSUES

There are additional external barriers that may contribute or hinder the development of inclusive education in Italy but they do not only concern the Italian setting. These crucial issues, in fact, reflect more generalised transformations and globalising trends characterising and influencing Western industrialised countries as a whole (Barile, 2003). As examples of this, two of the most debated current issues are concerned with the introduction of the International Classification of Functioning, Disability and Health (WHO, 2001), and the development of contemporary market-oriented economic policies.

The International Classification of Functioning, Disability and Health (ICF) belongs to the family of the international classification tools published by the WHO in 2001 and subsequently adopted by 192 countries. Italy was among the 62 countries that finalised the revision of the first classification tool known as ICIDH (1980). The purpose of the ICF is to provide a common language to collect and compare international data and to measure conditions concerning health and health related domains. These domains encompass both environmental and personal conditions that may hinder or facilitate the quality of life of an entire population. The tool has been considered as an innovative clinical, educational and research tool. For the first time, it focuses the attention on the individual's potentialities and the environmental determinants that may cause participation restrictions (contextual and personal factors) in addition to limitations in terms of activities (person's capabilities). It thus concerns the entire population since 'everyone at some point in their lives may find themselves with a health condition which, in a negative environment, develops into a disability' (WHO, 2001, p. 1).

As a lecturer on a Master's course on the use of ICF, I was faced with a series of dilemmas concerning the introduction of the ICF in the Italian context. On the one hand, the ICF represented a real opportunity to promote a change in the Italian culture of dis-ability. Those advocating the use of ICF were genuinely attempting to challenge the long-standing negative philosophical approach to disability which focused on what the person could *not* do, rather than focusing on what the person *could* do if a series of environmental modification were envisaged. I think, however, that despite the attempt to move towards a positive interpretation of the individual abilities of disabled people, the ICF perspective still maintains an individualised view of disability and consequently the issues to be faced are addressed at the individual level (Arnot and Barton, 1992).

The ICF publication itself (WHO, 2001) tries to reconcile the medical model with a more socialised model of disability:

> The ICF is based on an integration of these two opposing models. In order to cap-
> ture the integration of the various perspectives of functioning, a 'biopsycho-
> social' approach is used (p. 23).

The Italian disability community (including for example the FISH federation) accepted the ICF unanimously seeing it as a means of persuading policy makers and politicians to look at disability as related to functions outside the individual's intrinsic features. In contrast, some scholars of the English (Thomas, 2002) and the American Disability Movements (Pfeiffer, 2000) have instead, clearly indicated the possible risks deriving from the introduction of the ICF. In order to understand the different approaches is necessary to consider that in Italy, in contrast to the UK, there has been little sustained sociological and political theorisation of disability as social oppression (Oliver, 1990).

Moreover, although some Italian disability associations raised people's consciousness about the rights of disabled people, they never became politically active and never really embarked in the fight for human rights. However, the discussions about the introduction of the ICF, allowed some disabled activists such as Barbieri, and Griffo to promote the development of a more structurally organised disability movement in order to give voice to all disabled people and overcome its internal division into many different small associations, each one representing a particular 'category' of impairment.

My critique of the introduction of the ICF is based on the consideration that despite the fact that social and contextual issues are taken up in the assessment procedure, it seems that the medical model would continue to play a dominant role. In fact, medical personnel will still control eligibility and access to services, job placement and other financial aids. It is necessary to also critically engage with positions that oppose its usage and investigate these stances from an international perspective (D'Alessio, 2002).

The Ministry of Welfare and Labour and the participants at the second conference on Disability held in Bari in 2003, recommended the introduction of the ICF to overthrown the current culture of disability. Certainly, the ICF will contribute to the modernisation of the legislative language, in particular the outdated language of the Framework Law 104/92 (Massi, 1996):

> A handicapped person is someone who has a temporary or a permanent physical, sensory or mental impairment, which causes difficulties in learning, social relation and employment and consequently leads to a social disadvantage or marginalisation (Section 3.1, p. 207).

This disabling language will be substituted by 'activities restrictions' and 'participation limitations' in the ICF (WHO, 2001):

> Disability is the umbrella term for impairments, activity limitations and participation restrictions. It denotes the negative aspects of the interaction between the individual (with a health condition) and that individual's contextual factors (environmental and personal factors) (p. 168).

But, it seems to me that the concepts of disability and of impairment are being confused and are being treated as if they are the same thing, and that there is still a causal relation between the impairment (bodily functions and structures) and disablement.

Drawing from the works of Pfeiffer (1998, 2000) and Thomas (1999, 2002), I would argue that the ICF is still governed by two major assumptions: the first is a concern with the notion of deviance from a normal standardised human condition, whereas the second assumption is concerned with the idea of universalism. The existence of standardised taxonomic principles of normal functioning implies that disablement is a deviation from them as indicated in the document itself (WHO, 2001):

> Impairment represent a deviation from certain generally accepted population standards in the biomedical status of the body and its functions, and definition of their constituents is undertaken primarily by those qualified to judge physical and mental functioning according to these standards (p. 10).

I think that in order to be more inclusive we should challenge the idea that there exists a normality, to be 'judged' by professionals, even if only intended for statistical reasons (WHO, 2001:168). With the implementation of the ICF there will be only one accepted way of functioning and a globalising language to define that condition. Thus, the 'stigma' would be transformed into a code. I agree with those who indicate that the ICF unifying language will allow different professionals to come to an agreement and communicate throughout the country in a way that is understandable to them and that will take into account the role played by environmental barriers. It will also reduce the number of 'illegal' statements that sometimes are requested by educational and health care experts to obtain additional provision for the school through means of diagnosing more children. At the same time, the family may be comforted by the issue of an intelligible and comprehensive documentation. However, I wonder if the child will, ultimately, really benefit from a widely understood statement (or stigma). There is an attempt to broaden the scope of disablement by including the insights of disabled people that participated in the revision of the original text, but as Pfeiffer (1998), indicates, the globalising language is a Western World utopia that dismisses the experience of other cultures in favour of dominant ideologies.

I am grateful to the work of Morin (2000), that in recent times, helped me to consider that each single event cannot be considered separately from what is happening in the rest of the world, that a way of thinking that separates, also atrophies possibilities for reflection and for seeing the long-term developments. For instance, the way impairment is understood in Maori society is different from in European society (also different). Moreover, it seems to me that the ICF takes into account this multi dimensional and multi-cultural approach only marginally. Disability does not exist as a unique category; rather, it changes across cultures, histories and contexts. The need to classify it, and to provide people with additional specialisations is an attempt to address the social complexity of reality and, eventually, control it. Although the ICF envisages the overthrowing of attitudinal barriers, such as the idea of disability as a disease, it provides no indications of how this might be brought about.

There is still a long way to go to understand whether the ICF can be deplored as a more sophisticated social model that incorporates the personal and the experiential promoted by Shakespeare and Watson (Shakespeare and Watson, 2002). An investigation beyond the rhetorical usage of the language that defines diversity as a resource, should encapsulate the analysis of socioeconomic factors (e.g. poverty). Moreover, as Pfeiffer (1998) indicates, once we classify subgroups, it is easier to eliminate them. I recall the writing of Bauman (1992) who indicates how German Nazism made use of technicism in the holocaust tragedy.

As far as the current economic policy thinking is concerned, the Moratti reform is not an isolated example of educational change but it responds to contemporary economic and political tendencies. From an economic perspective national economies are undergoing 'structural adjustments' that have a crucial impact on education (Carnoy, 1995). Reform agendas tend to be dominated by cuts in public expenditure, the evaluation of the education system by means of students' performance (as the INVALSI system in Italy), the increased autonomy of schools and municipalities (e.g. Law 275/1999) and the privatisation of secondary and higher education. These actions, usually associated with the right wing government, have also been fostered by 'left wing' parties (Whitty, 1999) to provide alternative responses to the highly bureaucratised institution of post-war mass education.

My view is that those advocating this reform in Italy, as those advocating similar reforms in the studies reported by Whitty (1999), for example, claim that devolution, parental and individual choice and market-oriented systems may improve the level of responsiveness and efficiency of schools. They hope that by means of competition schools will enhance the overall quality of education and that all pupils' needs will be met with the adequate response. I think that we should counterbalance school decision making with goals regulated from the centre that take into consideration learning not only in terms of students' academic achievements (Whitty, 1999). This is particularly true for *integrazione scolastica* where students' achievement are to be measured also in terms of socialisation and communication skills (Nocera, 2001).

I am grateful to the reading of educational policy analysts such as Barton and Slee (1999) who helped me to understand that due to the increasing role played by individualism and selection, current governments construct the concept of failure as resulting from a problem located within the child and that consequently:

> Children who are already experiencing discrimination and disadvantage in many
> forms encounter further practices of exclusion and marginalisation within the
> school situation (p. 6).

Those advocating 'deficit thinking' should instead focus on the way schools can be organised to prevent learning inequalities and fight against the transformation of schools into market oriented businesses (Barton and Slee, 1999).

Furthermore, what education reform can be 'successful' if financial resources are reduced? For example, in Italy, according to the Financial Act 2004, only 40 million euro will be allocated for *integrazione scolastica*, with an inevitable reduction in the number of support teachers appointed and the resources provided to each school. The reform, as it is now, risks exacerbating already existing inequalities, between the Northern and Southern regions for example, but also between social classes by reproducing differences in terms of social justice.

NO GOING BACK

The European Year of People with Disabilities 2003 coincided with the Italian Presidency in the European Commission. As a consequence of this, many initiatives were organised in the year 2003 to discuss disability issues and the future of *integrazione scolastica*. On many occasions data were presented with the goal of showing the progress of *integrazione scolastica* and social legislation. For instance, the Ministry of Education reported that 148,737 disabled students (i.e. with statements) were attending regular schools. Moreover, each initiative listed a set of priorities necessary to overcome the barriers to *integrazione scolastica* and the quality of schooling as a whole. For example, the Bari conference on Disability, focused on the issues related to the enactment of those legislative measures concerning disabled people and their families

(Law 162/98). It also addressed issues such as actions to be taken to increase mobility for disabled people, how to finance the development and the use of assistive technologies and the enactment of the 'targeted employment' regulation (Law 68/99). In contrast, the national conference on the quality of *integrazione scolastica* in Rimini, focused on the need to increase the life long training of support teachers and the training of all curricular teachers in relation to the use of ICF, the introduction of *integrazione scolastica* indicators in the national assessment system and more strict budgetary control in the way funding is used to provide resources to *integrazione scolastica*. Furthermore, the recently re-constituted National Observatory on Handicap (sic), originally created in 1991, discussed the need to monitor the quality of *integrazione scolastica* and conduct quantitative research in the field of disability issues, and finally, after ten years, the passing of a State act that creates a historically important new post of the '*amministatore di sostegno*' (Law 6/2004) to safeguard the rights of disabled people lacking personal autonomy, totally or partly

Considering the many priorities set by different organisations and institutions, I wonder what my priorities should be in terms of challenging barriers to inclusive education? Despite the important role played by the many issues highlighted in documents and legislation, I wonder why we keep focusing attention on what is not working within the child, and in the setting immediately around the student, rather than understanding what is happening in the wider socio-cultural context. With a legacy of 30 years of *integrazione scolastica*, it is time to look for more ambitious long-term projects that encompass both the collection of successful technical examples of the 'best' practices of *integrazione scolastica* but also the investigation of those cultural, political and socio-logical forces that have made those practices possible beyond the initiative of the individuals and of the local situation.

I hardly believe that words such as 'special' and 'vulnerable' can be transformed into neutral adjectives to identify all members of the population who may experience difficulties during their school career. Language matters and as Corbett argues, definitions such as 'special educational needs' and 'vulnerable' are becoming more and more unacceptable (Corbett, 1996). I envisage the need to modify a language that still hides a 'significant degree of patronage' (Corbett, 1996, p. 15) and labels students. Maybe we should emulate the experience of the 'Index for Inclusion' (Ainscow and Booth, 1999) used in the English setting and where the term 'special educational needs' has been replaced by 'barriers to learning and participation', hence shifting the attention from the individual/medical approach to disability, to the social approach. In my opinion, a medical approach is still strongly embedded in the Italian culture, despite the camouflaged language of the ICF.

In my research diary I listed a set of reflections and actions that drive my investigation into the Italian context in relation to the realisation of inclusive education. For instance, I wish we could look at the person, not as a problem and a scapegoat of societal dysfunctioning, but as an individual. Thus, we should confront the problems of the school's out-dated teaching styles, the lack of state funding and possibly come to terms with our cultural fears of engaging with our own human and mortal fragility. I wish we could forge an education system that creates a school starting from the students and their learning and not on the basis of standardised achievements and future job careers. I wish

I could speak of an inclusive pedagogy, rather than special education, whose aim is to identify those forces that influence the daily actions of those teachers really committed to inclusive thinking rather than focusing only on provisional responses. I think we should investigate and unveil those personal manoeuvres and 'escamotage tactics' that allow people, occupying strategic roles, to oppose the actual realisation of inclusive education, though they appear to comply with social legislative measures. I wish I could speak of students, rather than disabled students, of inclusive POF (Piano dell'Offerta Formativa) rather than Individual Educational Plans based on a medical diagnosis. I envisage a Welfare State in terms of human rights rather than compensatory assistance measures, enabling the disability movement to challenge still existing power relations that distinguish between disabled and non disabled people. I think that we should start to consider *integrazione scolastica* not as a separate educational process, but as part of a wider societal process of transformation.

There is still a long way to go before we can realise a generalised and more inclusive way of thinking, but to avoid the risk of going backwards in relation to what has been already achieved, I want to emphasise the need to investigate the following key issues:

- The importance of counteracting the managerial state and the neo-liberal international trend of market-led and finance driven reforms that are not only detrimental for *integrazione scolastica* but for the quality of school as a whole. Perhaps we should start by clarifying the purpose of 'education' and what education is for.
- The need to investigate the possible dangers of an unconditional adoption of the ICF, in particular considering that the ICF will regulate people's eligibility to services and financial aids. Certainly, the ICF dislodges the central role that physical and mental dysfunctioning have played as the prior condition of disablement, but I argue that there is very little attention focused on the possible challenges lying beneath or hiding behind the linguistic change. Much attention should be given to the risk of a dichotomous separation between normal/disabled, the concept of deviance and the lack of information about other cultures, the deployment of medical discourses by professionals and consequently the maintaining of established power relations. Finally, we should investigate the link between disability and impairment with those political and economic factors, that the ICF does not mention, that strongly contribute to their uneven distribution in society.
- The crucial requirement of fostering inclusive thinking in the teacher training sessions and for all school actors, from the curricular teachers, the specialised teachers, the principals to the school personnel. The inclusive education training courses should aim at identifying two main questions: what are the cultural, organisational and political barriers that prevent a school from being inclusive? And subsequently, what are the provisions being offered to students in order to develop their potentialities? An inclusive thinking and pedagogy envisage structural and organisational changes that go beyond the within-the-child deficit view of special education. A form of teacher training is necessary, that counteracts the danger of re-creating segregated teaching inside the mainstream, as well as the isolation of the support teacher[2].

- The need to critically engage with a revision of the legalese language of anti-discrimination policies and legislative measures, such as the Framework Law 104/92, that risks perpetuating the very forms of discrimination they should be reducing, by claiming to be in favour of independence, emancipation and autonomy of disabled people. An essential way forward will be to increase the participation of and the consultation with disabled people (Corker, 2000) in the policy making process and, in general, to promote the participation of the NGOs of disabled people, rather than for disabled people, in the decision making process. Significantly, the role of the disability movement will gain more power if disabled people's associations unify under a unique political flag rather than maintaining internal differences due to the kind of impairments they represent.
- The need to identify dominant ideologies that are embedded in official policies and laws and that can result into the enactment of discriminatory practices. In order to detect such ideologies I argue that we should investigate existing discourses being deployed at different levels, such as those of 'charity', 'assistance', 'care' and also what Benjamin describes as the insidious discourse of 'valuing diversity' (Benjamin, 2003). That is to move beyond the individual discourses of disability and of school failure and explore the understated role of the society and of the education system in constructing them (Moore, 2004).

CONCLUSIONS

It was with trepidation that I have expressed my voice, sometimes articulating ideas which are in contrast with current perceptions in the Italian academy. As I have already mentioned, what I write is from my personal and intellectual experiences and is not intended as an attempt to provide a final and authoritative statement of the state of the art of inclusive education in Italy. It is instead, an attempt to offer some particular ideas that will hopefully contribute to developing debates within Italy and other countries. The strength of the biographical element lies in the fact that it can be fully understood, shared, known and set against some of the filters imposed by institutional and political forces. It does not aim at being reproduced, transferred and generalised, but it enters the mind and the imagination of the reader to promote that internal understanding and change across nations and language, that official legislation and policies often fail to achieve. It is possible to foster understanding beyond rhetorical speeches, but the road to it is long. Inclusive education could be a way to it starting from the education of the new generations.

I envisage a reform of the education system in terms of ways of thinking. A reform of the minds that abandons the disjunctive paradigm typical of our modern and western societies (classificatory, separating, ordering and controlling) to move towards a more complex thinking modality (linking, summarising, connecting and contextualising) and that Morin indicates as the 'complex thought'. It consists of a paradigm integrating the differences by emphasising and verifying the peculiarity of the individual differences (Morin, 2000).

Although inclusive education and *integrazione scolastica* do not correspond, an inclusive approach to education cannot be exclusive, in the sense that it cannot dismiss the experience of the Italian *integrazione* as part of the wider picture to promote more inclusive thinking. Within the struggle for inclusive education, the legacy of *integrazione scolastica* is that it was one of the first historical responses used to fight prejudices and social injustice. It was the first attempt to face practical issues including the rights of disabled people being seriously addressed. Moreover, *integrazione scolastica* was 'made in Italy' in the sense that it is strongly rooted in the historical and economic tradition of the country but as a symbol of uniqueness, rather than as a symptom of perfunctoriness.

Attempts to define what inclusive education means in different countries is a very problematic task and the personal data are endeavours to provide a closer understanding of local contradictions and issues. Certainly, it is necessary to remember that inclusive education is not to be considered as a new term to define *integrazione scolastica*.

Ultimately, inclusive education, is a way to challenge the assumed norm of mainstream schooling, beyond the paradigm of integrating disabled students in ordinary classes. When the *integrazione scolastica* of disabled students in ordinary classes was first implemented, it had among its main purposes the overall transformation of the education system that is, organisational, curricular and pedagogical changes (Malaguti Rossi, 2004). In contrast, it seems that *integrazione scolastica* never really impacted the traditional education system and I also argued that it rarely questioned the assumed 'norm'.

Likewise, to promote inclusive thinking, *integrazione scolastica* would require an ultimate, apparently utopian, intervention from an ideological perspective. It must contemplate the struggle against those ideological and discursive forces that legitimate discriminatory policies and practices, sometimes even unintentionally. For example it is important to explore current discourses of disability which rely on the idea of disability as a 'personal tragedy' (Oliver, 1990; Armstrong *et al.*, 2000) and that contribute to the development of compensatory policies that do things 'on behalf' of disabled people, rather than enabling them to do things for themselves (Armstrong *et al.*, 2000), even if in a condition of interdependence with others (Canevaro, 2004).

At this stage it is necessary, to engage with more ambitious and theoretical issues. Drawing on the pedagogy of hope as expressed by Freire (1996) combined with Morin's 'complex thought' (2000), we could conceive an 'international index of inclusion' that takes into account the different theorisation and strategies to implement inclusive education from a cross cultural perspective. In conclusion, *integrazione scolastica*, drawing on recent conceptualisations of inclusive education, appears to have acquired a new vision, that of an ongoing process of societal and educational changes. It is with this in mind that current research in the field should be conducted.

NOTES

[1] The Italian Education system is in a continuous flux depending on the political party on Government. Thus, the Moratti Reform was not fully implemented because of the overthrowing of the Berlusconi Government in 2006. Only the lower secondary education undergone the changes envisaged by the Law 53/2003.

² Currently a new decree has passed (Decree 227/2005) which envisages the development of a new teacher training requiring all curricular teachers to attend specialised courses in the field of *integrazione scolastica*.

REFERENCES

Ainscow, M. and Booth, T. (eds) (1998) *From Them to Us: An International Study of Inclusion in Education*. London: Routledge.

Ainscow, M. and Booth, T. (1999) *Index for Inclusion: Developing Learning and Participation in Schools*. Bristol: Centre for Studies on Inclusive Education (CSIE).

Aprea, V. (2003) 'Inserimento e integrazione delle persone handicappate nella scuola. Relazione al Parlamento del Sottosegretario Aprea'. *L'integrazione scolastica e sociale*, 2, 35–41.

Armstrong, F. (2003) *Spaced Out. Policy, Difference and the Challenge of Inclusive Education*. Dordrecht-Boston and London: Kluwer Academic Publishers.

Armstrong, F., Armstrong, D. and Barton, L. (eds) (2000) *Inclusive Education. Policy, Contexts and Comparative Perspectives*. London: David Fulton Publisher.

Armstrong, F. and Barton, L. (2001) 'Disability, Education and Inclusion'. In L. Albrecht, Gary D. Seelman, Katherine and M. Bury (eds) *Handbook of Disability Studies*, 693–710 Thousand Oaks, London and New Delhi: Sage Publications.

Arnot, M. and Barton, L. (eds) (1992) *Voicing Concerns: Sociological Perspectives on Contemporary Education Reforms*. Oxford: Triangle.

Ball, S. J. (1993) 'What is policy? Texts, Trajectories and Toolboxes'. *Discourse*, 132, 10–17.

Barberio, N. (2002) 'L'inclusione: un nuovo modo di concepire e gestire la diversità nella scuola negli USA'. *Orientamenti Pedagogici*, 49, 27–38.

Barile, M. (2003) 'Globalisation and ICF Eugenics: Historical coincidence or connection? The more things change the more they Stay the Same'. *Disability Studies Quarterly*, 23, 208–223.

Barton, L. and Slee, R. (1999) 'Competition, selection and inclusive education: some observations'. *International Journal of Inclusive Education*, 3, 3–12.

Bauman, Z. (1992) *Modernità e Olocausto* (M. Baldini, Trans.). Bologna: Il Mulino.

Benjamin, S. (2003) *The Micropolitics of Inclusive Education. An Ethnography*. Buckingham and Philadelphia: Open University Press.

Canevaro, A. (1999) *Pedagogia speciale. La riduzione dell'handicap*. Milano: Bruno Mondadori.

Canevaro, A. (2002) 'Il progetto Moratti per la riforma: scuola superiore e formazione professionale'. *L'integrazione scolastica e sociale*, 1, 229–234.

Canevaro, A. and Ianes, D. (eds) (2001) *Buone prassi di integrazione scolastica. 20 realizzazioni efficaci*. Trento: Erickson.

Canevaro, A. and Ianes, D. (2003) *Diversabilità. Storie di dialoghi nell'anno europeo delle persone disabili*. Trento: Erickson.

Canevaro, A. and Mandato, M. (2004) *L'integrazione e la prospettiva 'inclusiva'*. Rome: Monolite Editrice.

Carnoy, M. (1995) 'Structural adjustment and the changing face of education', *International Labour Review*, 134, 653–673.

Corbett, J. (1996) *Bad Mouthing*. London: Falmer Press.

Corker, M. (2000) 'The U.K. Disability Discrimination Act. Disabling language, justifying inequitable social participation'. in L. P. Francis and A. Silvers (eds), *Americans with Disabilities. Exploring Implications of the Law for Individuals and Institutions*. New York/London: Routledge.

D'Alessio, S. (2001) 'Addressing Diversity: the challenge of the handicap'. *Perspectives. A Journal of Tesol Italy*, XXVII, 55–69.

D'Alessio, S. (2002) 'Osservazioni sull'utilizzo dell'ICF nei Paesi intervenuti al seminario della Commissione Europea'. *L'integrazione scolastica e sociale*, 1, 452–455.

de Anna, L. (1998) *Pedagogia speciale. I bisogni educativi speciali*. Milano: Guerino.

de Anna, L. (2002) 'La riforma Moratti e l'integrazione scolastica degli alunni in situazione di handicap'. *L'integrazione scolastica e sociale*, 1, 11–14.

Faloppa, M. (2003) 'Riforme scolastiche e processo d'integrazione'. *L'integrazione scolastica e sociale,* 1, 14–21.

Freire, P. (1996) *Pedagogy of the Oppressed.* B. M. Ramos, trans., New Revised 20th Anniversary Edn., New York: Continuum.

Fulcher, G. (1999), *Disabling Policies? A Comparative Approach to Education Policy and Disability.* Sheffield: Philip Armstrong Publications.

Hart, C. (1998) *Doing a Literature Review. Releasing the Social Science Research Imagination.* London, Thousand Oaks, New Delhi: Sage Publications.

Ianes, D. (2002) 'La riforma Moratti e l'integrazione scolastica degli alunni in situazione di handicap'. *L'integrazione scolastica e sociale,* 1, 14–16.

Ianes, D. (2003) 'Integrazione scolostica: un intreccio tra speciale e normale'. Rassegna – Periodico dell'I stituto Pedagogico provinciale di Bolizano, XI, Editoriale.

Ianes, D. (2005) *Bisogni Educativi Speciali e inclusione. Valutare le reali necessitdà e attivare le risorse* Trento: Ericson.

Ianes, D. and Cramerotti, S. (2003) 'Gli alunni con Bisogni Educativi Speciali: dal Piano educativo individualizzato al Progetto di vita'. *L'integrazione scolastica e sociale,* 2, 395–409.

Iosa, R. (2002) 'La Riforma e l'integrazione scolastica degli alunni in situazione di handicap', *L'integrazione scolastica e sociale,* 1.

M.I.U.R. (2003) *2003: l'handicap e l'integrazione nella scuola* (Report). Rome: Ministero Istruzione, Università e Ricerca (MIUR) and Servizio di consulenza all'Attività Programmatoria (EDS Italy).

Malaguti Rossi, E. (2004) *Handicap e rinnovamento della didattica. Esperienze e riflessioni dell'Autonomia.* Roma: Anicia.

Massi, D. (ed.) (1996) *Handicap e legislazione. Diritti in gioco.* Rome: Presidenza Consiglio dei Ministri e Dipartimento per l'Informazione e l'Editoria.

Mills, C. W. (1959) *The Sociological Imagination.* London, Oxford, New York: Oxford University Press.

Moore, A. (2004) *The Good Teacher. Dominant Discourses in Teaching and Teacher Education.* London and New York: Routledge Falmer.

Morin, E. (2000) *La testa ben fatta. Riforma dell'insegnamento e riforma del pensiero* (S. Lazzari, Trans.). Milano: Raffaello Cortina Editore.

Nocera, S. (ed.) (2001) *Il diritto all'integrazione nella scuola dell'autonomia. Gli alunni in situazione di handicap nella normativa scolastica italiana.* Trento: Erickson.

Oliver, M. (1990) *The Politics of Disablement.* Basingstoke: Macmillan.

Pavone, M. (2003) 'L'integrazione scolastica in una fase adulta'. *L'integrazione scolastica e sociale,* 2, 7–14.

Pfeiffer, D. (1998) 'The ICIDH and the need for its revision'. *Disability and Society,* 13, 503–523.

Pfeiffer, D. (2000) 'The devils are in the details: the ICIDH2 and the disability movement'. *Disability and Society,* 15, 1079–1082.

Shakespeare, T. and Watson, N. (2002) 'The social model of disability: an outdated ideology?', *Research in Social Science and Disability,* 2, 9–28.

Thomas, C. (1999) *Female Forms. Experiencing and Understanding Disability.* Buckingham and Philadelphia: Open University Press.

Thomas, C. (2002) 'Disability theory: Key ideas, issues and thinkers'. in C. Barnes, M. Oliver and L. Barton (eds), *Disability Studies Today* 38–57, Cambridge: Polity Press.

Whitty, G. (1999) 'Creating quasi-markets in education: a review of recent research on parental choice and school autonomy in three countries'. in J. Marshall and M. Peters (eds), *Education Policy* 219–263. Cheltenham, UK; Northampton, MA, USA: An Elgar Reference Collection.

WHO. (2001) *Classificazione Internazionale del Funzionamento, della Disabilità e della Salute.* Trento: Erickson.

ABDELBASIT GADOUR

5.   THE RHETORIC OF INCLUSIVE EDUCATION IN LIBYA: ARE CHILDREN'S RIGHTS IN CRISIS?

INTRODUCTION

For me, the area of special educational needs, particularly in the developing countries, has been a subject of concern for a number of years, not only because of the lack of research by which to inform policies and practices within those countries in general, but also because of educational, social, political and economic constraints. These concerns are also integral to identifying the educational needs of children and therefore providing relevant provision within the mainstream system. Although the argument of Barton and Tomlinson (1984) that there is a lack of comparative research in special education is still valid, it is not my intention to compare educational policies and provision for children with special educational needs in Libya with those elsewhere.

This chapter aims to discuss the Libyan literature on special educational needs (SEN). Additionally, in the following pages I shall explore ways in which the notion of 'education for all' is perceived in the Libyan context; and the origin of the notion of special educational needs. I also aim to examine the current position and function of special education in relation to the existent policies and practices. It is hoped that this will provide some significant insights into the Libyan situation with regard to construction of categories, educational policies and teachers and schools' concerns.

EDUCATION FOR ALL: A HISTORICAL PERSPECTIVE

Generally in Libya, there are three main stages of education prior to the tertiary level: primary from the age of 6 to 12, preparatory from the age of 13 to 15 and secondary from the age of 16 to 18. Previous to the early nineties only the primary level was compulsory. Within the schools, a system of promotion based solely on passing end of year examinations prevailed. Thus if a child failed at one level, they had to repeat that level for another year. As a possible consequence of this, legislation was later passed to combine the first two stages, thus extending the age at which an individual could legally leave school to 15. Despite being given this additional time to complete compulsory schooling, this system of promotion based on academic success did not adequately meet

73

L. Barton and F. Armstrong (eds.), Policy, Experience and Change, 73–90.
© 2008 Springer Science + Business Media B.V.

the needs of pupils. Children may still have been expelled either by the schools for failing the same level twice, or through the sheer frustration of being unable to cope with the demands of school. This would not have been the end to their educational careers though, as many of them simply enrolled in another school based on their parents' relationships with teachers and school administrators. There is little to indicate, however, that all the educational needs of these pupils were met. Having identified this problem, and armed with information and policy statements from the World Conference on Special Needs in 1994, the Libyan Educational Authorities (LEAs) moved forward to achieving 'education for all'.

The search for education for all is a worldwide phenomenon but it is particularly important in developing countries, where education is widely viewed as a key to individual and collective success. The 'World Declaration of Education for All' (1990) Article 3 urged that steps be taken to provide equal access to education for all disabled persons as an integral part of the educational system. Following this testimony, the Salamanca Statement (1994) asserts similar rights:

> We the delegates of the World Conference on Special Needs Education representing ninety-two governments and twenty-five international organisations, assembled here in Salamanca, Spain from 7–10 June 1994, hereby reaffirm our commitment to education for All recognising the necessity and urgency of providing education for children, youth and adults with special educational needs within the regular school system. (p. iii)

At Libya's independence in December 1951, enormous effort was directed toward the education sector and particularly toward primary education for all. However, due to economic problems and extreme shortage of teachers and professionals, the government found it difficult to achieve this target. It was not until the present government took over in 1969, when the country became financially secure and educationally well established as a result of the oil revenue, that education reached almost every child (Ministry of Education, Directory of Planning, 1974; The National Educational Report, 2000). Education was then viewed as a process of human liberation that should be provided by the state for all its citizens. Thus, education from 6 to 15 was made compulsory and free of charge for all children at the basic educational level (The Libyan National Commission for Education, Culture and Science, 2001).

Currently the number of children enrolled at the basic educational level has reached 1,160,315 in 1998, compared with 560,798 in 1968 (Ministry of Education, Directory of Planning, 1974; The Libyan National Commission for Education, Culture and Science, 2001). The Libyan national educational report on education for the year 2000 states that the rate of enrolment for the first preparatory grade has reached 100 per cent, and sometimes exceeds this rate because schools accept children who are younger or older than six years of age. In comparison with the total population in 1998, which was 5,270,000, all children who are of school age and adhere to the compulsory laws of education are enrolled (The Libyan National Commission for Education, Culture and Science, 2001). Moreover, the Libyan educational authorities have emphasised that the national curriculum should be flexible and meet the educational needs of all learners so that they will be able to contribute to the formation of their society (The Libyan National Commission for Education, Culture and Science, 2001). National educational provision was, therefore, based on the principle of education for all and its principal aim was to secure equal educational opportunities for all children (see Law No. (5) for 1987 concerning disabled people).

Despite all the initiatives of the Libyan government to ensure universal education at the basic educational level, it seems that there has been a greater concern with the quantity (enrolling more children) rather than with the quality of education delivered to these children. This appears to be an overwhelming feature in relation to the current trend toward education for all. Abdelhameed (1996) attributed the problem associated with quantity as opposed to quality in education largely to the limited budget that is often allocated to educational provisions within underdeveloped countries. This has, in his opinion, put policies and decision makers in Libya under unnecessary pressure to choose between whether they want to continue having a high number of pupils at mainstream schools or maintain a high standard of schooling. While both have looked appealing in Libya, it is often the case that effective schools are constantly measured by the number of children who are promoted to the next year as opposed to the number of children achieving academic success in terms of their own development (The Department of Educational Supervision, 1998). Certainly the educational system in Libya is exam-oriented with a focus primarily on those who are likely to pass their exams and get transferred to the next stage of their education. This has caused, in turn, the quality of teaching and learning received to deteriorate and consequently allows room for some pupils to be held back and eventually excluded. To illustrate this further, schools in Libya are reluctant to allow pupils to continue studying after they have repeated the same academic year twice in a row. Likewise, some pupils may find it extremely hard repeating the same academic work, while their classmates are promoted to the next stage of their education. Thus, some pupils may feel disadvantaged in the sense that they can no longer study with their peers and face the additional stigma of being the 'repeaters' in the upcoming year group.

Currently, in the Arab world, there is a growing concern with the increasing number of pupils who are held back and prevented from being promoted each year (Abdelhameed, 1996; The National Educational Report, 2000). According to Abdelhameed (1996) the holding back system has led to many pupils giving up school at an early age. While countries such as Libya have already begun to create a system that guarantees automatic promotion for pupils, it seems that the real deficiencies within these schools, that is, poor quality of teaching and learning, are still ignored (see The National Educational Report, 2000). Although this may reflect a lack of educational support in general, there is a belief among Libyan educators that pupils do benefit from the holding back system. Despite the fact that this has proved on the national scale to be expensive and very damaging, it has prepared the ground for pupils to be totally excluded from their schools. Equally, one would argue that the automatic promotion system, which is implemented in years 1 to year 3 of primary education, is loose and very underdirected. Unquestionably, the needs of children at this stage should be properly scrutinised and addressed within the context where the problems occur rather than holding them back from promotion. This, in my view, should take into account children's and parents' opinions of the difficulties and what may have contributed to them.

The Libyan National Report concerning Education for All (2000) acknowledged the need to include the excluded in mainstream schools in Libya. The report also suggested that children who fail more than once in the same class should still be expelled; further Al-Shapani (2000) noted children with deviant behaviour continue to present teachers and schools with great problems and consequently teachers find themselves spending more time controlling children's behaviour than actually teaching. Thus, the quality of teaching and learning is again affected in a negative way. This situation is paradoxical in that there seem to be a contradiction between the aims of the education for all policies and the actual practices of LEAs. Thus, it seems that there are still efforts necessary to make progress towards achieving education for all.

Although Libyan legislation is in accord with UNESCO's principles concerning education for all (The Libyan National Commission for Education, Culture and Science, 2001), it is not yet evident whether the initiative of education for all is fully appreciated by LEAs. Interestingly, while the LEAs seem to welcome integration of a large proportion of children labelled as having special educational needs in mainstream classrooms, they seem to have failed to ease the pressure imposed on both children and teachers by the requirements of the national curriculum. This anxiety in turn means pupils are still segregated because they fail the academic requirements for achievement as measured by school exams (Al-Shapani, 2000). It has also been found that the current sanction system used by teachers in mainstream schools contradicts the Geneva Convention on children's rights (The United Nations Report, 1998). Indeed, the current educational practices in Libya suggest that the fate of children lies in the hand of professionals, namely, teachers and head teachers, who are entitled by the LEA to make all the decisions regarding children's schooling problems. It is the regulations of LEAs which further allow teachers and head teachers to exercise their power in order to make children conform to school rules, while jeopardising the welfare of children and making parents reluctant to participate effectively with schools in the education of their children. This reflects the considerable need for a clear framework for children and parents to consult in times of crisis with teachers and schools, particularly when the school is violating their interests.

Indeed, the real question then is not whether it is sensible to continue struggling for education for all, but rather how to ensure that education for all responds adequately to the educational needs of those who are very often marginalized within mainstream classrooms. Thus, I strongly believe that the educational needs of children in Libyan mainstream schools need to be clarified before the target of education for all can be achieved.

THE NAME GAME – AN ANALYSIS OF THE ORIGINS OF
CATEGORIES AND IDENTITIES IN EDUCATION IN LIBYA

A review of the Libyan literature on the categories of special educational needs revealed that very little formal research has been done (El-Samman, 1993; The National Educational Report, 2000; The People's Committee for Education and Scientific Research, 2000; Al-Shapani, 2001). The seven categories recognised by the Ministries of Health and Social Security as requiring special educational provision include: mental retardation/severe learning difficulties; emotional and behavioural disturbance; visual impairments; hearing impairments; language disorders; physical disabilities; and learning disabilities (Ministry of Education, 1979; El-Samman, 1993). Yet the educational needs of children classified in this report are neither explicitly nor educationally defined. Although a great proportion of these children are still educated in mainstream classrooms, this does not ensure that their specific needs have been addressed properly. In fact, the LEAs have failed in their legislation to reach an agreement on common terms that actually describe the educational needs of these children. This is also the case concerning educational policies and regulations covering the general education of children.

There is still some ambiguity concerning the notions of special educational needs and special education (SE). In fact educators often use these terms interchangeably to describe the same complex phenomena. The origin of this misnaming can be traced to the origin of the terms themselves. These expressions have been imported from the west, namely the UK and USA, mostly by postgraduates studying in foreign contexts. While understanding the foreign contexts in which they study, it must be pointed out that the principles and policies underpinning educational practices in the West vary greatly from those in Libya. Indeed, these terms are alien to the Libyan culture and as such have done more harm than good to our children and education system than actually anticipated by their importers. This is often because they tend to focus on classifications rather than remediation and as such create tensions between schools and homes in general. Regrettably this problem has become widespread and affected many educational policies. Hence it has become quite legitimate to refer to children as having special educational needs as 'slow learners', 'disruptive' or 'maladjusted' children both in school documents and national educational reports, instead of genuinely attempting to contextualise children's educational needs and consequently responding to those needs within the mainstream classroom (The People's Committee for Education and Scientific Research, 1994). Moreover it could be argued that educational policies in Libya have failed to address children's educational needs because they were not informed by actual research conducted in the relevant context, but rather influenced by individuals' findings and ideas which were merely brought from abroad. Therefore, it is not uncommon to see teachers like other school professionals in Libya carry out their assessment with children experiencing learning and behaviour difficulties in the absence of a clear framework.

Another controversial issue concerned with the creation of special educational needs is the use of labelling to describe children's difficulties. There is a growing concern with the subjectivity of labels used by school professionals in Libya to identify the needs of children as opposed to actually trying to understand the needs of children (Gadour, 2003). Although labels are often used generally as a vehicle to secure resources for the school (Farrell, 1995), it seems almost impossible to have the children's needs officially assessed without the referral of their teachers. This issue remains to be addressed by Libyan educators. Interestingly enough, like elsewhere, in Libya there are political and socio-cultural factors influencing the label attached to the referral. On the political level, there will always be a threat to the general budget if the educational needs of children are identified and met within the mainstream system. This would require extra resources for spending on preparing and training specialists. While on the socio-cultural level schools are fully aware of how serious the problem is when labels are exposed and used by classmates, similarly, parents of children with special educational needs would condemn schools for having certain labels for their children. This is similar to the perception of parents of children in England. Although children are statemented so that the school can get additional money to hire support staff, many parents fight this as they think it will stigmatise their children (Blaize, 2000). This is not to say that mislabelling of children as 'slow learners' or 'disruptive' does not exist in schools, but rather that the needs of children are poorly defined. It is also worth mentioning here that mainstream schools in Libya no longer make provision for personal and social education, yet are ready to hold pupils responsible for failing to conform to its rules and regulations.

OBSTACLES TO SPECIAL EDUCATIONAL PROVISION

Research into the educational policies in Libya concerning the support available within schools highlights the lack of educational provision for children with special educational needs (Al-Shapani, 1996). In fact, the new educational structure in Libya has once again failed to explicitly lay down the procedures by which the educational needs of children are identified and consequently addressed within mainstream schools; despite the existing policy of encouraging integration of pupils with special educational needs into mainstream classrooms (The People's Committee for Education and Scientific Research, 2000).

The National Conference on Education, 1996, was set up partly in response to the public's concerns with the lack of having educational provisions for children classified as having special educational needs in schools in Libya. Al-Shapani (1996) highlighted the increasing lack of response to children's emotional and behavioural difficulties in Libyan schools, while at the same time he was concerned with the growing pressure on teachers to pass on academic knowledge rather than actually enhancing children's personal and social education. In fact, the majority of papers delivered by the participants in this conference underline the overwhelming need for schools to have enough resources to respond to pupils' educational needs on day-to-day bases.

The subsequent report (The National Educational Report, 2000) showed there is a strong link between those who failed to get promoted and the lack of resources available at schools. In a similar way, the report showed that those pupils who were prevented from promotion because of academic reasons have also had behaviour difficulties of one sort or another. In line with these problems, the report described the number of pupils who gave up school during the last decade as unprecedented and alarming, reflecting children's accumulated frustrations in complying with the schools' and classrooms' expectations. In addition, the report showed a tendency to label children's behaviour as casual, disaffected and sometimes disruptive to the classroom routine. Indeed, there are an increasing number of children labelled as having behaviour problems whose failure to comply with the school rules and regulations reflects learning pressures imposed by a restricted national curriculum (Gadour, 2003). While this appears to reduce children's self-confidence and hence make them over-anxious, it confirms that the current educational programme implemented in the primary school is too formal. Likewise, children's anxiety was also associated with copying constantly from boards, putting up with teachers' instructions and attitudes, being disadvantaged by the standard examination format (often finding it easier to learn in groups) and assessment results which do not reflect the amount of effort they put into their study.

Nonetheless, recent research suggests there is a wide range of support available to mainstream schools with respect to children experiencing learning difficulties – additional pedagogical support and access to visiting specialists to monitor pupils' progress (El-Hassain, 1996). El-Hassain noted an extensive use of individual educational plans (IEPs) in schools used as a means of responding to pupils' academic difficulties. In a similar way, teachers are expected to identify individual learning needs and inform their educational supervisors of the need to set up a particular plan that would respond to the needs of pupils (The Department of Educational Supervision, 1998). Nonetheless, it is important to note that only a small percentage of mainstream schools in Libya provide adequate IEPs for pupils (Gadour, 2003). Similarly, experts in the field of education have noted that the IEP does not involve those with various behavioural difficulties, though their behaviour may only be a reflection of their learning problems (Al-Shapani, 1996). Instead, children with anti-social behaviour are identified as either troubled or trouble makers and are normally left to their own devices (The People's Committee for Education and Scientific Research, 2000). As an alternative to the remedial procedures mentioned above, schools may on occasion use various forms of sanctions including corporal punishment. Although all forms of punishment against children in Libya are denied in the Committee Report on the Rights of the Child, this does not mean that children will not be physically punished in schools (The National Report, 1991; submitted report on education in Libya to the UNESCO). In fact, corporal punishment is still, in effect, the ultimate way to make pupils conform to school rules; thus, some teachers still maintain tradition and perceive the cane as the most effective means of imposing discipline (Al-Shapani, 2001).

Al-Shapani (2001) has found the relationship between school rules and the way children react to these rules to be strong. He described the current role of the school in dealing with pupils' behaviour problems as more complex and difficult than it was in the past. He also highlighted the increasing lack of shared understanding about standards of 'good' and 'bad' behaviour for both pupils and teachers within the school. In exemplifying this, Al-Shapani observed that pupils would no longer stand up when teachers entered the classroom; while he argued that this is because pupils want to show disrespect to teachers, he stressed that teachers' attitude to this traditional symbol has become casual, and consequently this change has influenced their attitudes as much as those of the pupils. This echoes the PCESR's Report (The People's Committee for Education and Scientific Research, 1994) which deemed that the current school system of reward and punishment, counselling and attitudes of its professionals towards pupils' personal and social education can have a direct influence on students' behaviour.

Similarly, Al-Shapani (2001) expressed concern over pupils' current lack of academic achievement and with the level of disruptive behaviour within Libyan schools. In fact, these problems appeared to cause the teaching-learning process to suffer (Al-Shapani, 2001). Interestingly while teachers in the United Kingdom also faced a common problem, its origin is very often attributed to factors beyond teachers and school control (Croll and Moses, 1985, Wheldall and Merrett, 1988; Garner, 1991, Farrell, 1995). While this can be true, Al-Shapani (2001) held that the lack of resources including teachers' training programmes, revenue and the nature of the national curriculum were responsible for teachers' frustration and failure to meet pupils' educational needs. This suggests that pupils' difficulties in schools are caused by factors that fall beyond their control. Although it is beyond the scope of this chapter to locate the origin of pupils' special educational needs, it should be noted that there would always be different causes beyond the individuals' control to which their particular difficulties could be attributed. A more recent published report by PCESR (2000) on 'Educational Objectives for The Twenty First Century' highlighted the growing concern with the lack of educational provision in mainstream schools. Although the PCESR suggests that teachers within schools should address pupils' educational needs, nothing has been publicly formulated on how this can be done, a problem that is often noted in the annual educational reports. Certainly the use of IEPs falls short of parents' and children's expectations and hence does not fulfil the required educational goals. In the absence of written policies on special education/provision each school appears to develop its own policy in line with their own mission statement. As a result of these circumstances there are neither legislation nor clear school policies to regulate how and when special education services should be provided.

POLICIES AND LEGISLATIONS

The Libyan National Commission for Education, Culture and Science (1994, p. 31) defined special education as 'the kind of education that enables certain groups of the population to obtain the kind of teaching and training most appropriate to them'. Like many educational policies in Libya, the Libyan National Commission for Education, Culture and Science links special education with disabled pupils and likewise classifies them as pupils with special educational needs, though the needs of these pupils have not been explained educationally. Generally there are more government policies concerned with disabled people namely those who are blind and deaf, than with any other forms of disabilities. Although the actual reasons behind the government's inclination to support particular groups of disabled people, as opposed to others are not clear, it appears that the long social and political struggles by the blind and deaf volunteer members for equal rights led to the development of specific legislation concerning their educational needs. The most distinctive legislation concerned with disabled people's civil liberties was released after the General Libyan Congress gathered in 1986 to endorse the establishment of the National Committee for the Disabled People (NCDP). This was done after deep consideration of both the popular congresses' and committees' decisions and the Law No. 3 for Disabled people in 1981. Following this resolution the NCDP issued Act No. (5) in 1987, which consisted of thirty-nine decrees, all of which underpinned the rules and regulations for disabled people. The first decree stressed that 'measures to prevent disability occurring is a responsibility which falls equally on the individual, family, communities, local authorities and the society as a whole'. Decree No. 2 defines a disabled person as 'anyone who suffers from permanent deficit that prevents him/her partially or completely from working, or from "practising normal behaviour" as perceived in society, whether it manifests itself in physical, mental or psychological impairments, or is caused by external or congenital factors'.

Decree No. (3) classifies disabled people into four main categories:

- Mentally retarded.
- Those who suffer from impairment which prevents them from 'practising normal behaviour' as perceived in society, even though this may not be necessarily associated with apparent impairment that stops them from working
- Those who suffer from chronic or long-term illnesses which prevent them from working, even though this may not be necessarily associated with an apparent deficit that stops them from 'practising normal behaviour' in society.
- Those who have had one or two of their limbs amputated or those who suffer from permanent deficit in one part or more of their bodies.

My personal reservation concerning the above definitions stems from the fact that the terms 'deficit' and 'behaviour' are ambiguous words. Also, the definition implicitly suggests that abnormal behaviour is contrary to 'normal behaviour', both of which are poorly identified in the 1987 Act. (The Arabic League for Social Workers (1981).) In fact, decree No. 3 has done little, if anything, to clarify previous legislation, particularly with regard to the type and nature of deficiency that prevents people from behaving in a 'normal way'. Similarly, both decrees failed to identify the needs of disabled people, though the Act emphasised in more than one place that the needs of disabled individuals should be addressed in spite of the extent and density of the disability. This, on the other hand, suggested that disabled people should be granted proper access to accommodation, education, work and rehabilitations under the 1987 Act. (The Social Security Association, 1987.) These include subsidies, exemptions from taxes and a reduction of up to half price on flights and bus tickets. However, despite the fact that the 1987 Act stressed the right of disabled people to obtain the necessary equipment and facilities in order to be able to adjust their behaviour and integrate into society; it legitimised, under the decree No 15, exclusion of disabled pupils from regular classrooms where integration with their counterparts is not deemed possible.

Additionally, decree No. 15 continues to legitimise and follow a 'medical model of diagnosis', treatment and cure, which has dominated the assessment of children labelled as having special educational needs. The fact that this view appears to characterise behaviour problems as being inherent in the individual consequently constructs two separate categories of people, 'normal' and 'abnormal' and thus reinforces this limited law. As a result of this model, a service delivery system has emerged which removes deviant behaviour from the regular education classroom by providing specialised services. Thus, several medical centres for children with severe learning and behaviour disorders have been established, mainly in the large cities of Libya, to respond to the wider needs of those children. This includes 'maladjusted' children whose emotions and behaviour become either disturbing or disturbed, though the borderline between these terms remains problematic. Maladjusted children have often been described in educational terms in Libya as reflecting deficiencies within their personal and social education (see Al-Shapani, 1996). It is implied that they are ineducable within the mainstream school setting. In fact, this concern has been highlighted in the Educational Reform Act (1974) indicating difficulties experienced by teachers and schools in meeting the needs of maladjusted children within the normal classroom (cited in The Ministry of Education, 1979). Consequently, new decrees were created by the Ministry of Education in 1974 recognising the rights of these children to more accessible and sociable education in the public schools. In line with this, the Ministry of Education (1974) also authorised some social organisations run by the Ministry of Social Security to coordinate day and boarding schools designated for children with various behaviour disorders – more qualified experts, for example, paediatricians and psychiatrics, were imported from neighbour countries, such as Egypt, in order to respond to the needs of such children.

In line with many previous Acts and other government documents, the 1987 Act was not conclusive in identifying the educational problems encountered by pupils in schools. There are still substantial numbers of pupils with various educational requirements unknown to the LEAs. This is usually because of two main reasons: one of which is poor diagnosis of the problem, which in my judgment has contributed significantly to the cursory response to the educational needs of these children. Secondly, through the influence of parents networking within the school administration, the child remains within the regular classroom, even though this may lead to his/her educational needs being neglected. This also has an effect on the implementation of school and educational policies which are also very often manipulated by the parents' relation with professionals. While this may reflect parents' power to affect the decision making process in ways which allow their children to stay in the setting they choose, it does not ensure that the educational needs of children are properly addressed. The problem, therefore, seems to lie quite often in the abuse of the educational system by both parents and school professionals, rather than the lack of decent educational policies in Libya. Likewise, it should not be surprising to note the public perception of the educational policies as of little significance in terms of contributing to the overall development of the welfare of children. It is within this problematic framework that special education seems to have to function. Therefore unless serious measures are taken by the LEAs to see educational practices determined by policies, the education of children in Libya are at risk.

Parents of disabled children are entitled by the LEAs to choose whether they wish to bring their children to mainstream schools or send them to special centres and schools. This opportunity is restricted to certain groups of disabled children such as those who are partially blind, hard of hearing or those with mobility impairments. It is highly unlikely that children with anti social behaviour will be allowed to stay in any settings, let alone mainstream schools (El-Samman, 1993). This is often because they are perceived as a threat to the interest of schools and as such provide particular challenges to the system of education. There is also much less interest among parents to send their children to schools renowned for using ineffective procedures with pupils who display anti social behaviour. Hence, there is a general tendency to remove the problem child from the classroom regardless of the location of the setting or of the child's abilities. While this is often against the wishes of parents and children, it is justified by rationalizing the problem as being the child's unwillingness to conform to school rules and regulations as opposed to an admission of failure on the part of school.

Children are frequently excluded from schools on the grounds that they will benefit greatly from special provision in special schools, but very few, who were often orphans and boys who come from disadvantaged families, were found to willingly accept being educated in special schools (see Ministry of Education, 1979). Interestingly El-Samman (1993) found children with deviant behaviour difficult to manage in special schools and consequently they are excluded from special schools too. Although El-Samman claimed that these children are at higher risk and therefore require more individual attention, he highlighted the lack of expertise available to determine their specific needs and in turn capacity to respond to those needs. Children are often encouraged to join the vocational departments within these special schools (El-Samman, 1993) in an attempt to encourage them to remain. This 'solution' is further compounded by the stigma and sense of devaluation which follow those who attend special classes and schools wherever they are as they are seen as being less competitive than those who stay in ordinary classrooms. This has indeed made the chances of such provision succeeding in a traditional society such as Libya, very slim. Thus, it is essential to recognise these traditional barriers alongside other factors, which contribute to the exclusion of these children.

INTEGRATION VERSUS INCLUSION

In general, educational policies in Libya reflect a tendency toward integration of all children at the basic educational level by promoting the notion of education for all (The Libyan National Educational Report On Education, 2000; The National Educational Report, 2000; The People's Committee for Education and Scientific Research, 2000, 1994). This has also emerged clearly from the educational report submitted to the United Nations in Geneva, 1998. However, the report indicated that inclusion in Libyan schools is far from being achieved as there are some children, particularly those with challenging behaviour who are either excluded or discriminated against within the mainstream settings. Indeed, there has been a move toward integration of more children experiencing learning difficulties than with behaviour difficulties, though the requirements of the former have not been addressed properly within classrooms (Gadour, 2003). Despite this progress, children with learning difficulties are very often left to their own devices in terms of assimilation into the mainstream classrooms. Hence, integration seems to fall short of learners' expectations and more often than not exposes them to unnecessary pressure. Thus, it is hoped that within the inclusion framework the curricula and pedagogy in mainstream schools in Libya will be moulded to suit the diversities and requirements of classroom learners.

The Ministry of Education (1979) has defined the term 'inclusion' as giving opportunities for all pupils regardless of their disabilities to equal access and participation in all activities in the total school environment. Al-Qadhafi (1990) further perceived inclusion in general social terms, as the main solution to our problems in Libya Al-Qadhafi (1991) used the word inclusion to include the poor, difficult, disadvantaged, disabled and those deemed 'ineducable'. However, this rhetoric of inclusion is not yet implemented in schools. In fact, there are still many obstacles preventing inclusive education from developing in Libya. Similarly Al-Qadhafi (1990) believed that there were still some people marginalised by the state for a variety of reasons. In the early nineties he was concerned with the practices of educational assessment in schools, which in his opinion, are based on rigid criteria of methodised curriculum (Al-Qadhafi, 1990). While he held this process responsible for pupils' exclusion in general, he described it as:

> ... compulsory obliteration of a human being's talents as well as a forcible direction of human being's choices. It is an act of dictatorship damaging to freedom because it deprives man of free choice, creativity and brilliance (Al-Qadhafi, 1990, p. 110).

Indeed, for many pupils, exclusion has been an inevitable path from an early stage in their schooling. This is often because of their failure to meet the expectations of the classroom which are frequently determined by competency criteria based upon the national education curriculum. In relation to this, the National Educational Report, 2000 showed the number of those who had left education before the school leaving age has increased rapidly over the last decade, though the actual figure and reasons accountable for that remain unknown. However, the report does identify a correlation between those who give up school and low achievement. In fact, the report classified those who quit school, in particular, as 'low achievers'. The fact that these children are labelled as low achievers does not necessarily reflect the pressure imposed upon them to score high marks for promotion within a large class size that make individualised attention very difficult, where teachers look for consistency of pupils rather than diversity.

This situation has forced schools to run extra, special classes in the afternoon, taught mainly by experienced teachers. These had the aim of benefiting slow learners in small and well-organised classes using special materials although there is no evidence demonstrating that these segregated special classes have significant benefits for learners. Interestingly, this seems in direct contradiction to the 2000 Educational Report which emphasised the right of slow learners to more inclusive and appropriate education. In a similar way, the report requires alternative programmes of education and training to be available for such pupils, where placement in public school was preferable to placement in any other type of programme of education and training, and placement in a regular public school class was preferable to placement in a special class in a public school. Despite these recommendations, in practice, there is a general tendency among teachers to remove the problem from the main setting although this means the education of the pupils suffer and that they may be held back.

Nonetheless, Al-Shapani (1996) stressed the pivotal role of teachers in fulfilling pupils' wishes or in hindering them, also noting the extreme shortage of resources available for teachers to cope with day-to-day classroom pressures. Al-Shapani used resources to encompass teacher training, income support and the school's ethos in general. Whilst, Abdelhameed (1996) argued that there is not conclusive evidence to suggest that pupils were excluded or forced to leave schools from an early age because of insufficient resources within schools. Instead, he insisted that schools which frequently motivate and expect a high level of achievement among their pupils do encourage them to stay longer and consequently overcome their difficulties. In this respect, Abdelhameed appeared to give much more weight to the role of teacher as a facilitator whose attitude and knowledge of the subject is important in the process of teaching and learning. Likewise, he depicted teachers' roles as both manipulating and influencing the classroom activities which in turn shape pupils' approaches and attitudes toward learning rather than external factors, for example, textbooks and other school facilities.

While Abdelhameed's arguments may be true in that the teacher is an essential figure in the whole approach toward promoting inclusion in schools, inclusion cannot be achieved without the necessary ingredients such as: appropriate teacher training, adequate financial support for teachers, effective teaching aids, a balanced and flexible national curriculum, proper home-school communications and adequate provision for children. These issues need in my opinion to be addressed by the LEAs. Thus, what seems to be present in mainstream schools is a shadow form of integration, as opposed to inclusion, merely for those who are perceived as less disruptive, less noisy, and withdrawn, suffer in silence and basically demand less attention from the teachers. Of course, there will always be room for some children with challenging behaviour to stay in mainstream schools, regardless of the difficulties encountered by teachers, empowered by the influence of their parents on the school administration. On the other hand, in Libya, it will take a long time to fully realise the objectives of inclusion, not least because the current educational reform fails to readdress the notion of education led by assessment. Indeed, as long as the present system of 'holding pupils back' is still applied within mainstream schools, there will always be pupils excluded from schools. Therefore, for inclusion to take place, there should be a total revolution of the education system in which schools are required to replace their old approaches, based on segregation and exclusion, with the new principles of inclusion.

One way of moving forward is to question the notion of exclusion. In this respect, experts from the United Nations Office at Geneva have expressed concern with regard to the increasing number of children who are excluded from public schools in Libya (The United Nations Report, 1998). In this respect, the committee of experts asked stakeholders in the educational system whether under Libyan legislation and in practice children's voices were heard concerning procedures affecting them in such cases as expulsion from school and corporal punishment. Although no accurate response was given by the Libyan delegation to the United Nations Office on this issue, it has been stressed that traditionally children must respect the opinions and decisions of adults: parents, teachers and head teachers, and consequently express no contradictory views to their elders. The delegation also appeared reluctant in the report to comment on the increasing use of corporal punishment both at home and in school as a means of dealing with children's antisocial behaviour. In spite of the existing law which forbids parents and teachers from using corporal punishment, this has not guaranteed that children would not be abused. Furthermore, although the United Nations Report (1998) showed that Libya has for many years had a children's congress encouraged by the leader

Al-Qadhafi to allow them to voice their opinions and inform adults of children's issues, little has been done to really familiarise parents and teachers about this convention.

Indeed, the above practices appeared to contradict the underlying principles in the social basis of the third universal theory advocated by Al-Qadhafi, where it is seen that an individual's needs, rights and demands should be responded to collectively (see the Green Book by Al-Qadhafi, 1991). In line with this Al-Qadhafi believes that learners in schools all over the world (including pupils in Libyan schools) are still being denied the chance to choose freely the place, type of education, subjects that they wish to learn and the criteria of assessment. In the same manner, Al-Qadhafi stated that inadequate schools restrict pupils' freedom of choice and consequently put them under unnecessary pressure to accept what is merely available; while on the other hand denying them natural right of choice of where they want to be and what subjects they want to study. Moreover, with this argument, Al-Qadhafi (1990, p. 112) portrayed societies which prevent and monopolise knowledge, and therefore deny the right to learn, as 'reactionary and biased towards ignorance, and hostile to freedom'; therefore knowledge is a 'natural right of every human being which nobody has the right to deprive him of under any pretext'.

In making these allegations, Al-Qadhafi was especially concerned with the disempowerment of pupils in the decision making process in Libyan schools, which he believed was responsible for marginalizing the voice of learners and hence leading to much less meaningful education. In fact, he depicted schools which fail to meet learners' educational needs as 'dysfunctional' and 'ignorant'. Likewise, he perceived the exclusion of certain groups from full participation in education based on their lack of adjustment and intelligence as 'reactionary' and 'backward'. Although this often emerged as a result of a lack of understanding of what pupils' educational needs actually were, it is interesting to note Al-Qadhafi attributes pupils' difficulties to factors within the educational system and schools: pedagogy and lack of supervision. Thus, unless these problems are clearly identified and addressed within mainstream schools by LEAs, pupils' liberties are at risk.

CONCLUSION

For a number of reasons, this chapter was not an easy one to write. In particular I must emphasise the difficulties in finding sources on special education in Libya, where there are no clear policies on inclusive education and integration. Although I am informed by the wealth of information on special education in western society, I did not want to fall in the same trap as my predecessors, and impose western values into the Libyan context. On the educational grounds I felt that engaging with non-Libyan literature, especially where the philosophy and educational practices differ considerably from those in Libya, would have jeopardised the legitimacy of the arguments in this chapter. Perhaps what struck me more than anything else is the fact that children and parents in Libya seem to accept the rules and regulations of the school and those of LEAs, though these more often than not act against their wishes.

Despite the claim by LEAs to have moved towards a more liberal approach to empower children in their schools, there seems to be a problem in achieving social objectives especially the welfare of the child as opposed to social exclusion. The educational practices, in Libya, suggest that LEAs need to think long and hard before meaningful education for all can be achieved despite the efforts made to enable a large proportion of children to receive education at the basic educational level. However, there is a considerable need for more desirable education, which is based not on segregation and exclusion. Education at the primary level does not need to be led by rigid assessment that routinely produces children with poor educational qualities. In my view, this factor alone has caused the idea of education for all to suffer, because it allows some children to be categorised and excluded from receiving proper education in the setting they want. It is within this ineffective framework of assessment, which constantly prepares the ground for some children to be excluded from schools from an early age, mainstream schools appear to function. This, in turn, limits the opportunity for children, especially those with specific learning, emotional and behavioural needs, to stay within a regular classroom. Thus, if true inclusion is to become a reality, serious consideration needs to be given to the focus of education. This suggests that the current educational system in Libya, particularly at the basic educational level, should move away from the focus mainly on those who are likely to pass their exams and get promoted toward more inclusive education concerned with the overall development of all children.

Similarly there should be clear procedures for assessment and intervention with children experiencing special educational needs. Currently, there are no specific procedures in place to respond to children's personal and social needs within the mainstream schools, nor are there identified roles for children and parents in the assessment process (The National Educational Report, 2000). It remains the decision of the school, in consultation with the LEAs, to determine whether special placement or exclusion of children labelled as having special educational needs is necessary. Therefore, it is essential for successful assessment and subsequent intervention with children to take their views on board. This process should also operate from a structured and systematic instructional base in order to identify the nature of children's needs and consequently address those needs within the setting that includes all children.

The argument in this chapter has been that education as practised in Libya, particularly at the basic educational level, is divorced from the relevant concerns for many children classified as having special educational needs and as such tends to expose children to unnecessary pressures. While this is due to many reasons explained earlier in the chapter, it is predominately because education focuses mainly on academic promotion rather than being concerned with the interests of all children.

At present, there is strong belief among Libyan educators that the idea of education for all is not without problems. The time has come, in my opinion, for the Libyan ministry of education through the LEAs to identify the real barriers to education for all at the basic educational level and to make more explicit their views of the actual problems, in terms of children's educational needs and consequently act upon them. This would include rerouting funds traditionally subordinated to other technical and technological projects to basic education, and a more vigilant management of these funds at the micro level where there sometimes exists misappropriation and abuse of allocated funds (Al-Shapani, 2000). Most importantly there is a need for a clear vision of education for all, clearly narrated policies which articulate this vision is enforced by an official body to which schools would be accountable.

Although the above arguments are based on my experience and understanding of the education system in Libya, the fundamental inconsistencies contributing to these issues are yet to be addressed by educational research on policies in Libya, even though they are embedded in the recommendations of The National Educational Report (2000). While these issues remain politically oriented in their concerns and therefore virgin territory for researchers, it is interesting to note that the National Educational Report (NER) attributes the lack of legislations on special educational needs in general to shortage of research on this topic. Thus, a critical perspective of the present situation of special education based on actual research would enable us to focus our interventions more effectively and in turn inform educational policies and practices.

ACKNOWLEDGEMENT

The research reported in this chapter was supported by the cultural department of the Libyan Embassy, London. I would like to give special thanks to professor Derrick Armstrong and professor Jerry Wellington at the School of Education, Sheffield University, for enabling me to use the university facilities to see this post doctorate research through.

REFERENCES

Abdelhameed, A. (1996) The factors that affect students' achievement: Reading in educational research, paper presented at the National Conference on Education Facing The Twenty First Century: Tripoli.

Al-Qadhafi, M. (1990) *The Green Book: The First Part*, Libya: Tripoli Press.

Al-Qadhafi, M. (1991) *The Green Book: The Second Part*, Libya: Tripoli Press.

Al-Shapani, O. (1996) *The problems That Face Education in Libya and Ways of Overcoming Them:* Tripoli: Tripoli Press.

Al-Shapani, O. (1996) A Philosophical educational project for Jamahiriya Arabia Elbiya, paper presented at the National Conference on Education Facing The Twenty First Century, Tripoli.

Al-Shapani, O. (2000) *Educational Psychology*, Tripoli: Al-Fateh University Press.

Al-Shapani, O. (2001a) *Principles of Social Research*, Libya: Al-Fateh University Press.

Al-Shapani, O. (2001b) *The History of Education in Libya*, Libya: Al-Fateh University Press.

Barton, L. and Tomlinson, S. (1984) *Special Education and Social Interests*, London: Croom Helm.

Blaize, L. (2001) Psychopedagogy explored: An investigation of the psychological approaches used to manage behaviour in Sheffield schools, unpublished MEd thesis, University of Sheffield. United Kingdom.

El-Hassain, S. (1996) Pupils teach each other within limited time and by using organised groups, paper presented at the National Conference on Education Facing the Twenty First Century: Tripoli.

El-Samman, M. (1993) Social relationships, adaptive behaviour and achievement in a school for the blind. unpublished thesis, University of Cardiff. United Kingdom.

Farrell, P. (1995) *Children with Emotional and Behavioural Difficulties: Strategies for Assessment and Intervention*, London: Falmer Press.

Gadour, A. (2003) An investigation into perspectives on children experiencing emotional and behavioural difficulties with special reference to the Libyan context. unpublished thesis, University of Sheffield. United Kingdom.

The Arabic League for Social Workers (1981) The final report on the first conference for the disabled people in Libya: Benghazi.

The Department of Educational Supervision (1998) The supervisors' Annual Report on Education: Basic Education Level. Libya: Derna.

The Libyan National Commission for Education, Culture and Science (2001) The development of education in the Great Jamahiriya, The Great Socialist People's Libyan Arab Jamahiriya, Tripoli.

The Libyan National Report concerning Education for All for the year 2000, the Arabic Regional Conference on Education for All, The evaluation of the year (2000), January 24–27, 2000, Cairo.

The Ministry Of Education (1979) The Jamahiriya Schools Guide: 1978–1979, Ministry of Education Publication: Tripoli.

The National Committee for the Handicapped (1987) The Social Security Act 5, Libya: Tripoli.

The National Educational Report (2000) Education over the years 1996–2000, Libya: Tripoli.

The National Educational Report (1991) Education over the years 1989–1991, Libya: Tripoli.

The People's Committee for Education and Scientific Research (1994) Annual Report by the Legislative Congress: Tripoli.

The People's Committee for Education and Scientific Research (2000) Annual Report by the Legislative Congress: Tripoli.

The Social Security Association (1987) The Libyan Congress Resolution: The National Committee for Disabled People: Tripoli.

The United Nation Report (1998) Education in Libya: Geneva.

UNESCO (1994) The Salamanca Statement and Framework for Action on Special Educational Needs: Paris. UNESCO.

MITHU ALUR

6.   THE LETHARGY OF A NATION: INCLUSIVE EDUCATION IN INDIA AND DEVELOPING SYSTEMIC STRATEGIES FOR CHANGE

In this chapter I describe how we, a group of activists, challenged the systemic failure and exclusion of disabled children within existing Indian Government programmes, and the contributions we made as one of the largest Non-Governmental Organisations (NGOs). The chapter describes how we have begun to evolve from supporting a special school system towards supporting an inclusive one, and how we have developed a unique 'macro-micro' model of inclusion with a top-down bottom-up approach. The chapter focuses on an analysis of disability issues within the policy framework of India and moves on to the mechanisms of change that have been introduced on a macro, mezzo and micro level. The chapter examines the role played by national and international NGOs and agencies over the years and concludes by examining the transformation and change we brought about.

A REFLECTION

Reflecting on issues related to oneself are 'important determinants in providing [readers with] a frame of reference' for a researcher or a writer (Clough and Barton, 1995). Constructs held by us in our personal and professional life shape our thinking, the way we view life and the way we act. Like many people, I guess, I have had to play several roles in a country where there is a systems failure as far as services for disabled people are concerned. I have been an activist, working with families and disabled people to change social attitudes and policy related to disability. I have also been a practitioner, involved with setting up a series of segregated special schools. I have been involved in mass communication, writing in the media, making films and documentaries, and also in advocacy work, participating in rallies, meetings, discussions, conferences and courses, often working with the Government and frequently critiquing government policies. I am not an academic attached to an institute or university; my work is done at grassroots level. Activists are emotional, passionate people. We are not interested in semantics and words but in action and change. From a personal perspective, my interest in the field of disability is part of a long-standing concern for disabled children and their families which began after my daughter was born with an impairment. The role I have enjoyed most of all – and which taught me a great deal about barriers and adversity – is

91

L. Barton and F. Armstrong (eds.), Policy, Experience and Change, 91–106.
© 2008 Springer Science + Business Media B.V.

being a mother and living with my disabled daughter. Day after day I have learned about
the oppressions, large and small, faced by disabled people.

It was in 1966 at a private nursing home in Kolkata, India, where my daughter Malini,
who changed my life so dramatically, was born. At that time very little was known about
her condition, which was a multiple impairment associated with cerebral palsy, and
there was no provision at all in the way of special schools. Finding little understanding
about her needs in India, my husband and I moved with her to England, so that she
would have access to services. Consequently, my life became an ongoing East-West
journey between India and England. I was fortunate to come from a family which had
close links with England, so we were able to take up residence there. My husband found
work and Malini went to an excellent special school in London, called the Hospital for
Sick Children, where she flourished.

At this time I began my professional life at the Institute of Education, the University
of London, where I undertook a diploma in teaching children with physical impairment.
In 1969, the concept of integration was still in its infancy, and my fellow students and
I did not observe any schools where integration was being practised. The teaching continued to be about disabled children in segregated special schools, and visits included
some excellent schools. On my return to India in 1972, together with a group of
colleagues I was able to establish the first special school for children with cerebral palsy,
which combined education and treatment under one roof. It was similar to the special
schools I had observed in England but within an Indian cultural context. We called
the organisation The Spastics Society of India. On the macrolevel we achieved the
following:

- Technical support was provided which offered a strong base for children with
  cerebral palsy and other physical disabilities.
- For the first time the Government recognised neurological disorder as one of the 11
  classifications of cerebral palsy.
- Holistic programmes, combining education and treatment under one roof, were set up.
- The voices of parents were heard and they were empowered to carry on effective
  home management.
- Educational reforms, needed for the Board Examination System, were introduced at
  both the policy formulation and policy implementation level. All over the country,
  several concessions for children were agreed, allowing them to have amanuenses
  and extra time in school. These concessions were introduced at both the school and
  university level.
- Pedagogy on a national level helped to decentralise the services.
- Strong, effective links were established with the Government and with NGOs at both
  the national and international levels.
- The replicability of the model is evident from the fact that several spastics societies
  adopted the first socio-educational model. In 1974, the Spastics Society of Eastern
  India was opened in Kolkata; in 1978, the Spastics Society of Northern India was
  launched in New Delhi and in 1982 and 1985 respectively, the Spastics Society of
  India, Bombay, opened branches in Bangalore and Madras. Each of the societies is

today independent and well known for their innovative work for the disabled. Currently 18 of the 31 States of India have been able to replicate this model (see Bowley and Gardner, 1980, p. 220 for more detail).

Since then our students have pursued careers in accounting, journalism, finance and computing. Some have set up their own successful businesses, others have pursued academic work, achieving Masters degrees and doctorates, demonstrating that – with a few modifications – they are able to undertake the same examinations as regular students in the mainstream. Our experience shows that services can be spread to a larger domain by the sharing of knowledge with other interested parties and, above all, it shows that governments are willing to change.

This took two decades to accomplish. However, although the spastics societies had an enormous impact, this was only the tip of the iceberg in terms of what was needed. Even after two decades of work, I found that children with disability were being excluded from Government programmes, and Government statistics reported that 90 per cent of people with disabilities were not receiving any services (GOI, 1994).

I began to critically examine my own position on a broader level and became a student once again, this time of policy. It was an opportune moment for me, as in 1994, I was invited by the London School of Economics to carry out research as a visiting academic. Here I began a doctoral study of the policy concerning disabled people in India, which I completed at the Institute of Education, the University of London, in 1998. My research focused on a Government of India policy known as the Integrated Child Development Scheme (ICDS). Today the ICDS is considered to be the world's largest preschool service for women and children. It functions on a mammoth scale, providing health checkups, immunisation and nutrition, referral services and informal preschool services, for children from 0–6 years. Although it may have been the intention to include all children, I found that, in practice, disabled children are being overlooked. In examining how this had happened in the world's largest preschool service, I found that many factors had contributed to the non-inclusion of children with disabilities in the Government's mainstream programmes.

THE INTERNATIONAL CONTEXT

Historically, the lives of children and adults with disabilities, and their family members, have been neglected and devalued, their rights as citizens of their countries unrecognised. They have been excluded from schools, isolated from their neighbours and community and been excluded from employment. In response to this history of oppression, a paradigm shift in characterising disability has occurred in the last twenty years. Towards the end of the 1960s, organisations of people with disabilities in the Northern countries started to formulate new conceptions of disability as a form of social oppression; a result of pathology within societies rather than individuals. Today law, policy and programmes tend to reflect two primary theoretical approaches that treat disability either as an individual pathology or as a social pathology (Oliver, 1990; Barnes, Mercer and Shakespeare, 1999). A human rights approach has taken centre stage. International human rights initiatives decree that the exclusion of people with disability in any sphere is a contravention of their human rights. In this context recommendations may involve the provision of support, services and other forms of aid to enable social and economic integration, self-determination and the enforcement of legal and social rights. The emphasis is not merely on the environments which enable or restrict people from participating as equals in societies, but also on policy and law, and on broad systemic factors. International declarations, such as the Convention on the Rights of the Child (UNICEF, 1989) and the Salamanca Statement Framework of Action (UNESCO, 1994), have stipulated that the inclusion of all children with disabilities in mainstream schools should be mandatory. The guiding principle is that ordinary schools should accommodate all children, regardless of their physical, intellectual, emotional, social, linguistic and other differences.

The Dakar Framework (UNESCO, 2000) also made similar stipulations that all children with disabilities should be a part of mainstream schools, and that Education for All (EFA) goals and targets must be reached and sustained. Broad-based partnerships within countries, supported by co-operation with regional and international agencies and institutions, were seen as the best way to achieve this. It was recommended that these plans be integrated into a wider poverty reduction and development framework, and should be developed through more transparent and democratic processes, involving stakeholders, especially peoples' representatives, community leaders, parents, learners, NGOs and civil society. However, Booth (2000) writes that 'Education for All' should be clarified through a transformative inclusion agenda concerned with all learners, which recognizes the particularities of exclusion, barriers to learning and participation within local communities, and seeks to mobilize local resources to overcome them. EFA should also involve mutual learning between Northern and Southern countries. Reporting on the Dakar Conference, Booth (2000) observes that the term 'Education for All' was used as if it only applied to economically disadvantaged countries or countries in the South, falsely conveying the impression that Northern countries have succeeded in including all students equally. Policy is not made in a vacuum. Writers have argued that a wider value system underlies policy discourses. A society's values are reflected in its broader socio-cultural, ideological and political framework (Bachrach and Baratz, 1970; Barton and Tomlinson, 1984; Hudson, 1993). The education system as a whole and the attitudes of professionals working within that system must be examined; we must not simply focus on the needs of individual children (Barton and Tomlinson, 1984, pp. 65–80). Turning to India, we find that while the Government has signed up to all the major international declarations and there are many policies in place, in practice there has been significantly more rhetoric than action.

HISTORICAL BACKGROUND TO THE INDIAN CONTEXT

When India attained independence in 1947, she inherited the education system prevalent under British rule. In 1835, Lord Macaulay formulated the British policy on education, which governed the Indian system for more than a century and does so, to some extent, even today. Lord Macaulay rejected all that was oriental: Indian culture, Indian languages, literature and Indian history. He stated:

> ... a single shelf of a good European library was worth the whole native literature of India and Arabia ... it is, I believe, no exaggeration to say, that all the historical information which has been collected from all the books written in the Sanskrit languages is less valuable than what may be found in the most paltry abridgements used at preparatory schools in England (Macaulay, 1935, p. 349).

The idea behind education seems to have been to create a cadre of Indians who would think and express themselves like the British. This is reflected by Lord Macaulay's famous statement:

> We want a class of persons Indian in blood and colour, but English in tastes, in opinions, in morals and in conduct (Sharp on Macaulay's Minute, 1852).

Education in colonial India was restricted to the upper and upper middle classes, excluding the vast majority of citizens, resulting in a split and in alienation of the masses (Naik, 1975). Primary and mass education did not receive any serious attention; only higher education was considered important (Tilak, 1990, p. 6). This created a dichotomy between the elite upper classes, whose sons and daughters were educated to be anglicized – 'more British than the British' – and those who could not speak the 'Queen's English', who were considered to be of a lower social level. Many missionaries, charities and voluntary organisations set up schools and colleges; however the curricula had a British orientation (Naik, 1975). This imported model of education created divisions which dominated the country. Additionally there was a wiping away of indigenous forms of education and anything 'native'. And while Indian forms of education did continue for the broad masses, these were limited by a scarcity of resources. The initiatives of enlightened educational philanthropists such as Gokhale, Tagore, Tilak and Radhakrishna were only able to create small ripples. The structure and philosophy of colonial India continued to dominate the Indian education system and determine its basic shape. The tilt towards higher education – which produced a galaxy of eminent scientists, lawyers, doctors, economists, writers and the IT revolution – has been at the heavy cost of the neglect of primary education.

Universal education still remains an unfulfilled dream. This has had an impact on the education of the girl child, of children caught in difficult circumstances such as dire poverty and of children with disability. Professor Amartya Sen has written:

> ... underdevelopment of Indian school systems, especially in socially backward regions of the country and particularly for disadvantaged groups, has been both deeply inefficient and amazingly unjust (Dreze and Sen, 1996).

International comparisons give a useful but bleak view. The average adult in India has spent a little over two years at school, compared with five years in China, seven years in Sri Lanka and over nine years in South Korea. India appears in a poor light even compared with regions that are often considered here as 'backward' for instance, female literacy rates are much lower in India than in sub-Saharan Africa (The Probe Report, 1999).

John Sargent, an eminent British Educational Commissioner, recommended as far back as 1944 that children with disabilities must be brought into the mainstream system.

This recommendation was backed up by the Kothari Commission in 1964, which called for the education of children with disabilities to be the responsibility of the Ministry of Education. These recommendations have yet to be adopted. Today we find that while the Ministry of Human Resource Development (HRD) is responsible for the formulation and implementation of education policy and programmes, the Ministry of Social Justice and Empowerment (formerly the Ministry of Welfare) is responsible for disabled children. Despite this, it has been reported that a high level of informal integration has been occurring and the number of children with disabilities who have been integrated into the mainstream now far exceeds those in special schools.

In 1987, Dasgupta, the former Secretary for Education in India, wrote:

> India has witnessed a phenomenal expansion of educational opportunities in the post-independence period. However, disabled children have not benefited substantially from this growth in educational facilities. This is not to say that no work has been done in the field of disabled welfare. Considerable work has been done over the years both by the Government of India and the voluntary sector with substantial increases in the allocation of funds over different Plan periods. The special education system has done pioneering work in the field of educating children with disabilities. It is however faced with several problems like limited coverage, lack of qualified teachers and a sheltered environment. It was to overcome some of these problems that the Ministry of Welfare launched the scheme for IEDC.

Government Teacher Training departments do not include the education of children with disability within their pedagogy and curriculum. According to Jangira (1995):

> The failure to develop a sizeable human resource is untenable not only as an equity and human rights issue, but also from the point of view of sustainable economic development.

The objective of the Ministry of Social Justice was and still is to 'rehabilitate' rather than to 'educate'. This has become a major barrier to inclusion, resulting in a systems failure to address the educational needs of disabled children. Similarly, in the critical formulation stage of the ICDS, the issue of educating children with disabilities was not clearly defined resulting in massive exclusion with universal education an unfulfilled dream. In the wider context, the ICDS policy of non-inclusion of disabled children reflects the wider malaise that exists and demonstrates a lack of cohesion, convergence and ideological commitment within India's National Policies on Education with no clear directives for inclusion to take place we find that, even within an anti poverty programme such as the ICDS, disabled children do not get nutrition or other components of the programme. The result is the exclusion of four to five million under-five-year-olds in the rural, tribal, and poverty stricken areas. Writers have argued that 'demands for inclusion should be concerned not only with the rights of disabled children but also part of a wider critique of that which constitutes itself as normal' (Armstrong, et al., 2000).

In all its policies and projects on integrated education, the Government has encouraged and supported voluntary effort in the expectation that it would supplement the public sector (Department of Education, 1986). Evidently, it suits Government budgets to let NGOs raise much needed resources for children with disablilities. But by delivering services within a charity framework, we have inadvertently moved away from a rights approach and disempowered the Disability Group. Furthermore there is overwhelming evidence that voluntary agencies tend to establish special schools, not integrated programmes (Taylor and Taylor, 1970; Chaturvedi, 1981; Rao, 1983; Jangira, 1984). And, valuable as all our efforts as NGOs have been, with our very limited capacity to raise funds, our limited outreach and our increasing dependence on grants, we have been unable to reach large populations in remote parts of the country.

Venkatesh (1995), a disabled activist, argues:

> Political manifestos of the last 45 years in India have not included disability as an issue. The scattered disabled population does not have political clout, as it is not organised to campaign for its rights (ADD India, 1995).

It has been argued that the history of children with 'special needs' does not indicate their inability to adjust to the education system but highlights the rigidity of that system and its inability to adjust to their differences (Fragou, as cited in Armstrong, Armstrong and Barton, 2000, p. 39). Further, by 'emphasising the pupil's failure, the fundamental issue of the failure of the system to meet the needs of all pupils is masked' (Barton and Oliver, 1992, p. 14).

THE ROLE OF INTERNATIONAL AGENCIES AND
THE LEGACY OF COLONIALISM

A key issue is the ambivalent role played by international agencies. Scrutiny of documentation of the ICDS in the policy formulation stage indicates that the matter of including children with disabilities was not even brought up for discussion. Although there were several ministries, child development authorities and international agencies involved with the formulation of ICDS, a former education secretary who was present during the talks said 'they did not figure'. International agencies such as UNICEF, the World Food Programme, CARE (US) and the World Bank remained and still remain silent on the matter of inclusion in their programmes of children with disability. Representatives of international agencies – although aware of international policy declarations – failed to raise the issue from the outset. Non-decision making can be a subtle process by which issues remain latent and fail to enter the policy agenda. One can only infer that it suited the vested interests of experts from the West to remain silent and avoid controversy. Morally, national and international agencies engaging in development issues have a responsibility to ensure the inclusion of all children in all education and health programmes on the grounds of human rights. They can remain silent spectators to these matters no longer. A failure to act or a deliberate decision not to act can, as we have seen, nurture segregation and oppressive practices. The current orthodoxy and best practice, international reforms legislation and laws should be openly debated in policy discussions, enabling each country to develop awareness of prevailing trends and to interpret these within their own cultural context. Ultimately I believe that the principal responsibility for policy formulation remains with countries themselves.

I am not suggesting that all methods of attaining goals should be homogeneous the world over nor that Northern paradigms are transferred and implanted by national and international experts as happened during the colonial and the post colonial period.

Policy implementation and methodology will differ from region to region and from country to country. Inclusion is the challenge of addressing diversity, and this must involve the differences between countries and their people. It is important to see beyond our own context and to try and set aside what we 'know' in order that we can learn from our understanding of other cultures. This is one of the most important and difficult demands made on cross-cultural enquiry. That the perspective of the affluent 'North' has to be rejected in favour of one which appreciates the position of the countries of the 'South', as Stone further argues:

> Malnutrition and poverty are the principal causes of impairment in the South. It is clearly impossible to separate impairment from the politics of underdevelopment ...(Stone 1996, p. 480, 481).

Colonialism may officially have come to an end but a new era of neo colonialism has taken over. This has been engendered not only by Western 'experts' but by sectors of Indian society too. One legacy of colonialism is a deeply entrenched belief that 'West is best' and consequently there is a tendency at every level to turn to the Western consultant for help. The situation is compounded by Western advisors who fail to point out that informed expertise exists within India itself.

The biggest divide in the disability movement is between the agenda of the countries of the North and South. While Northern countries have provided entitlement regimes which are based around the individual, Southern countries have at most provided institutional supports. Consequently, disability groups in southern countries are still struggling to obtain basic services and at the same time are having to work within an inadequate policy framework. Our international collaborators have made a point of trying to understand our cultural background and develop paradigms within the Indian context. Furthermore, they have helped to put our problems on an international level collaborating in a true exchange of ideas, where each country has contributed and benefited from the partnership.

LEGISLATION AND POLICY IN INDIA

As a result of the ESCAP Proclamation for the Asia Pacific Region, the Government enacted landmark legislation in 1995 known as The Persons With Disabilities Act (PDA) for Equal Opportunities, Protection Of Rights and Full Participation. This Act encompasses a broad vision for people with disabilities in India and has directed attention to all the issues that impinge on their lives. Chapter V of the Act, which deals with Education, states that the Government will ensure that 'every child with a disability has access to free education in an appropriate environment till he attains the age of 18 years'. It adds that 'the appropriate governments and the local authorities shall endeavor to promote the integration of students with disabilities in the normal schools'. It also puts forward measures for the restructuring of the curriculum for children with disabilities.

The Constitution of India provides for the education of children in two domains: firstly, a directive principle providing for early intervention for children under six years; secondly, a fundamental right accorded to every child which guarantees eight years of schooling from the age of 6 to 14. The preschool period of early inclusion still remains a directive not a mandate. In 2001 the 93rd Amendment to the Constitution of India was passed by the Government. A clause was added to include children with disabilities.

Article 10 of the Free and Compulsory Education for Children Act (2003) leaves the decision as to whether a child with disabilities should be in mainstream school to the Basic Education Authority and fails to assert the rights of disabled children to access the 'normal' school system. The principal flaw is the inherent ambiguity and lack of commitment to the provision of school services for children with disabilities. There is an urgent need to introduce principles and procedures for the inclusion of disabled children in the mainstream school system with the necessary support systems in place.

There are many policies in place in India which are commensurate with international standards. However, the structural changes that are needed to put policy into practice have still not been implemented. It is now vital to challenge this systemic failure.

THE NATIONAL RESOURCE CENTRE FOR INCLUSION

A number of changes have taken place in the Spastics Society, both in policy and practice. The National Resource Centre for Inclusion, India, was set up in 1999 in partnership with the Roeher Institute, Canada, supported by the Canadian International Development Agency (CIDA). This joint project was a unique two-dimensional one, based on an action research approach developed within an accountability framework referred to as a 'Results-based Management Structure'. We redefined and reorientated our goals and activities. The term inclusion is being used with a distinctive and broader perspective, including children who are socially disabled through poverty, the girl child who faces formidable cultural barriers to participation and the disabled child facing systemic bias. With this move a major paradigmatic shift from a segregated special school system to an education for all model has been initiated. Over 300 children have been placed in regular schools (NRCI Report) and there are over 50 organisations and schools who are our local partners. The National Resource Centre for Inclusion (NRCI) is committed to creating mechanisms for implementation that are culture specific and provide a framework for developing inclusive educational practices together with existing infrastructures. This code of practice is called Culturally Appropriate Policy and Practice (CAPP). Consultations have been carried out with key stakeholders such as disabled activists, families with disabled children, NGOs and professionals both in the national and international arenas.

Various scholars in the field of inclusion have put forward their different theories and perspectives on how inclusive education can be put into practice. The most effective of these is the Index for Inclusion which has been developed to assess participation in schools and to assist schools in planning inclusive development. It provides some insight into the overall context for inclusive education and emphasizes the need for a comprehensive and systemic approach (Booth and Ainscow, 2000). The development of the Index had been influenced by the collaborative research project: 'Developing Sustainable inclusion policy and practice: India, South Africa, Brazil and England'. This four-nation project, like the Index itself, is concerned with the cultures, policies and practices of learning centres. The Index has three equally important dimensions, which are closely linked to school life: creating inclusive cultures, producing inclusive policies, and evolving inclusive practices. Creating inclusive cultures involves not only building a shared, secure community, but also creating inclusive values. Inclusion in the school is assured through supporting policies that increase the capacity of the school to respond to student diversity so that 'learning for all' becomes active and participatory.

NRCI has focused on how inclusion can be actualized through change at three levels:

- the micro – at the level of classroom and school values, culture, policies and practices
- the mezzo – at the community level
- the macro – including policy, legislation, and culture at the local, state, national, and global levels.

In 2001, the organisation set up an international exchange of knowledge and experience through a series of conferences called the North-South Dialogues with the purpose of exploring models of inclusion in education, which are culture and context specific, within the framework of each individual country. The aim is to use the Dialogues as a platform to build partnerships between organizations, to learn from each other, exchange ideologies and support each other in this journey towards inclusion. A further aim of the Dialogues is to document the issues that emerge and to use these as a part of a code of practice being written up by the National Resource Centre for Inclusion.

The first Dialogue, held in Mumbai in 2001, turned out to be most meaningful, with experiences from diverse cultures, contexts, resources and policies shared. Speakers from both North and South countries such as Canada, the UK, Hong Kong, Europe, Brazil, South Africa, Bangladesh and different regions of India participated. There was a large gathering of government officials at central, state and local levels, Donor Aid agencies, NGOs, school principals, teachers, parents, volunteers, activists, medical and paramedical professionals, people from the print and electronic media, university academics and policy makers. Culture specific issues were addressed, highlighting the barriers to inclusion and possible approaches to overcome them. The second North-South Dialogue, *Moving from Rhetoric to Practice*, which took place in Kerala in 2003, focused on the problem that whilst governments and international institutions were appearing to make commitments to education for all (e.g. Dakar, Salamanca, G8), these commitments were not being transformed into policy. To move towards facilitating this action, all delegates convened to advance a global agenda for inclusive education that is consistent with international commitments to Education for All as set out in the Dakar Framework for Action (2000), the Salamanca Statement and the Kochi Declaration (2003) which affirm that segregation is a violation of human rights. These declarations state that all children, including children with disability, have a fundamental human right to be included in mainstream local schools. Education for All will not be achieved without inclusion; inclusion will not be achieved outside Education for All. To achieve inclusion, the systemic barriers people and learners face in accessing education – as a result of differences arising from religion, race, gender, poverty, class, caste, ethnicity, language and disability – must be removed. The voices of disabled people, emphasizing their exclusion and isolation, must play a leading part in the struggle for inclusion of all in the education system (Kochi Declaration, 2003).

The third North South Dialogue was held in New Delhi in 2005. The Dialogues have provided opportunities for bringing people together and to form a network of warm and close relationships, where people listen to the voices of different and diverse groups and reach out to support each other in overcoming difficulties which transcend territorial barriers. Other outcomes of the conferences, and discussions during the dialogues have lead to the formation of certain groups and alliances. A disabled activist group or the Rights Group has been formed called ADAPT which stands for Able Disabled All People Together. The main aim of ADAPT is to transform the organisation from one which focuses on delivery to one which promotes a rights and entitlements agenda with a focus on adults and their needs. The other aim of ADAPT is to move towards keeping so called 'able' and disabled people together within a broader framework where academics, parents and activists all play a part. To reach people all over India, an All India Regional Alliance has been formed made up of many of the spastics societies, with a charter to move towards inclusion in each of the regions. To involve an even wider region, an Asia Pacific Course for Master Trainers has been set up. This three-month certificate course prepares Master Trainers and Management personnel to train others to promote inclusive education in response to the particular contexts and cultures of the Asia Pacific regions outside of India. Master Trainers from Nepal, Bangladesh, Mongolia and different parts of India have completed the course.

THE EARLY INTERVENTION PROJECT

At the community level, to address the exclusion of children from the ICDS, the Early Intervention Project (Spastics Society of India/UNICEF Action Research) was started. The project demonstrated how children with disabilities could be included in ICDS preschool programmes, under the aegis of The Canadian International Development Agency (CIDA), UNICEF and the Spastics Society of India (SSI). The aim was to study the mechanisms or intervention strategies needed to include children with disabilities into existing Government programmes. Research consultants were brought in from outside the organisation. The team was seeking to learn from the actual experience of inclusion and to evaluate and validate the factors that contribute to it. Situated in the inner city slums of Mumbai, the project focused on a sample of 6000 families living in extreme poverty. Six sites were identified within which all disabled children between the ages of 3 and 6 years were put into newly created inclusive nurseries with non-disabled children. The project had two key components: intervention and research. The former aimed to demonstrate the 'how' of inclusion, and the latter to track the changes in the children and the community over two years. Development Scores for children (DS) were created for the above purpose, based on a review of child development and early education literature. The parameters for DS included the defining of components of well-being. A Likert-type rating was used for each of the DS scales, with higher scores implying a more advanced stage of development. Factors that impede development, and the achievement of full potential, lie not just within a child but also in external sources.

The Barriers to Inclusion List (BIL) was a new tool created to identify and quantify these factors/barriers. Intervention involved strengthening the community and building support with a top down bottom up approach; we called this process a whole community approach.

Substantial work was undertaken with key persons from the community. The most important need, initially, was to sensitise ourselves about the community and understand their aspirations, suffering, fears and anxieties. Some of the barriers we faced arose in relation to the community, local anganwadi or nursery teachers, and what we have termed the 'I am the Professional syndrome'. Schooling for disabled children, according to traditional special educational perspectives, is seen as a technical problem to be solved through diagnosis and remedial intervention. Dominated by a highly professional attitude, it has its roots in a technical and specialist approach cloaked in the medical model. Typically this generates policies which involve the use of professional experts to identify the nature and extent of disability. What follows is a highly bureaucratic process of assessment to calculate the human and material resources needed to support the disabled child in the mainstream school or classroom. This creates a barrier and causes the teacher in charge to feel deskilled.

Professionals were reoriented to take into account both the environmental and individual conditions in their approach to disabled children. They were encouraged to reframe the context of their own professional knowledge in a way that recognised the expertise of parents, community-members and others involved in the inclusive classroom and community. I have called this process the Three R's for the training of professionals in inclusive cultures. They were:

- Retraining into a new context and culture of the community.
- Relocation away from the institute and towards the community, which means developing more community-based initiatives.
- Redeployment of time, involving the introduction of new priorities which allow professionals to work in the community.

Local teachers were employed from the slums or development sites. They were not highly educated but had graduated from high school. They lived in the slum settlements and were aware of the cultural diversity and the social mores of the community, their regional, caste and religious differences. The training merged theory and practical sessions to cover early childhood development issues, classroom management and the value and use of teaching aids. An interactive participatory approach was used to develop the curriculum in which teachers were involved as key participants.

An ecological inventory was conducted to make the teachers aware of the kind of objects and animals, for instance, that the children were familiar with and these were used as teaching aids. The routines, tasks and activities commonly undertaken by the children in their daily lives were also identified and used to inform the content of the curriculum. An 'Ecological Inventory Observation Guide' was prepared for this purpose; it consisted of items eliciting answers on various environments and activities: the home, kitchen, toilet, play and geographical boundary.

The findings of the ecological inventory survey provided a foundation for the development of an enrichment programme that is culturally appropriate and ecologically valid.

The ten-point programme focuses on social, emotional, linguistic, cognitive and motor development. It is a detailed curriculum covering activities, teaching methods and teaching aids used in the anganwadis based on the findings of the ecological inventory. The cultural continuity between the child's home and school life has enabled learning to progress more effectively and the programme provides a nurturing environment for all children.

Inclusion in this context involved a shift in the kinds of responsibilities a specialist has and the way they use their skills. Rather than providing primary interventions in specialized settings, inclusion involved moving away from this model to one based in the community. It also involved a greater emphasis on the environmental barriers to learning and development, recognizing that families, communities, teaching methods and attitudes all play a significant part (Alur and Rioux, 2003). Listening to the voices of the community was another input which was critical. Initially the parents themselves were not fully convinced and felt apprehensive.

Street level administrators and other locals also had their apprehensions; fears and prejudices which presented barriers that needed addressing. The kinds of comments made by the local street level bureaucrats were:

'Disabled children are best in special schools.'

'The Anganwadi teachers will not know how to deal with our children.'

Intervention included workshops and discussions, folk dramas or *yatra* (an Indian term for a short play), rallies and street plays focusing on children's needs and rights. Inclusion involved a shift from a specialist role to an expanded role which included empowering the community and the community-based workers to handle diverse situations and provide support. Such a shift also involved introducing a more cooperative and collaborative partnership instead of an authoritarian and hierarchical approach. A major indicator of good practice appears to be the involvement of the community; a whole community approach was critical in creating an inclusive environment and allowed the community to take ownership of the programme. Shifting the onus from specialists to the community, empowered the workers enabling them to provide support and information and, indeed, to handle most situations.

The overall results of the evaluation have been very positive. The research findings showed a reduction in the barriers to inclusion and an improvement in children's development scores. It showed that the community teachers had grasped the principles of inclusion. They were also very creative in designing educational aids and toys from cost effective recycled material. In fact the success we have had in training the community workers has indicated that 'special needs' can be addressed without too much specialization. More than 1000 children, with a special focus on the girl child and the child with disability, have moved into inclusive classrooms in state schools.

From this evidence-based research, emerged a series of instructional resource materials: the 'How to' series of inclusive education, flip charts, manuals, CD ROMs, audio visual material and films are now available.

The manuals are relevant for any organization or agency working to address the crucial need of bringing children with disability into inclusive settings. They recommend a whole community approach to inclusive education and, although the research was carried out in India, it can be used anywhere in the world. This project showed that inclusion can be implemented with limited resources if there is a commitment to do so and a continuum of support given in the right spirit. Education through example of inclusion is necessary for local administrators and street level bureaucrats to understand the changes in culture and practices that are needed. Yet the larger goal of achieving full inclusion through changing state programmes to include children with disabilities still lies ahead. The removal of systemic barriers requires a commitment from top levels of government, and such a commitment is beginning to emerge (Alur and Rioux, 2003). It is hoped that the results from this micro initiative will help in developing the model at the macro level through the Government's infrastructure. If and when that happens the needs of four to five million children, aged under five, will be met.

CONCLUSION

In conclusion, there are four factors which have been crucial in the work of SSI in developing inclusive opportunities and practices.

- It is important to demonstrate what inclusion means in practice. This was achieved by developing models of inclusive education at school and community levels that are culturally appropriate and context specific. It has also been achieved by developing models of inclusive early childhood care and education within a larger existing national programme. Policy needed to adopt a bottom up top down approach. Clarity in policy formulations at the top ensured that the policy objectives were matched at the community level.
- The efforts of civil society are valuable and micro initiatives can generate macro outcomes. Macro change can be difficult and slow, especially in resource strapped developing countries. The social sectors are not given priority in government policies or in spending. As we have seen, in a country like India, where universal education has not been achieved, where there is a lack in the delivery system and an unhealthy reliance on NGOs to provide services, micro efforts of civil society are important catalysts and can lead the way for Government action.
- It is important to bear in mind that inclusive education is not just a 'recipe' for the rich affluent countries of the North. Inclusion is not about funding, it is about ideology, changing attitudes and challenging assumptions. Lack of funding should not mean that certain children are segregated. Tapping into existing resources and working with the community are valuable ways of advancing change. The ideology of inclusion and the methods to achieve it differ with each situation and each country must develop its own practice. The experiences related in this chapter have shown that change can take place within the poorest communities in a cost effective way. In countries of the South, where there has been relatively little investment in segregated educational provision for disabled children, inclusive education programmes tend to be more successful. In fact, wealthier nations have arguably created greater, more insurmountable obstacles to inclusion because of their relatively vast material resources. In the South, by contrast, the rehabilitation and 'special needs' industry is much smaller and less powerful and human resources can be harnessed to bring about inclusion. Here, implementation of

inclusive education may simply involve the positive reinforcement of well-established, community-based and inclusive attitudes and practices.

- Inclusion is the challenge of addressing differences and diversity. For international professionals, it is essential to be sensitive to the ways these are expressed in each region and to the fact that inclusion needs to be culture and context specific. It is essential to break the entrenchments of colonialism and enable each country to develop their own indigenous models, encouraging networking and building alliances within the country. Disabled activists differ from region to region depending on the context they are in. Their voices need to be heard and professionals need to be sensitive to their different ideas. For macro level change it is critical to engage with Government. In our case, unless structural fragmentation is corrected, disabled children will continue to remain uneducated and unempowered; an underclass of people buried in a debris of institutionalized and systemic discrimination. We who are involved in this journey will go down in history as people who colluded in a kind of apartheid as not being able to legitimize their needs.

The journey is not over. Having started an organization which has spearheaded action in many areas, I feel strongly that civil society has a crucial role to play in changing social attitudes and moving towards social change. The many roles I have played sometimes blur my strong belief that the most important role for me has been that of a mother, a parent and the proudest moments have been to see my daughter go from strength to strength as she finished her second Masters degree with one finger, determined to fight and hope for a change towards a more equal, more humane and just world. Because without hope, without fighting for change, one might just as well be dead.

REFERENCES

Alur, M (2002) *Invisible Children: A Study of Policy Exclusion*, New Delhi, India: Viva Publications.

Alur and Rioux, M. (2003) 'Included: An Exploration of Six Early Education Pilot Projects for Children with Disabilities in India', The Spastics Society of India/UNICEF Project. available at the National Resource Centre for Inclusion, Mumbai, India.

Armstrong, F. 'Differences and Difficulty: *Insights, Issues and Dilemmas*', Sheffiled: Department of Educational Studies, Sheffield University.

Armstrong, F. and Barton, L. (1999) (eds) *Disability, Human Rights and Education: Cross Cultural Perspectives*, Buckingham: Open University Press.

Armstrong F., Armstrong, D. and Barton, L. (eds) (2000) *Inclusive Education – Policy, Contexts and Comparative Perspectives*, David Fulton Publishers.

Bachrach, P. and Baratz, M.S. (1970) *Power and poverty: Theory and Practice*. New York: Oxford University Press.

Barnes, C., Mercer, G. and Shakespeare, T. (1999) *Exploring Disability: A Sociological Analysis*, Cambridge: Polity Press.

Barton, L. (ed.) (1996) *Disability and Society: Emerging Issues and Insights*, Longman Publishers.

Barton, L. and Tomlinson, S. (eds) (1984) *Special Education and Social Interests*. London: Croom Helm.

Booth, T. and Ainscow, M. (2000) *Index For Inclusion*, CSIE – Centre For Studies For Inclusive Education.

Bowley, A. H. and Gardner, L. (1980) *The Handicapped Child*. Reprint 1989. Edinburgh: Churchill Livingstone.

Chaturvedi, T. N. (ed) (1981) 'Administration for the disabled: policy and organisational issues', (Special Issue) *Indian Journal of Public Administration*, 27, 3.

Christensen, C. (1996) Disabled, handicapped or disordered: 'What's in a name?' in C. Christensen and F. Rizvi (eds) *Disability and the Dilemmas of Education and Justice*. Buckingham: Philadelphia: Open University Press: 63–78.

Christensen, C. and Rizvi, F. (eds) (1996) *Disability and the Dilemmas of Education and Justice*. Buckingham: Philadelphia: Open University Press.

Clough, P. and Barton, L. (eds) (1995) *Making Difficulties: Research and the Construction of Special Education Needs*. London: Paul Chapman.

Dasgupta, P. (1997) 'Education for the Disabled', in S. Hegarty, and Alur (2002) (eds) *Education and Children with Special Needs – From Segregation to Inclusion*, India: Sage Publications.

Dreze, J. and Sen, A. (1996) *India ... Economic Development and Social Opportunity*. Bombay: Calcutta: Madras: Oxford University Press.

Government of India (1994) Directory of NGOs receiving Grants-in-Aid under various schemes of Ministry of Welfare. New Delhi.

Government of India (1999) Education at a glance, Department of Education, Maharashtra.

Hudson, B. (1993) 'Michael Lipsky and street-level bureaucracy, a neglected perspective', in Hill (ed.) *The Policy Process, A Reader*. London: Harvester Wheatsheaf.

Jangira, N. K. (1984) 'Role of central government to meet the educational needs of the young disabled', *Indian Journal of Integrated Education*, 1, 72–77.

Jangira, N. K. (1995) 'Rethinking teacher education'. *Prospects*, June, 25, 2, 261–272.

Macaulay, T. B. (1935) 'Minute on Indian Education', in M. Alur (2002) (ed.) *Invisible Children: A Study of Policy Exclusion*, New Delhi India: Viva Publications.

Macaulay, T. B. (1852) *Minute on Indian Education*, reprinted in Prose and Poetry, Cambridge: Harvard University Press.

Miles, M. (2002) 'Community and individual responses to disablement in South Asian Histories: Old traditions, new myths?' a cited in Asia Pacific Disability Rehabilitation Journal: Selected Reading in Community-Based Rehabilitation, Series 2, Disability and Rehabilitation in South Asia.

Naik, J. P. (1975a) *Elementary Education in India: A Promise to Keep*. reprint 1979. Bombay: Allied Publishers.

Naik, J. P. (1975b) *Policy and Performance in Indian Education*. New Delhi: Asia Publishing House.

Oliver, M. (1990) *The Politics of Disablement*. London: Macmillan.

PROBE in India (1999) Oxford University Press, New Delhi.

Rao, V. (1983) 'Services for the handicapped persons: organisation and policy implications', *Indian Journal of Social Work*, 43, 351–368.

Siraj-Blatchford, I. (1994) 'An evaluation of early years education and training in the ICDS in India', *International Journal of Early Years Education*: Spring 2, 1.

Sood, N. (1987) An evaluation of non formal preschool education component in mangolpuri ICDS block, *NIPCCD Technical Bulletin*, April, 1.

Stone, E. (1996) 'A law to protect, a law to prevent: Contextualizing disability in legislation in China', *Disability and Society*, 11(4), 469–484.

Swaminathan, M. (1996). 'Innovative child care programmes in India', *International Journal of Early Years Education*, Summer, 4, 2.

Taylor, W. W. and Taylor, I. W. (1970) 'Services for the handicapped in India'. New York: International Society for Rehabilitation of the Disabled.

Tilak, J. (1990) *The Political Economy of Education in India*. Buffalo, New York: Comparative Education Center, State University of New York at Buffalo in co-operation with the Department of Educational Studies, Curry School of Education, University of Virignia.

UNESCO (1994) Salamanca Statement and Framework for Action on Special Needs Education, Paris. UNESCO

UNESCO (2000) The Dakar Framework for Action – Education for All Meeting Our Collective Commitments, Dakar, Senegal, 26–28 April 2000.

UNICEF (1989) UN Convention on the Rights of the Child, New York UNICEF.

Venkatesh, B. (1995) in *ADD India Newsletter*, Bangalore, India.

Verma, A. (1994) 'Early childhood care and education in India', *International Journal of Early Years Education*, Autumn, 2, 2.

JENNIFER LAVIA

7. INCLUSIVE EDUCATION IN TRINIDAD AND TOBAGO

INTRODUCTION

This chapter gives me the opportunity to examine inclusive policies and practices in Trinidad and Tobago and to reflect upon my own involvement and understanding of developments that have taken place within the broader contexts of education policy development locally and in the Caribbean region. Indeed, such an examination seeks to articulate connections between current perspectives on inclusion and the historical circumstances that have influenced current practice.

Admittedly, the perspective taken in this chapter draws upon my own experience within the education system in Trinidad and Tobago, my evolving ideas about the aims, purposes and meaning of education within a small island state that has been affected by five hundred years of colonialism, and current research on education in the region. Consequently, reference to the colonial condition signifies recognition of the impact of 'colonial imagination' (London, 2002) on the territory (and all other Caribbean territories) in which 'colonial imagination' became the apotheosis of 'habit, law, psychology, religion and education' (Millette, 1985, p. xv).

My first experience as a teacher was in primary education. I was the beneficiary of a rather archaic and illogical practice, which allowed recent schools-leavers who had gained a full G.C.E Ordinary Level Certificate[1] to be appointed in the primary school system without formal teacher training. I considered myself fortunate to be placed at a primary school within my community since I had already begun to formulate ideas about teaching that resonated with concepts of 'giving back to the community' and 'being of service' to students. I was convinced that the role of the teacher went beyond classroom interactions. I was assigned to a class that had been without a teacher for a few weeks; that teacher had been away on extended sick leave. Very little information was forthcoming about my new class, but as a youthful, optimistic, and progressive minded neophyte, I was ready to 'teach', 'to mould minds', 'to impart knowledge' and to shape my students into good citizens. Not having any formal teacher training, I resorted to using methods that I remembered from how my teachers taught me with a few innovations that I gained by asking family members who were teachers. Yet,

L. Barton and F. Armstrong (eds.), Policy, Experience and Change, 107–122.

I found that I spent much of my time in the classroom situation repeating tasks and instructions and trying to 'control' a particular student who would spontaneously erupt into fits of anger and violence in the classroom. It took two weeks of me using my limited range of strategies to figure out that I had not been told the real story about my group of students nor was I adequately prepared to address their needs.

Over lunch one day, with some of my more experienced colleagues, they told me that the class I was assigned was one in which were placed those students who were perceived as having a learning difficulty. At that time, there were no policies, rules or guidelines at a national level to address students who were experiencing learning difficulties, and so, the creation of an unresourced 'special' class was the best that the school could come up with.

I was again reminded of that first teaching experience, when I entered teaching at the secondary school system. By then, I had developed my thinking about educative practices and had become very concerned about two groups of students at my school. One group consisted of seven male students who, after five years of secondary education were still unable to read. The other was a group of five students who were continually being excluded from classes.

These two groups, as was the case in the primary school setting, remained part of the school but were excluded from quality teaching and did not benefit from any coherent programme that was designed to support their learning. Indeed, these cases raised for me questions about the interplay between policy and practice and the continual barriers they present for inclusive education. Further, these cases illustrate examples of how a system that is attainment driven marginalises vulnerable groups. Finally, these cases demonstrate that any system of inclusion whether by default or by design will have implications for teacher training.

This chapter therefore, draws upon historical circumstances that have impacted upon educational policy and practice and provides an analysis of some of the challenges to inclusion within current policy frameworks. Beginning with a discussion of the historical development of the education system in Trinidad and Tobago, I consider continual barriers to inclusion within the context of current policy developments in education and the impact of global policy agendas upon local initiatives. The discussion then continues into an identification of key barriers to inclusion posed by a system that places high value on attainment and its significance to the provision of systems to support learning. The chapter concludes with an examination of the inclusion and its implications for teacher training.

INCLUSION IN CONTEXT

Prior to 1834, the islands of Trinidad and Tobago were separate slave societies. By 1834, with the coming of the Act of Emancipation and multiple changes in colonial rule mainly between Spanish, French and British colonisers, the complex nature of the society started to emerge. What became apparent was the transformation of 'a backward Amerindian colony governed by Spain into a Spanish colony run by Frenchmen and worked by African slaves' (Williams, 1962, p. 41) and then, a British colony which was predominantly non-English speaking, worked by indentured labourers from India (and to a lesser extent China) and freed Africans.

The movement towards industrialisation in the metropolitan centres and its impact upon colonies, brought with it the need for varied skills and a more educated, propertied class. This generated some movement toward the development of education. The new requirements of the colonial society became evident therefore, after the Act of Emancipation. A Creole society had developed and its consolidation would rely on the organisation of education. Brereton (1986) proffers the argument that the organisation of a system of education came about because of the disposition of the colonial government towards education. The colonial government was of the view that education was the business of the state and that, in some way, the state had a responsibility to educate the children of those who were enslaved. Liverpool (2001) contends, however, that it was not so much a fundamental shift in colonial ideology, rather, it was a policy shift to maintain control of an emerging (and massive) working class; a huge labour force that had to be contained.

In the case of the former notion, Green (1991, p. 328) suggests that 'metropolitan views on West Indian education were influenced by domestic English conditions where attention to the needs of the poor was traditionally a charitable concern'. Notwithstanding this position, Liverpool (2001, p. 214) argues that 'even though the Africans were freed, the Eurocentric idea that a population of imported labourers should produce staple crops to create wealth for the privileged classes, who in turn dominate the society, did not end'. Thus, the development of colonial education, based on values, interests and interpretations of Western colonialism, was the response to the questions – who was to be educated, by whom, where and what were they to learn. A system was designed to 'educate young colonials' and school them, in the ways of the colonial masters.

Two highly divergent schools of thought had emerged within the period of transition from colonial rule to self-governance. On the one hand, the masses were mainly exposed to primary education, as it was felt that there was no need for any further education for them. On the other hand, there was the thinking that the new nation state required an educated mass that would drive the process of social, economic and political development. Indeed, education was seen as the means by which a process of decolonisation would take place.

As a commitment to the latter position, the nationalists, who successfully led the independence movement, prepared a contract between their political party,[2] and the masses in what they called the People's Charter (People's National Movement,1956). In articulating the direction for education within the new nation state, the Charter advocated a policy of *integration* in which the diversity of the complex society would be harnessed as an asset to modernisation. Further, attention was to be paid to ensuring 'the highest possible academic and other standards in all schools'; 'the provision of an adequate number of schools at all levels, well designed, with appropriate alterations to existing unsuitable buildings' and 'the enforcement of the compulsory education ordinance at the primary level with the extension of assistance to necessitous children'. Such sentiments influenced several major policies which impacted on the modernisation of the education system.

The rhetoric of 'integration' and 'modernisation' however did not resolve the historical circumstances of disabled people and individuals who were perceived as having learning difficulties. Indeed, these individuals, as Armstrong *et al.* (2005, p. 72) have argued, 'have historically been marginalized ridiculed and seen as burdens to the society'.

Prior to 1981, voluntary, non-governmental organisations provided educational programmes for disabled individuals and in many cases, special schools were set up to provide for their education. These organisations developed out of the philanthropic endeavours and were organised around categories of disability and as such there was one association each that undertook the care and education for the visually impaired, hearing impaired, physically challenged and the mentally challenged.

Added to the work of these organisations, were private efforts that were conducted by individual teachers, some of whom were qualified but many were not. These 'teachers' ran private schools and would be well known within the communities as places where children who were perceived as having learning difficulties would go.

While these private initiatives went unaided by the state, non-governmental, voluntary organisations received financial assistance. The assistance given was in two forms. A subvention was given to them by the state for administration and provision of specialist services. In addition, their schools became assisted schools and were incorporated as part of the public education system.

By the 1980s government began to rethink its approach to educational provision in light of international concerns about education as a human right and educational expansion in the developing world based on the development of human resources. The terminology 'special educational needs' emerged as a progress on educating children with disabilities. However, the convolution of policy intent, practice and increased demands with regard to inclusion resulted in a plethora of state led policy initiatives. These initiatives included a 'National Survey of Handicapped Children and Youth in Trinidad and Tobago' (1984). The findings of that survey were that an estimated sixteen per cent of the school population were in need of 'special education provision'. This percentage represented approximately twenty-seven thousand students who were in the school system but for whom adequate and appropriate learning support was not provided.

Since the 1980s, thinking about inclusion has developed to incorporate a much broader remit. Government has become more responsive to global debates and has included themes of 'social inclusion' and 'Education for All' (Armstrong *et al.*, 2005, p. 73) to the national agenda. Evidently, for developing states, the impact of globalisation with its rapidly developing technologies and policy frameworks cannot be ignored.

The Salamanca Statement (UNESCO, 1994) for example, proclaims the fundamental right of every child to education in inclusive learning environments which are based on child-centred pedagogies and organised for successfully educating all children. The Statement also calls on governments 'to adopt as a matter of law or policy the principle of inclusive education'. Further, the Statement advocates inclusive education as 'the most effective means of combating discriminatory attitudes, creating welcoming communities, building an inclusive society and achieving education for all (UNESCO, 1994, p. ix)'.

Calls for inclusive education in Trinidad and Tobago had earlier been echoed by the 1990 Pilgrim Report which had seen inclusion as a development of special education and which had called for one system of education for all children. Additionally, influenced by UNESCO's goal of Education for All in 1990 and later in 2000, government embarked on a comprehensive review of the education system by setting up a National Task Force on Education.

The National Task Force on Education produced the 1993–2003 report in which it identified several major issues that needed to be addressed. One of these issues was the challenges imposed by 'the learning systems over the last two decades' which the report states, 'did not cater efficiently as they might for those who are "educationally at risk", as well as for those individuals in our community with special needs (Ministry of Education, 1993, p. viii)'.

Specifically, the report noted that levels of academic achievement were unacceptably low and loose or absent and curricula arrangements for personal and social development outcomes left a lot to be desired (Ministry of Education, 1993, p. 1). The report also highlighted the submission by Trinidad and Tobago to the Meeting of 1991 of the UNESCO/CARNEID and Ministry of Health's special education task force. This report stated that 'most special needs children are in regular schools' and that the conditions were thus:

> 80 per cent of children who have special education needs identified by referral to and assessed by the Child Guidance Clinic are receiving inappropriate education and their special education needs are not being met in the existing system. The research further reveals that 13 per cent of the special needs children were attending no school at all; 5.8 per cent were at pre school; 5.1 per cent were attending special schools and 6.7 per cent other facilities, while 67.2 per cent were in primary and secondary schools. (Ministry of Education, 1993, p. 62)

It was therefore recognised that to redress such 'symptoms of organisational pathologies' systemic change was required. Systemic change in this context meant moving towards a decentralised mode of education provision where the school would have greater autonomy to develop internal structures including the development of 'clearly articulated plans and programmes' for children with disabilities and learning difficulties, similar to what had been proposed earlier in the 1990 Pilgrim Report.

The policy framework that developed out of the new plan included a new, multi-disciplinary orientation based on prevention, identification and placement. Attention was drawn to the need for early detection and intervention procedures that were community based. A placement strategy was also to be implemented where the preferred route for placement of children with learning difficulties would be based on educational practices as opposed to clinical approaches. A multi-disciplinary team would then be responsible for the placement after carrying out student assessments. The ideal therefore, was to promote the inclusive school, the inclusive community and the inclusive society in which a major goal would be establishment of a seamless and inclusive education system.

Current policy developments that have emerged within the last two years have advanced the commitment of government to consider the notion of social inclusion as a fundamental element of national development. In this regard, social inclusion is being advanced as having wider aspirations than the provision of appropriate education for disabled individuals and children with learning difficulties. Rather, the government's framework for action recognises the need 'to provide care and education for the most vulnerable' (Ministry of Education, 2004, p. 13) and includes a commitment to widening participation at all levels of education, eliminating gender disparities and promoting social cohesion.

Despite the rhetoric of inclusion, however, 'the reality is that the goals of equity and equality of opportunity remain distant for the majority of Caribbean people (Armstrong *et al.*, 2005, p. 74)'. Marginalised groups remain marginalised; those who are vulnerable and disadvantaged remain excluded from economic and educational activities.

BARRIERS TO INCLUSION

Beneath the rhetoric of inclusion lies a range of dilemmas and barriers. On the one hand, the problems of systemic failure have made clear the need to improve learning systems and to set targets in specific areas such as literacy, numeracy and essential life skills. On the other hand, the current system of funding brings with it conditionalities and priorities which may conflict with national aspirations. These two dilemmas set up a scenario where the barriers to inclusion can be more fully explored.

ACADEMIC ACHIEVEMENT AND CITIZENSHIP

In response to the requirements of the new nation state for educational change, the Draft Education Plan (Ministry of Education, 1968, p. 5) raised the key question for government and generated its own response thus:

> What are we educating for? We are supposed to produce citizens who are intellectually, morally and emotionally fitted to respond adequately and productively to the varied challenges of life in a small multi-racial developing country and to the changes which are being brought rapidly in the economic foundations of civilisation.

Evidently, the construction of curricula within the new nation state would represent an inherited system of schooling that was attainment oriented and examination driven.

In Trinidad and Tobago prior to 1962, the education of individuals who were disabled and who were perceived as having learning difficulties was largely ignored. As the state gained central control of education after political independence in 1962, access to education became more of a concern, although in the Education Act of 1966 the state allowed itself only discretionary power with regard to setting up special schools.

The first major policy was the Education Act of 1966 which recognised the authority of the state and established the parameters for the management of education by three 'partners': central government, education boards of management and a regulatory body for the teaching service. The Act was the state's response to the issue of human rights and equity, democratisation of the education system and a commitment to systemic administration.

Democratisation of the system was also to be seen by the way in which schooling was defined. First, the Act retained the notion of compulsory education. Second, assisted (denominational) schools were to be considered as public schools albeit with an autonomous management structure that respected their historical development and at the same time bringing them under the authority and control of the state. This notion of joint management became the subject of further negotiation in the 1970s. Joint management also allowed for the state to have discretionary powers over the placement of children after the Common Entrance Examination, a negotiated position which assisted the state in its expansion programme for secondary education. Third, a diversified curriculum was to be implemented with the different types and forms of post primary education. These included intermediate schools; junior secondary school for children aged 12 to 14 years; the traditional grammar school, (modern) secondary schools, comprehensive schools and technical or vocational school (Government of Trinidad and Tobago, 1966, p. 13).

Indeed, the promise of political independence came with much anxiety and hope for increased places at the secondary education level. But the newly independent state inherited a system of education in which academic success was measured by gaining full certificates at the external Cambridge based General Certificate Examination at Ordinary Level and Advanced Level. Even when these examinations were taken over by a regional assessment body, the Caribbean Examination Council (CXC),[3] the criteria were based on the GCE except that the content of the examination was decidedly more relevant to life in the region. Five subjects were considered a full certificate including Mathematics and English.

Systems like ours in Trinidad and Tobago (and indeed the Caribbean) which are driven by examinations form a definite barrier to inclusion. In fact, it can be said that children are driven out of the system by examinations. The report of the National Task Force (1993, p. 2) supports this point thus:

> performance on one major test in the primary system supersedes genuine learning achievement; and curricular arrangements linked to the attainment of a basic minimum of five CXC passes subvert the goals of a sound general education at the secondary level.

The major test that is referred to in the above quotation is the Common Entrance Examination which is a selection examination taken by children at around 11+ to determine where they will be placed at secondary level. Prior to the year 2000, it was estimated that over 10,000 children per year were excluded from secondary school because of insufficient places at secondary school. Vena Jules (1994) in her Study of the Secondary School Population in Trinidad and Tobago: Placement Patterns and Practices, also noted that of those children who do receive a place at secondary school many of them actually fall out of the system in the first three years of their secondary schooling and these go largely undetected.

Added to these scenarios is the fact that selection for secondary school is based on an elitist system whereby different types of schools are placed within grading bands. Traditional grammar type schools enjoy the top grade and the Form One special classes receive the lowest grade. Consequently, the examination system selects the highest performing students who are usually placed within the preferred category of the grammar type schools and those scoring below 30 points are distributed among the Junior Secondary Schools and Form One special classes.

Despite the fact that each strand in the secondary school hierarchy is required to maintain a basic core curriculum of Mathematics, English and Science, the curriculum in the Junior Secondary Schools and Form One Special Classes tend to steer in the direction of vocational subjects.

The Jules study also revealed that there is a strong correlation between social class, ethnicity and demographics and placement patterns in secondary schools. Children who are from low socioeconomic status households and are of majority of the population (descendants of Africans and Indians), tend to be in the majority at the Junior Secondary and Senior Comprehensive Schools and Form One special classes. Children who are descendants of plantation owners and of the wealthy are invariably found in the grammar schools. There is yet another factor that is of recent vintage that has added another tier to the hierarchy that is the recent introduction of international schools which are private schools that offer either Canadian or American education.

According to Baksh (1986, p. 8), 'students in the less prestigious tracks are likely to have lower estimates of their ability and lower educational and occupational expectations'. Further, Mark (1993, p. 68) argues that the entrenchment of a schooling hierarchy brought about by the retention of the old system (grammar schools) and the new system (junior secondary schools and senior comprehensive schools) has given rise to 'new-school factors' where 'attainment levels of the students, the size of the school and the nature of the curriculum had a negative effect on the students'.

Despite the genre of secondary school, educational success is still largely measured by the level of attainment at the regional CXC examinations. Many children who are experiencing learning difficulties, if they manage to get into secondary school, often leave school before completing their studies. Consequently, individuals who are disabled and who experience learning difficulties are excluded from those aspects of education that are valued and which in turn would allow them to take up full citizenship. Given the current system of schooling, Armstrong et al. (2005, p. 76) are correct in assessing that 'nowhere is this tension between the role of education for academic achievement and the role of education for citizenship more pronounced than in the area of special and inclusive education'.

FUNDING

The experience of Caribbean states is that education policy has always been externally funded. The reality is that small states like Trinidad and Tobago do not always have the necessary financial resources to undertake the much needed reforms in education that are desired and needed. In its strategic objectives for 2002–2006, government has again reiterated its intention to achieve (inter alia) 'accessibility to educational opportunity for all and delivery of quality education (Ministry of Education, 2004)'. To achieve these goals requires funding for the construction of new physical structures as well as recurrent resources. As a consequence, implementation of strategic goals towards inclusive education would be limited by the extent to which much of the policies can be funded.

For example, in order to implement the Education for All goals, in 1996, the Trinidad and Tobago government negotiated with International Bank for Reconstruction and Development (IBRD) a loan which funded four main components of the systems (Ministry of Education 2004). These included increased provision in Early Childhood Care and Education, improved teaching and learning quality a the primary level, upgrade of the physical environment for teaching and learning and provisions for educational management an institutional strengthening for the ECCE sector. Continuing with the funding, the period 2002–2006 according to government's policy statements is focused on the modernisation of 'quantitative and qualitative aspects of education provision' where secondary education would be primarily targeted.

The danger here is that given the extensive and ambitious policy agenda towards Education for All, priority can only be given to what is or can be funded. Constraints to realising the goals, therefore, reside in a range of complex factors. These factors include (1) the risk of reform initiatives being uncoordinated where the range of funders make provision for various aspects of the reform; (2) poor methods and ineffective of implementation; (3) tensions between local need and funders' priorities; and (4) role confusion and the development of a more complex education bureaucracy where, new technical units with specific mandates for particular funded projects are established and where these supersede the existing bureaucracy.

Miller (UNESCO 2000, p. 8) identifies these constraints by highlighting that 'debt remains a major constraint on Caribbean countries in sustaining previous investments in education and making new ones'. As a consequence, concern was raised about the inclusion of the International Monetary Fund (IMF) in the process on Education for All where there are tensions that were 'related to structural adjustments, debt and their impact on public and private funding (ibid)'. The case presented by Miller was that on the one hand international lending agencies were participating in a solution oriented endeavour to bring about full citizenship globally yet, these international lending agencies were themselves the architects of conditionalities against loans that tied the hands of developing countries from making appropriate, adequate and sustained investment to develop their local and regional social systems.

SCHOOL SYSTEMS

The Education for All agenda has generated much debate about how schools are to be reorganised to provide quality learning support. In advocating for inclusive schools the Salamanca Statement (UNESCO, 1994, p. 6) recognises that schools should 'accommodate all children but that these conditions create a range of different challenges to school systems'.

While the new system of schools provided additional secondary school places, as I have previously stated, what developed was a highly stratified system of schools which placed value on academic attainment. In practice, the much touted differentiated curriculum did not materialise and it was felt by many educators that what was emerging was a system of 'warehousing' students, that is holding them until they either dropped out of the system or until the end of secondary schooling.

As a result, one of the barriers to inclusion is the way in which schools are organised for learning. In citing the problem of schooling in Trinidad and Tobago, the report of the National Task Force states thus:

> Many schools in our nation are run down, not only in the physical and social sense, but also from the perception of the organizational, administrative and professional qualities that are expected to exist therein. Schools, like the rest of the

system exhibit low levels of academic attainment; disproportionate learning disabilities; inefficiencies and ineffectiveness in teaching methods used; inappropriate curriculum; teacher and student indiscipline; poor motivation, morale commitment, loyalty, etc. (Ministry of Education, 1993, p. 31).

In order to realise the global agenda for inclusion and inclusive education, a key requirement is the reorganisation of schools. However, progress in this direction is hampered by well entrenched practices of school management which have been centrally controlled by an education bureaucracy. The aspiration of developing inclusive schools therefore presents a number of further dilemmas to an already complex set of circumstances. On the one hand, inclusive education requires that there is a flexible curriculum which can suit children with different abilities and interests and in so doing provide quality learning support programmes for all children. In this way student success is achieved based on a collective effort of home, school, community liaisons. On the other hand, what has been implemented in the local context as 'school base management (Ministry of Education, 1993, p. 31)' has been the source of much tension and conflict.

In practice, school autonomy is subject to the public purse and calls for greater accountability are being influenced by the global trend in education management towards 'performativity' (Ball, 1999). Constraints on resources on schools are further compounded by the fact that schools are called upon to supplement shortfalls in their income and many of the schools are in communities that are in challenging circumstances. The ideal of the inclusive school therefore cannot negate the fact that there is an inherited inequality in resourcing of schools and this inequality does influence the extent to which schools can attract the necessary resources required.

TEACHER EDUCATION AND INCLUSION

'Teachers play a key role as the managers of the educational process, supporting children through the use of available resources both within and outside of the classroom (The Salamanca Statement, UNESCO 1994, p. 24)'. One of the barriers to inclusion therefore, is the extent to which the teaching profession is mobilised around shared goals and are themselves included as active participants in the decision making process and the development of policies.

In providing specific elements of the problem, the report of National Task Force on Education (Ministry of Education, 1993, p. 2) has stated thus:

> The delivery system is adversely affected by [inter alia] a teaching corps in which morale has been affected negatively by the condition of the learning environment in some cases and by selection, recruitment, deployment, remuneration and promotion policies and practices which nullify the impact of professional formation and preparation and encourage the establishment of a mediocrity norm in the Teaching Service.

Like the other territories in the Caribbean, Trinidad and Tobago has also experienced trends that have negatively affected the achievement of the goal of Education for All. These trends include: many teachers opting for early retirement; high turnover of teaching staff; non replacement of staff on official leave; entire staffs being comprised of untrained and unqualified teachers; and the migration of specialist qualified teachers to metropolitan centres and other islands in the Caribbean through aggressive and direct recruitment schemes.

The greatest loss to the system in Trinidad and Tobago was among those teachers who were specialist in learning difficulties and who provided support to classroom teachers in developing appropriate learning support programmes to children. Many of these teachers cite greater professional development opportunities, more professional autonomy, and increased income as reasons for their migration.

As a corollary, another barrier to inclusion is the extent to which there is incoherence in the system of teacher training, and more so, the extent to which this incoherence results in wastage, and underutilisation of a trained cohort. I will recount a specific case that traces the history of teacher training in inclusive practice. In one sense it reflects government's commitment to improving learning systems and pedagogical practices. In another sense it also represents a case of teacher agency, which underscores the case for teacher participation in the decision making process.

PIONEERING EFFORTS

The training of teachers that included sensitisation about issues of inclusion was given a fillip in 1981 with the declaration of that year as the International Year of the Disabled by the United Nations. This declaration allowed the issues of disability and inclusive education to be brought to the forefront and to be related to the conditions in education in Trinidad and Tobago. The state's commitment to teacher education in regard to inclusive practice began in earnest with a workshop for teachers as a joint venture between the government of Trinidad and Tobago and the University of Manitoba and was sponsored by CIDA.[4] A large number of teachers which included teachers from special schools attended this workshop. It marked the beginning of an intensified period of teacher education in which teachers would be able to challenge and rethink current pedagogical practices.

Shortly after the workshop, a young educator from Trinidad and Tobago was pursuing a Masters course in Special Education at the University of Sheffield and, at the time of writing his dissertation, he had picked up on the gap in teacher education that had been identified in the Education Plan 1985–1990 where over five hundred teachers needed to be trained in special and inclusive education in order to provide quality education for students with disabilities and learning difficulties that had be earlier identified through the Marge Report of 1984.

One thing was a given. Since many children experience learning difficulties at some time in their school life and since increasing numbers of children were being perceived as having learning difficulties, previous notions of 'special education' had to be challenged. Most of the children who were perceived as having learning difficulties were in the schools.

Disabled children, on the other hand, approximately one thousand of them (Ministry of Education, 1984) were educated at special schools. Many of them did not receive any education since they were kept at home under the care of their families. However, in his criticism of the provision of special schools, a local educator and chair of a reporting committee on Special Education stated that 'special schools as they are at present, do not meet the needs of many special needs children in Trinidad and Tobago (Pilgrim Report, 1990, p. 37)'.

Given these circumstances, this young educator, who had established strong and collegial links with his supervisors and academic staff at his university, was given a local forum through the Association for Developmental Education (ADE) to host a forum on Special Education. He invited two faculty members of the University to deliver the workshop and this spiralled into a further 'two-week workshop which focussed on Curricular Strategies in Special Education' (Namsoo, 1998, p. 9) jointly managed by the new unified teachers' union and the ADE.

As Namsoo points out 'this was a revolution about to happen (Namsoo, 1998, p. 10)'. The introduction of new ideas about the politics and practice of inclusion through the various workshops and seminars that were being held, generated a flurry of activity among teachers who were interested in promoting inclusion. This activity was demonstrated in a loose plan of action which saw these teacher activists forming alliances and associations and locating themselves within key strategic positions so that they could influence policy and effect change. Some of these teachers and community interests were incorporated into The Association for Special Education in Trinidad and Tobago (TASETT). These members would then mobilise support for a special education committee to be formed within the new unified teachers' union. They would also locate themselves within the existing 'old' voluntary organisations that were limping along in their attempts at making education provision for their students. The old way of doing things was about to change and teachers were the pioneers in the new revolution in inclusive education.

I became involved in 'the revolution' as an adult student on the first Diploma in Special Education course in 1989 that was designed and managed by a group of teachers 'who were intent on achieving the impossible and who worked virtually night and day for months to put the course together (Namsoo, 1998, p. 11)'. My own motivation was traced back to my initial encounters at primary and secondary school that I have recounted earlier in the chapter, where I had recognised that the education system had failed those students. Yet, at the time that I had signed up for the course I was not yet fully aware of the ways in which being on such an innovative programme would fashion and deepen a commitment to the politics of teaching.

Along with one hundred and nine other students I began a journey that would put me into contact with the best, most progressive and highly respected local lecturers, who themselves had now found a forum to articulate their concerns and recommendations for change within the existing state of affairs in education. These lecturers were mobilised from local and regional higher education institutions, the Ministry of Education, special schools (both public and private) and the University of Sheffield, who subsequently validated the Diploma Course.

The course provided a basis for different interest groups to work together. As students on the course, we were actively involved in developing curricular and determining forms of assessment. We were exposed to new ways of thinking and being and in the course of the 'struggle', we were developing the language that would allow us to advocate for change. I remember the excitement that was generated when we decided to prepare a submission for presentation to the National Consultation on Special Education in 1990. It was an opportunity that we took to develop a collective voice for better provision for all children and for developing a national policy framework for inclusive education. We advocated for the introduction of inclusive education at the teachers' colleges as an elective as well as for all student teachers to be exposed to specialised profession development that would have allowed them to develop inclusive classrooms. Mindful of what Booth *et al.* (2000, p. 12) propose, we adopted a notion of inclusion that involved 'restructuring the cultures, policies and practices in schools so that they respond to the diversity of students in their locality'.

The journey towards developing a movement for inclusive education was one that was marked by the pioneering efforts of ordinary classroom teachers whose passion for social equity and justice found political space through innovative teacher development programmes. Such developments could have only been maintained through a practice of collaboration and partnerships that provided stability, sustainability and legitimacy to the efforts of these teachers.

LESSONS AND FURTHER BARRIERS TO INCLUSION

The injection of the aforementioned case serves to highlight several lessons about the relationship between the pursuit of inclusive practice and its impact on teachers training. First, notwithstanding the highly innovative teacher education programme that was developed, the language of 'special education' itself posed a barrier to inclusive practice. To those teachers on the course, 'special education' was read as a movement towards inclusion; within the wider system of education 'special education' was seen as the education of persons with specific disabilities who could not fully participate within general education.

Second, what was obvious was the need to redress poor pedagogical practices. These practices are highlighted in two ways: the practice of recruitment into the teaching service on the basis of minimum qualifications, without any teacher training where these teachers are ill-equipped to provide quality learning support; and the quality and appropriateness of teacher training. In this regard, the Salamanca Statement (UNESCO, 1994, p. 27) recommends that inclusive education requires thus:

> Pre-service training programmes should provide to all student teachers, primary and secondary alike, positive orientation toward disability, thereby developing an understanding of what can be achieved in schools with locally available support.

Further, teachers should be allowed to exercise their autonomy when applying skills and adapting curricula and instruction (ibid. 27).

The third implication for teacher training that inclusive education poses follows from the previous point about teacher autonomy. In order to develop programmes for learning support requires a willing cohort of teachers who are prepared to be innovative and creative. It is not unusual therefore to find that some teachers will resist the movement towards inclusive classrooms. The levels of resistance will vary and are dependent on how the change is introduced, teachers' level of participation in the change, and the extent to which deeply entrenched values and beliefs about learning and teaching remain unchallenged.

Government policy makes recommendation for improved and expanded teacher education programmes. These include the provision of management and leadership training for school administrators, undergraduate and postgraduate courses for principals, vice principals and senior teachers. Recommendation is also made for the establishment of a Caribbean Centre of Excellence for Teacher Training (CETT) which is designed to 'provide innovative leadership in inspiring, empowering and equipping teachers in the first three grades of primary schools, to improve the teaching of reading and thereby assist students in mastering the fundamentals of reading (Ministry of Education, 2004)'. The intention is to extend the concept of teacher training to include best practice through evidenced based teaching in areas such as reading.

The way in which teachers' colleges currently operate lags behind the requirements of the education reform agenda. The mismatch between teacher college curricula, delivery systems at the colleges and transference of pedagogical practices on graduation presents yet another barrier to inclusive education. Many teachers will question whether their training in fact adequately prepared them for the realities the classroom and what invariably happens is that when they are confronted with learning problem that they are not prepared for and are unable to address they simply resort to the old practices or to strategies that were used when they were taught.

The final barrier to inclusion that has implications for teacher training has to do with funding. Given the need for a complete rethink of teacher education programmes in Trinidad and Tobago, consideration must be given to priorities that are associated with what is to be funded and the sustainability of programmes. Underlying the policy framework about teacher training are deeply complex issues about the role of state in teacher training and the status of teacher education in Higher Education.

With effect from 2005, it is anticipated that all teacher training will be pre-service and will be removed from the teachers' colleges and run by the newly established local university, the University of Trinidad and Tobago. This fundamental shift in teacher training responds to the recommendations of the National Task Force on Education (Ministry of Education, 1993, p. xv) for 'the necessity for pre-employment training, orientation and induction programmes'.

CONCLUSION

In this chapter, I have provided an historical framework within which to examine the development of different perspectives on inclusion and the different policies and practices that have been associated with these perspectives. Historical overviews are important because they provide the cultural and political contexts that shape given policies and practices. In my recounting these, it was my intention to be critical of perspectives that seek to locate inclusive education as an end in itself where children with disabilities and learning difficulties are placed within settings, unsupported and without the needed resources. I am also very wary of current, local proclamations about 'social inclusion', the rhetoric of which is enticing and appealing but which face many barriers and as such may not fare any better that previously failed recommendations of past education plans.

It is important nonetheless to uphold the ideal of inclusion as going beyond the bounds of educational provision that is school based. I concur with Barton when he states that 'questions of social justice, equity, human rights and non-discrimination are central to the issue of inclusion (Barton, 2001, p. 94)'.

In that light, many of the initiatives undertaken through current local policy are indeed progress in inclusion. The modernisation and expansion of learning systems are seeking to provide more access to all. However, the barriers to inclusion are essentially rooted in more fundamental issues that have to do with inherited economic and social inequalities that have not transcended the postcolonial condition. Tensions will exist between a global agenda in which policy solutions that are framed from outside the region are given preference over the local and regional needs and contexts.

Although there have been regional and national gains in areas of enrolment and increasing numbers of children participating in early childhood education, primary education, secondary education as well as in teacher training and reorganisation of the education bureaucracy, the challenge facing inclusive education is that of sustainability of effort and investment. Evidently, it is unlikely that inclusive education will become a reality in the small states like Trinidad and Tobago if global market forces continue to implement and reinforce policies that are designed to exclude 'entire peoples from economic and social opportunities (Armstrong *et al*, 2005, p. 86)'.

NOTES

[1] At that time, there were external examinations that were British based. Since then, these examinations have been changed to a regional school leaving certificate run by the Caribbean Examination Council (CXC).

[2] The political party was the People's National Movement (PNM). The formation of this party was largely influenced by a group of progressive teachers and hence the education agenda of the party was not surprising. They did not confine the definition of education to mean schooling but rather engaged in what they called political education of the people.

[3] The regional equivalent to A Levels is being introduced from 2005 in Trinidad, with Trinidad being the last territory in the region to adopt the new regional examination which is called Certificate of Advanced Proficiency Examination (CAPE). It is conducted by CXC.

[4] Canadian International Development Agency.

REFERENCES

Armstrong, A., Armstrong, D., Lynch, C. and Severin, S. (2005) 'Special and inclusive education in the Eastern Caribbean: policy, practice and provision'. *International Journal of Inclusive Education*, 9, 1, 71–87.

Barton, L. (2001) 'Inclusion, teachers and the demands of change: The struggle for a more effective practice', in A. Armstrong (ed.) *Rethinking Teacher Professionalism in the Caribbean Context: Conference Proceedings. School of Education*, The University of Sheffield.

Baksh, I. (1986) 'Education and equality of opportunity in Trinidad and Tobago', *Caribbean Journal of Education*, 13, 1, 6–26.

Ball, S. (1999) Global trends in educational reform and the struggle for the soul of the teacher! paper presented at the British Educational Research Association Annual Conference, University of Sussex at Brighton, September 2–5, 1999.

Booth, T., Ainscow, M., Black-Hawkins, K., Vaughn, M. and Shaw, L. (2000) *Index for Inclusion: Developing Learning and Participation in Schools*. Bristol: Centre for Studies in Inclusive Education.

Brereton, B. (1986) *A History of Modern Trinidad 1783–1962*, Port of Spain: Heinemann Educational Books.

Government of Trinidad and Tobago (1966) The Education Act 1966, Trinidad: Government Printery.

Government of Trinidad and Tobago (1968) Draft Plan for Educational Development in Trinidad and Tobago 1968–1983, Port of Spain: Government Printery.

Government of Trinidad and Tobago (1985) (Draft) Education Plan 1985–1990, Port of Spain: Government Printery.

Green, W. A. (1991). *British Slave Emancipation: The Sugar Colonies and the Great Experiment, 1830–1865*, Oxford: Clarendon Press.

Jules, V. (1994) *Study of the Secondary School Population in Trinidad and Tobago: Placement Patterns and Practices*, UWI, St Augustine: The Centre for Ethnic Studies.

Liverpool, H. (2001) *Rituals of Power and Rebellion: The Carnival Tradition in Trinidad and Tobago 1763–1962*, Chicago: Research Associates School Times Publications.

London, N. (2002) Curriculum Convergence: an ethno-historical investigation into schooling in Trinidad and Tobago, *Comparative Education*, 38, 1, 53–72.

Marge, M. (1984) Report on the Survey of the Incidence of Handicapping Conditions in Children between the Ages of 3 and 16 in Trinidad and Tobago, Trinidad and Tobago: OAS.

Mark, P. (1993) The Implications of the effects of expansion of the secondary sector of Trinidad and Tobago's education system for teacher education: Defining the problem *Caribbean Curriculum*, 3, 1, 61–76.

Millette, J. (1985) *Society and Politics in Colonial Trinidad*, London: Zed Books Ltd.

Miller, E. (2000) *Education for All in the Caribbean in the 1990s: Retrospect and Prospect*, Kingston: UNESCO.

Ministry of Education (1993) Report of the National Task Force on Education, Education Policy Paper 1993–2003. Port of Spain: Government Printery.

Ministry of Education (2004) National Report on the Development of Education in Trinidad and Tobago 2004: Quality Education for All young People: Challenges, Trends, Priorities. Country Report submitted to the UNESCO.

Namsoo, A. (1998) 'It's now all history' in J. Lavia, and D. Armstrong, (eds) *Teachers' Voices from the Caribbean, Sheffield Papers in Education*: University of Sheffield, Department of Educational Studies.

People's National Movement (1956) *The People's Charter – Statement of Fundamental Principles* Port of Spain: P.N.M. Publishing Company Ltd.

Pilgrim, E. (1990) Report of the Collation and Evaluation Committee for the Development and Implementation of a National Special Education System for Trinidad and Tobago. National Consultation on Special Education, Ministry of Education of Trinidad and Tobago.

UNESCO, (1994) The Salamanca Statement and Framework For Action on Special Needs Education. Salamanca, Spain: UNESCO.

Williams, E. (1962) *History of the People of Trinidad and Tobago*, Port of Spain: P.N.M. Publishing Co. Ltd.

ROBERT CHIMEDZA

8. DISABILITY AND INCLUSIVE EDUCATION IN ZIMBABWE

INTRODUCTION

My name is Robert Chimedza. I work at the Zimbabwe Open University as the Pro Vice Chancellor for Academic Affairs. My training and working background are in special needs education and disability studies and I am a professor in that area. I have worked as a teacher for deaf students, a lecturer in special needs education at college and university levels and an education official on policy and practices in Special Needs Education in Zimbabwe and abroad for more than twenty-five years. In the process I worked very closely with people with disabilities in various associations of and for people with disabilities. I have also done a lot of research and publications on disability issues. My research interests are mainly in sign language, inclusion, cultural and cross-cultural issues in disability, inclusive education and HIV/AIDS and disability. It is against this background that in this chapter I discuss disability and inclusive education in Zimbabwe.

It appears to me for many developing countries important policies and practices such as the inclusion of students with disabilities in regular schools are a spillover from developing countries with very limited understanding of local conditions. It is imperative that when such policies and practices are adopted they are adapted to fit in the cultural context and resource base of the developing countries themselves. This is critical for the success of any such initiatives. My approach in this chapter is to interrogate the cross-cultural understanding of disability in the context of inclusive education.

THE CONCEPT DISABILITY

Developing countries such as Zimbabwe continue to grapple with terms, concepts and phenomena that imply including people with disabilities in regular schools. Terms such as mainstreaming, integration and now inclusion that emanate from developed countries may not mean exactly the same across different cultures and, in particular to developing countries. As the socio-cultural perspective to disability correctly observes, disability is a social construct and not an objective condition (Sarason, 1985; Edgerton, 1993; Trent, 1994; Armstrong and Barton, 1999). The social context of disability helps to define disability

L. Barton and F. Armstrong (eds.), Policy, Experience and Change, 123–132.
© 2008 Springer Science + Business Media B.V.

itself and its related concepts. Tugstad and White (1995) observed that attempts to universalise the category disability runs into conceptual problems because such definitions should take into consideration the social and cultural contexts. For instance Mpofu in Chimedza and Peters (2001, p. 13) urges that the construct 'mental disability' as is understood in Western countries is not indigenous to any African country. He goes on to explain that the terms used do not mean the same as in the West. For instance, he cites Talle (1995) who observed that the Maasai of Kenya had no word for mental retardation, and the Western conceptualisation on mental retardation was equivalent to the Maasai term '*olmodai*' which translates to 'fool'. Similarly, Zimbabwe native languages such as Shona and Ndebele do not have words that match the Western meaning of mental retardation (see Mpofu in Chimedza and Peters, 2001, for more detail). It appears there is lack of cross-cultural transportability of the construct 'mental retardation' from Western to African countries. The same can be said for many other disability related concepts.

THE CONCEPT INCLUSION

The discussion above problematizes the cross-cultural understanding of disability and its related concepts in some developing countries. It emphasises the need to understand disability concepts and issues within socio-cultural and historical contexts in which they exist. This is particularly important in a country like Zimbabwe where we have elements of feudal, neo-colonial, capitalist and even post-modern eras, all existing in the same historical moment. It is therefore not unusual for us to find the concept of inclusion problematic.

The notion 'inclusion' might not mean exactly the same for people in Zimbabwe, Uganda, Great Britain and the United States. For instance, in Uganda they have adopted the policy of inclusion in their education for children with disabilities. They base this policy on the Education for All principle (Jomtien Conference, 1990) and the Salamanca Statement and Framework for Action (1994) where Article 3 states that governments should adopt as a matter of law or policy the principle of inclusive education. In practice in Uganda, this means all children with disabilities must go to the nearest school to their home. This is the school to which their siblings, friends and neighbours go irrespective of the accessibility in the school, the pedagogic appropriateness and how the students with disabilities commute to school. In other words inclusion may mean placing the child with disabilities in a regular school with or without support. This is why it becomes imperative to understand these concepts within their socio-cultural and economic contexts. The economic situation in most African countries is unable to support inclusion cases in the same manner as in the West. There is therefore need to adapt both the definitions and comprehension of the concepts and their implementations.

Zimbabwe has a well-developed tradition of special needs education based on the special school and integration concepts, the most common integration practices being those that use the resource rooms (e.g. visual impairment), self-contained integration units (e.g. hearing impairment) and special classes with partial integration (e.g. mental disability). It is within this context that inclusion should evolve and be practised. In universities, colleges, schools, government offices, and among academics, specialist teachers and special education officers it is clear to them what inclusion is and that it is the best option for the education of students with disabilities. However, in a study by Chimedza (2000) most parents of students with disabilities in Zimbabwe preferred sending their children with disabilities to special schools with boarding facilities. These are usually far away from home and students go away from home for three months (one term) before they come home for a one month break. Effectively, in a year they spend nine months in a boarding school and three months at home with their families. The parents' choices were based on the following arguments:

- In rural areas, especially for parents of students with severe physical disabilities that affected their independent mobility, parents carried their children on their backs to go and get services such as for example, those provided by the clinic. It becomes difficult for them to imagine carrying the child to school every day. The problem gets worse as the child becomes older and heavier. Also, the school might be as far away as five kilometres from home and the physical terrain is not always user friendly even for those who are privilege enough to have wheelchairs.
- In urban areas where transport is presumed to be readily available, most parents do not have a car of their own to take their child to and from school with. They may also not have the money for the public transport to transport the child daily to school. For most working parents they have problems collecting the child from school since most of the schools break for the day when parents are still at work. The Government does not have the policy nor the resources to provide transport for students with disabilities.
- Most parents felt a boarding facility would relieve them of the daily chores and 'burden' they go through attending to their child with disabilities. They complained of burning out, fatigue, tiredness and viewed their responsibilities more in the negative than the positive.

However, not all parents viewed inclusion in the same manner as discussed above. Some parents saw inclusion as providing opportunities for them to live with their children whilst they attend school and also as a means to widen access to education for the many children with disabilities that are otherwise not in school.

SPECIAL NEEDS EDUCATION, INTEGRATION/MAINSTREAMING AND INCLUSION

It is important for scholars, researchers, parents and those involved in the education of people with disabilities to understand and appreciate the meanings and differences of the concepts special needs education, integration/mainstreaming and inclusion to facilitate planning and also so that when discussing and using these terms we mean one and the same thing. We have noticed the general use of these terms as if they mean the same across cultures, even at professional presentations. The discussions below are aimed at trying to understand and appreciate this problem.

Special Needs Education

The concept of special needs education is based on the acknowledgement that there are two clearly distinguished groups of students in the school systems: normal students and special students. The normal students require a normal teacher, normal schools, normal curricula and normal pedagogy. On the other hand the special student requires a special teacher, special school, special pedagogy, special curricula and so on. Basically, the special student has 'special educational needs'. The focus in special education is the child with disabilities and not the system of education.

Integration

The concept of integration suggests bringing the students with disabilities to the mainstream of the school system so that they learn together with regular students. Hence in the United States of America the same concept is called mainstreaming. As in special needs education discussed above, in integration classes the focus is on changing the student with disabilities to fit into the mainstream school system. The student with disabilities is expected and assisted to adapt to the system by provision of back up support. In real terms in developing countries such as Zimbabwe, integration has often meant a 'geographical process of moving a child with disability physically into a mainstream school. It ignores issues such as whether the child is really learning, really being accepted or included (Stubbs, 2002, p. 24)'.

INTEGRATION UNITS/SPECIAL CLASSES AND SELF-CONTAINED CLASSROOM

Another facility that is common in Zimbabwe in terms of provision for the education of students with disabilities are small units attached to regular schools or self-contained classes or special classes of students with disabilities geographically located within the regular school and operating as part of the regular school with or without partial integration in regular classes. The argument is that because the students with disabilities are physically there at the regular school, integration takes place naturally as the students mix and play together at school, both in and outside the classroom.

INCLUSION

The concept 'inclusion' as used in the education of students with disabilities tends to focus more on inclusive schooling yet its meaning is much broader than that. Inclusion should include inclusive schooling, inclusive education and inclusive societies. Where there exist inclusive societies and inclusive education, inclusive schooling becomes much easier. In most African societies inclusion of people with disabilities is limited due to attitudes and stigma against disability that are prevalent.

In inclusive schooling the aim is not to change the student with disabilities to fit into the environment. The aim is to change the environment to accommodate the needs of the student. Inclusion recognises that students are different and that all can learn. The systems are flexible. The children with disabilities learn in the same classes with their age mates, at their local home school where their siblings and neighbours go to.

Inclusive education should not only be a policy but a practice. Students with disabilities and those others equally marginalized in society (e.g. street kids, girls, farm workers' children, working children, children infected and affected by HIV AIDS) should be included in the regular school system on an equal footing with regular children. It is most disturbing that in many cases such students are treated differently and less well than regular students.

A Policy of Inclusion

In the preceding discussion, I provided two scenarios as follows:

- The Ugandan situation, whose thrust is to include all children with disabilities in regular schools with or without support and in most cases without support.
- The Zimbabwean situation, where there is a strong tradition of special schools and the integration concepts with limited (few) inclusion situations.

Whereas educationists in both situations above are agreed that the best education provision option for students with disabilities is one of inclusion at their neighbourhood school, it appears there are differences in when and under what conditions inclusion should be implemented. The argument that countries should wait for resources to support inclusion to be available may mean inclusion will never take place because of the poverty in those countries. Very few developing countries are able to provide the required support. Also, very few African countries, for instance, have prioritised disability services in their national budgets. It appears more logical, given the statements above, to go ahead and include children with disabilities in regular schools whilst at the same time lobbying for support provision from both government and development agencies.

The laws and legislations of the country should guide the policy of inclusion. The constitution of the country should protect people with disabilities from discrimination of any nature. An audit of the Zimbabwean constitution on disability issues was done (Zigomo-Nyatsanza, 2000) and it was observed that Section 23(1) of the constitution speaks of the right of Zimbabwean citizens to live lives free from discrimination on the basis of race, gender, tribe, and place of origin or ethnic background. It does not prohibit discrimination on the basis of disability. The constitution acts as though everyone is equal in front of the law and that everyone has equal rights and opportunities, yet the reality is that people are not equal. In this case people with disabilities are not equal to other people even in the country's constitution because they are not included in the list of people against whom discrimination is illegal.

In Zimbabwe there is no specific law on inclusion. The Disability Act does not specifically address issues on inclusion. Although legislation exists to uphold the right of every child to attend school, children with disabilities remain excluded. As Kabzems and Chimedza (2002) observed even when the disabled child's right to attend school is recognised, inclusion of loophole phrases such as 'funds permitting' defeat the whole purpose.

Inclusive Education and Inclusive Cultures

Stubbs (2002) gives a definition of inclusive education based on the Agra Seminar and South Africa Policy that says inclusive education:

- Is broader than formal schooling. It includes the home, community, non-formal and formal systems.
- Acknowledges that all children can learn.

- Enables education structures, systems and methodologies to meet the needs of all children.
- Acknowledges and respects differences in children: age, gender, ethnicity, language, disability, HIV/AIDS status etc.
- Is a dynamic process, which is constantly evolving according to the culture and socio economic and political context.
- Is part of wider strategy to promote inclusive society (Stubbs, 2002, p. 21).

Kisanji (1996) observed that traditional Africa Education was inclusive. Every child in the community irrespective of their status, abilities or disabilities were taught under the social cultural system of the village by the elders. However, Addison (1986), Barnatt and Kabzems (1992), Phiri (1979) and Onwegbu (1977) have noted that traditionally and culturally there exists negative attitude among African people towards disability. Further observations (Chimedza, 2000) acknowledge that these attitudes are changing and salient but they still do exist. What this means is that while the education system could have been inclusive its content with regards to people with disability was negative. Also, it has been noted that the Bantu people of Southern Africa use referent terms meant for animals and things to describe people with disabilities (Devlienger, 1998; Mpofu, 1999; Mawadza, 2000). For instance among the Shona people of Zimbabwe nouns referring to people and indicating kinship usually begin with prefix 'mu'- in singular (Noun Class 1) or 'va'- in plural (Noun Class 2). However, for people with disabilities they use prefix chi- for singular (Noun Class 7) and zvi- for plural (Noun Class 8). Noun Class 7 and 8 are for objects and things and when used for humans are considered pejorative (Dale, 1981; Devlienger, 1998; Mpofu, 1999; Mawadza, 2000; Kabzems and Chimedza, 2002). Yet they are used for people with disabilities. This dehumanises them into objects and things.

We have noted in the discussion above, the cultural and traditional context in which people with disabilities in most African cultures exist. The question and challenge that as educationists, sociologists and anthropologists we need to untangle is how inclusive these cultures are to disability and how best they could be approached in terms of developing inclusive education.

Language is the vehicle of our thoughts, feelings, attitudes and ideas towards objects, ideas, relationships and people. The language that people use to term or describe other people if negative shows the enshrined negative attitudes and stigmas that have been accepted as normal in that society. Cultures that accept and continue to perpetuate such attitudes and stigma against people with disabilities need to change. Inclusive education should result in and also exist within inclusive societies. Whilst educationists are working on having inclusion in their schools and classes, they should simultaneously work on developing inclusive societies. The very child who is learning with a disabled child in school under very well planned and developed school programmes might be discouraged at home by the terms, language, attitudes and even parental intervention negative to disability that they experience at home. The bottom line is inclusive schools must exist in inclusive societies and should result in more inclusive societies.

This discussion would not be complete without discussing some of the challenges that developing countries meet in their attempts to include children with disabilities in regular schools.

Lack of Equipment

One of the greatest challenges of the developing countries is lack of adequate teaching aids, assistive devices and educational equipment to support inclusive education for children with disabilities. Poverty characterises many developing countries. Most national budgets cannot sustain provision of assistive devices for people with disabilities and teaching aids needed in the schools. Also, support from developing agencies is erratic and dependent on the political tone of the country at any given time. In Zimbabwe at the moment most development agencies pulled out their support for political reasons that have nothing to do with disability issues. The land reform programme that the Government of Zimbabwe embarked on had nothing to do with support in relation to disability issues and yet development agencies withdrew their support of the disability agenda in Zimbabwe.

As a result of the limited if not unavailable material resources, students with disabilities are being included in regular schools without support. In most cases the inclusion programmes fail to take place because of lack of the required support that makes inclusion successful.

Lack of Trained Personnel

Inclusion assumes that the teachers who teach the students with disabilities have the expertise to do so or are adequately supported by specialist teachers or consultants with the expertise. This assumption is not always correct in developing countries. Generally teachers in regular schools are not trained to teach students with special educational needs. It is only recently that the teachers' colleges began to include topics on disability and inclusion in their curricula. It is important to note that most of these teacher education programmes that purport to include disability education on their programmes do so at psycho-social level with nothing at the level of pedagogy. While it is important for teachers to understand the child with special educational needs, that child still needs to be taught. That link is missing and kills inclusion. Regular teachers that teach students with disabilities in their classes should have both the psycho-social and pedagogic knowledge of special needs and diversity in education to make inclusion work.

The regular schoolteacher is the one who spends most of the time with the included child. It becomes imperative for such a teacher to have the right orientation, positive attitudes and the pedagogy to be able to work with the included student with disabilities in relation to other students in the class. There is therefore a need for appropriate training for teachers to accommodate this requirement.

Parental Involvement

Parents of children with disabilities especially mothers want to participate in the welfare of their children with disabilities. They participate very well in organised rehabilitation and early intervention programmes. What is usually the limiting factor is the financial support required.

Where parents are not involved, inclusion can be a problem. Parents of children with disabilities may view inclusion as an easy way out of their predicament of placing their child into school. On the other hand parents of the non disabled children in the school may not want their own non disabled children to learn together with children with disabilities because of negative attitudes (Devlienger, 1988; Chimedza, 2000). For inclusion to succeed there is need for both parents to see value in it. This is difficult to sell to parents of the non disabled children as they may see inclusion differently. Some parents argue that pedagogically their children's learning will be slowed down as the teacher spends more time assisting the child with special educational needs. Such perceptions need to be managed. It therefore means parental participation should be much more than fund raising events but should include involvement in the students' curricula and pedagogy so that they see how both students benefit in inclusion.

Inaccessible Environments

One of the main barriers to inclusion is inaccessible environments in schools. Most schools in developing countries, if not all of them, are constructed with able bodied students in mind. There are high steps and no ramps. Toilet doors are too narrow for wheelchair users. The situation is worse in rural schools where they use pit latrines. These are very difficult to use for children with physical disabilities.

The architecture of schools should be inclusive. As school committees plan to build structures they should bear in mind students with disabilities. Schools should have ramps instead of steps. All common places such as the library, laboratories, dining halls, boarding places and classrooms should be accessible.

Inclusive Curricula

The school curricula should be inclusive as well. The regular school curriculum is the one that is generally used in inclusion. The common thinking is that students with disabilities who are in inclusion classes simply learn what other students are learning since they are just like any other students. Such thinking, while logical, does not always work to the best interest of the student with disabilities. In many cases students with disabilities need other courses or subjects that they should take to facilitate their access to the curricula. For instance students who are blind may need to have extra classes in braille reading, braille writing, mobility and orientation. Students with learning disabilities may need extra tutoring after the regular class teaching to fill in missed gaps. These adaptations and adjustments are critical for inclusion to succeed.

Inclusive Pedagogy

The pedagogy that most teachers use in regular schools is meant for the average student. Teachers tend to teach ignoring the diversity in learning abilities typical in inclusive education systems. In inclusive education if the pedagogy is not changed to accommodate the diversity of the class such as gender, ethnicity, disabilities, slow learners, then the disadvantaged student misses out and becomes a passenger rather than a participant in the education process. Because the teacher teaches for the average students, others will not benefit. They get segregated, frustrated and in many cases they drop out.

There is a need for teachers to use pedagogy that accommodates all learners in the classroom. Examination centred teaching ignores the child. In many developing countries there is a serious chase for the diploma at the expense of the child's actual learning. Teachers then teach for the examination. In the process they use inappropriate pedagogy and they ignore those who learn differently.

CONCLUSION

The purpose of inclusion in education is to develop inclusive societies. Discriminatory attitudes, stigmas and behaviours against disabilities that are found in some cultures in developing countries need to be challenged and corrected. There is a need to develop an accommodating society that embraces diversity. This can only happen through appropriate public and community awareness of disability issues including inclusion. Societal education on disability should be on the increase yet it appears to be on the decrease in some countries such as Zimbabwe. Such awareness campaigns need to be supported by the right national laws and policies both on human rights in general and disability in particular. Laws that list some disadvantaged groups and leave out disability are suspect in their commitment to addressing problems in that area.

For inclusive education to succeed in developing countries such as Zimbabwe a lot of support is required in terms of financial and material resources. There is a need to ensure that the teachers who work with the students with disabilities in the regular classes on a daily basis have the right pedagogy. There is also a need for community education that challenges wrong attitudes and assists in correcting them. Parental involvement is critical especially the involvement of not only parents of children with disabilities but also those of non disabled children.

REFERENCES

Addison, J. (1986) *Handicapped People in Zimbabwe*, Harare: NASCOH.

Armstrong, F. and Barton, L. (eds) (1999) *Disability, Human Rights and Education: Cross-cultural Perspectives*, Buckingham: Open University Press.

Barnatt, S.N. and Kabzems, V. (1992) 'Zimbabwean teachers' attitude towards the integration of pupils with disabilities into regular classrooms' *International Journal of Disability, Development and Education*.

Chimedza, R. (2000) *A Situation Analysis of children with disabilities in Zimbabwe*, Harare: UNICEF.

Chimedza, R. and Peters, S. (2001) *Disability and Special Needs Education in an African Context*, Harare: College Press.

Dale, (1981) *Shona Mini Companion*, Gweru: Mambo Press.

Devlienger, P.J. (1998) 'Physical disability in Bantu languages: understanding the relativity of classification and meaning', *International Journal of Rehabilitation Research*, 21, 63–70.

Edgerton, R.B. (1993) *The Cloak of competence*, revised and updated. Berkeley: University of California Press.

Ingstad, B. and Whyte, S.R. (1995) *Disability and Culture*, Berkeley: University of California Press.

Jomtien Conference (1990) World Declaration on Education for all, Spain.

Kabzems, V. and Chimedza, R. (2002) 'Development assistance: disability and education in Southern Africa', *Disability and Society*, 17, 2, 147–157.

Kisanji, J. (1996) Interface between culture and disability in the Tanzania context: Part 1, *International Journal of Disability Development and Education*, 42, 93–108.

Mawadza, A. (2000) *Shona-English, Shona Dictionary and Phrasebook*, New York: Hippocrene Books, Inc.

Mpofu, E. (1999) 'Social acceptance of Zimbabwean early adolescents with physical disabilities', unpublished doctoral dissertations, University of Wisconsin.

Mpofu, E. (2000) in R. Chimedza and Peters, S. (eds). *Disability and Special Needs Education in an African Context*, 98–137, Harare: College Press.

Onwegbu, O. (1977) 'The Nigerian culture, its perception and treatment of the handicapped', Unpublished quoted in E.O. Caulcrick (ed)., *Handicapped Children: Early Detection, Intervention and Education*, Geneva: UNESCO.

Phiri, N.L. (1979) *Problems of the Handicapped: An Assessment of attitudes Towards the Disabled and Implications for Rehabilitation in Zambia*, Lusaka Institute for African Studies.

Salamanca Statement and Framework for Action (1994).

Stubbs, S. (2002) *Inclusive Education: Where There are Few Resources, Oslo:* The Atlas Alliance.

Talle, A. (1995) A child is a child: disability and equality among the Kenya Maasai: In S.R. Whyte and B. Ingstad (eds), Disability and Culture, 56–74. Berkeley: University of California Press.

Trent, J.W. (1994) *Inventing the feeble mind. A History of Mental Retardation in the United States*, Berkeley: University California Press.

Zigomo and Patsanza, L. (2000) Audit report to the Disabled Persons Act (1992), Harare: National Association for the Care of the Handicapped.

VIANNE TIMMONS

9.   TOWARDS INCLUSIVE EDUCATION
IN CANADA

INTRODUCTION

Living in the smallest province in Canada, Prince Edward Island, has its advantages and disadvantages. As a researcher in education, focusing on family literacy and inclusion, it is a privilege to work closely with teachers and families in the province. It is a community built on relationships and respecting relationships is critical if one wishes to research in the community. One of the challenges is that often you work in isolation, as there is not a critical mass of researchers in your field, and you need to depend on community alliances. The alliances are often with the school districts, Department of Education and community groups.

The province has three school districts, two English and one French. It has an extensive French Immersion programme for Anglophone families who want their children to learn two languages. The province has a community college and a university. There are no provincial or standardized exams given in the province. There has been a trend in Canada to bring in accountability through standardized testing; however Prince Edward Island has not jumped on board yet. In the recent Programme for International Student Assessment (PISA) results Prince Edward Island students did the poorest in Canada. PISA is an internationally standardized assessment that was jointly developed by participating countries and administered to 15-year-olds in schools. More than 250,000 students in 41 countries took part in PISA 2003, the second three-yearly survey of its kind. The survey involves pencil and paper tests lasting two hours, taken in the students' schools. The main focus in PISA 2003 was on mathematics, but the survey also looked at student performance in problem-solving, science and reading and at students' approaches to learning and attitudes to school. Though Prince Edward Island students did well internationally, they did not perform well nationally.

Due to these performance results here is much discussion about the school system, with an education task force recently formed with a mandate of reviewing student achievement in the province.

Students are accepted into postsecondary education based on their high school marks which are teacher generated. The school system has implemented education which is whole child focused. It has an extensive music programme taught by specialists, teacher

133

L. Barton and F. Armstrong (eds.), Policy, Experience and Change, 133–146.
© 2008 Springer Science + Business Media B.V.

librarians, art and physical education programmes and, guidance counsclors in all schools. The province has maintained small schools and resisted amalgamation of these community schools. These factors are not considered in the PISA assessment.

The above description presents the context in which I work, a small province, with limited resources struggling to meet the needs of all students.

In this chapter I will explore developments in inclusive education in Canada. First, I will present an overview of the country and educational system to develop a context for the discussion on inclusive practice. Canada is the world's second largest country in land mass, encompassing six time zones. Canada has 24 people per 100 hectares; in comparison, the United Kingdom is almost 100 times as densely populated, with 2300 people per 100 hectares. Canada has ten provinces and three territories, the latter located in northern Canada. This great land mass creates challenges in communication, transportation and services to rural communities.

The population of Canada is 30.7 million people. The country is truly multi-cultural with only 19 per cent of Canadians reporting Canadian as their ethnic origin. Seventy-seven per cent of Canadians live in cities and 3 per cent of Canadians are Aboriginal. Over the last century, a steady migration from rural areas of the country to urban areas has taken place. This combination of cultures and languages creates challenges in the educational system. In all urban centres expertise in teaching English as a second language has been developed.

The educational system in Canada is under provincial jurisdiction. There is no national office of education or any federal power to dictate educational policy. Provinces are very protective of their authority over education. This provincial system creates considerable challenges in the development of a national picture of educational practices and policies. All provinces engage in developing curriculum and setting policy and standards for achievement for the children in that jurisdiction.

Inclusion is a term that is variously interpreted, and has different meanings for different people. An accepted definition of inclusion is where adults and children with disabilities learn, play and work in their community with their neighbours. Mittler (2000) notes, 'Inclusion is based on a value system that welcomes and celebrates diversity arising from gender, nationality, race, language of origin, social background, level of educational achievement or disability (p. 10)'. Inclusion is a philosophy which one embraces when teaching, working and communicating within a society characterized by diversity. Inclusion, therefore, encompasses all members of a community, not just those who historically have been most at risk of marginalisation and exclusion. This chapter, however, focuses particularly on education and disabled children.

HISTORICAL OVERVIEW

The history of education for children with disabilities in Canada followed a similar pattern to other countries. The first Canadian school specifically for students designated as 'mentally handicapped' was established in 1888, on the grounds of a government institution for 'feeble-minded' adults and children in Orillia, Ontario. Prior to the nineteenth century, children with disabilities were considered evil or possessed and were generally excluded or hidden from society. In the late nineteenth century, Canada opened a number of institutions for people with disabilities. They were located in grounds and buildings which had previously been used as hospitals or sanatoriums. Winzer (2001) notes some characteristics of this era:

> Residential schools – variously referred to as asylums, institutions, colonies, or training schools – were first established in Canada in the 1860s to serve children described in the parlance of the day as deaf and dumb, blind, and idiotic or feeble-minded. In the United States and Canada, these special schools were divorced from the general educational system and administered along with prisons, asylums, and public charities. Not until the early 1900s were special schools in most parts of Canada placed under provincial departments of education (p. 31).

During the twentieth century increasing numbers of day schools were created, led by groups of parents interested in having their children educated in their community. These day schools were often in basements of churches or community halls. The teachers were hired by the parent groups and the curriculum was a combination of arts, crafts, and life skills. Some communities built segregated schools to house children with disabilities. During this time institutions continued to flourish in Canada, often resembling large minimum security prisons.

In the late 1970s, I worked in an institution for children with disabilities to finance my way through university. The children slept in dormitory-style rooms, and spent much of their day in large day rooms. These day rooms were not furnished but had large foam shapes for the children and young people to sit on or mats for them to lie on. If the weather were pleasant, they would be allowed to go out in the fenced yard to sit on play ground equipment. The children and young people ranged in age from infants to young adults in their early 20s. The care was custodial rather than focused on development of the children's potential.

During the four years that I worked in the institution, I saw the belief emerge that children with mental handicaps could be 'educated'. A teacher was hired specifically to develop programmes which had some educational components. By my final year, in 1979, the children and young people attended classrooms (in the institution) rather than being housed in day rooms, and the teacher provided a number of life skills and communication programmes to the students. It was exciting to see children learn to communicate, help themselves and be encouraged to develop interests.

While working in the institution, I did not observe children overtly mistreated; however, nor did I observe a great deal of love and affection. The primary role for staff was custodial. They ensured that the children were clean, well fed and did not create any disturbances. I did observe children left in soiled clothing to teach them a lesson, and children tied down in bed at night to prevent them from wandering. In retrospect, these custodian practices were abusive, and have made me reflect on the nature of institutions and the culture that emerges in them. The workers, although possibly well-meaning, came to view the children as objects to maintain, not human beings who required stimulation, variety, play and love. Segregation leads to removal of humanity and dignity, as institutional staff focus on chores rather than children.

We have seen abuse in institutions emerge throughout our country. Residential schools for Aboriginal children were places where children experienced significant isolation and abuse. In Newfoundland, in the orphanages run by the Christian Brothers incidents of cruelty and sexual abuse occurred. Institutions seem to create their own rules and lose touch with the fact that children thrive in loving, caring environments. These incidents are shameful parts of our past and we need to ensure that they are not repeated.

In the later part of the 1900s, school boards slowly assumed the administration of the segregated schools. By the 1970s and 1980s, segregated classes were being established in regular schools. The institution I had worked in was closed, and the children were moved to group homes or smaller institutions, where they attended segregated classes in regular schools. The adjustment for many children was surprisingly smooth. They seemed to be resilient even with so few experiences outside the institution that had been their home most of their lives. In the institution, staff had changed on a regular basis, reducing opportunities for deep relationships and ties, and I think that this made it easier for the children to leave and move on.

In 1980, I was hired to teach a group of adolescents who were identified has having 'mental handicaps' who attended regular school. These teenagers had a classroom in the basement of an elementary school by the furnace room. They had a different start and leaving time than the other children so that they did not mix with, or frighten, the elementary schoolchildren. Their curriculum consisted of age inappropriate tasks, and lots of repetitive tasks such as pegboards and lacing. During their school day, they did not interact with children without disabilities. This move into integration resulted in the students being educated with a curriculum which kept them occupied at best, and provided little opportunity for growth and development. It was a pathetic attempt at integration. As I travel around the world, I still see examples of integration which are segregation under the name of inclusion. It is frustrating to see continued overt separation viewed positively by well meaning caregivers.

In the final decades of the twentieth century, important legislation on access to education emerged in the context of growing awareness and responsiveness, internationally, to the issues facing people with disabilities. The International Year of Disabled Persons in 1981 had a catalytic role in raising awareness and prompting action in Canada. That year a special House of Commons committee, the Committee on the Disabled and Handicapped, was established and made a series of recommendations. In the following year, Canada attained the distinction of being the first country in the world to include the rights of disabled persons in its constitution, through the inclusion of physical and mental disability under Section 15 of the Canadian Charter of Rights and Freedoms. Throughout the 1980s and 1990s, further measures were taken by Canada and by provinces and territories to advance the rights of people with disabilities. Jurisdictions placed particular emphasis on improving the inclusion of children with disabilities in the public school systems, and most reflected this emphasis through specific provisions in their education related legislation. In recent years, some provinces have moved to update and improve these provisions.

As a result, by, the late 1980s, mainstreaming and integration came to be widely considered as the appropriate way to educate children with disabilities in Canada. In 1982, I took a job in a segregated school in British Columbia. The children ranged in ages from 5 to 21 years. The school was located in a school complex which housed an elementary and a high school. Approximately 20 students attended the school at any one time. The students were on a life skills and academic programme and we attempted to arrange for the children to attend the adjacent schools for courses such as physical education and music. The children did get to interact with their age appropriate peers for very brief periods of time during the day.

I moved to another community in the mid 1980s and participated in the closure of a segregated school. During those years, there was a significant movement in Canada to close schools for children with disabilities, and to close institutions and move adults with disabilities back to their home communities into group home settings. Closing the segregated school was a challenging task, as the parents had worked hard to ensure its establishment and resources. It had a family atmosphere where parents came often and there were numerous school events which welcomed the families. The parents were confident that their children were well cared for and safe in this setting, and were apprehensive of having their child exposed and vulnerable in a school where they might be teased and ostracized. The school closure had to be carefully orchestrated to ensure that the receiving schools felt prepared and the parents felt their children would be safe. Extensive work was done with the staff and children at the receiving school. It became evident throughout this preparation that the more knowledge and strategies the receiving schools obtained the more positive and confident they were.

The transition was a positive one overall. The children became part of their new schools and the parents had to adjust to a new role with the schools. They were not as involved in the direct education of their child but rather had to assume an advocacy role. After a year the parents said they would not wish to return to the segregated setting for their children.

The 1990s brought continued reform of traditional special education practices. Many school districts adopted inclusive education policies and practices. More and more segregated classes were closed and children had the opportunity to attend regular classes in their neighbourhood schools. They were often involved in individualized or small group instruction through pull-out programmes. Some provinces moved more aggressively towards inclusive practice than others. A province like Ontario still features segregated schools and categorically grouped children. Provinces such as Prince Edward Island and New Brunswick are focusing on how to improve inclusive practices in the classroom. As Winzer (2001) observes:

> The 1990s are witnessing the inclusion movement, which seeks regular education advantages for all children with disabilities. Even the implementation of inclusion is changing. At first, it was connected intimately to a place; now it is more associated with a group of services and adaptations (p. 32).

As education is a provincial responsibility, there is no national approach to inclusive education in Canada. Each province develops its own policies towards inclusive education, and as mentioned earlier, some provinces are more progressive than others. The provinces which seem to hold on to segregated educational practices seem to also be the ones focused on provincial testing and accountability in education. Lupart and Weber (2003) state, 'Over-reliance on standardized testing as a measure of school quality is another obstacle to the improvement of schools ... A more complete picture can be observed by adding information garnered through parents and student surveys, interviews, observations, and case studies (pp. 29–30)'. Some provinces in Canada publish the results of these standardized tests, and schools become ranked based on the results. The socio-economic status of the school's neighbourhood or the make up of the school community are never included in the ranking; therefore schools become apprehensive of including all children in their regular classrooms as it could affect their ranking and reflect negatively on the staff. Based on the recent PISA results mentioned earlier in the chapter this may be a fall out for Prince Edward Island. Inclusion may be blamed for low PISA results.

The areas in Canada that have seemed to make considerable strides in inclusive education appear to be those that are more rural than urban. This may be due to the fact that it is difficult in sparsely populated areas to acquire a critical mass of a specific population to develop and set up segregated services. These communities tend to have more generic services and the children often attend classes with their age appropriate peers. In the urban centres the tendency is to congregate children with specific disabilities and provide *specialized* services. This expert model is one which promotes segregation.

In Canada, approximately 15.5 per cent of the Canadian school-age population is considered to have exceptionalities, which may include behavioural, communications, physical and intellectual differences. Among these children and adolescents, boys are more likely than girls to be identified as having disabilities (Winzer, 1991, p. 14). Services for children with special needs vary from province to province as do policies and practices. These variations range from segregated schools to schools without any segregated classes.

Even when inclusive education is adopted as a principle, teachers express apprehension at successfully educating all children in their classrooms. They often feel unprepared and at times inadequate for the task. Lupart and Snart (1994) found that despite considerable agreement on the principles that support inclusion, when faced with the philosophical, organizational and pedagogical implications, educators have often been overwhelmed by the magnitude and scope of change that the implementation of inclusive education requires. There continues to be agreement among parents, teachers, professors, and ministry officials that the primary purpose of schools is to ensure maximal development of learning potential for 'every' student through effective education. According to Horne (2001), this causes many concerns for teachers and parents, as supports are not always in place to teach all students in the class effectively. Over the past twenty years, the inclusion of students with exceptional learning needs within the education system has been a dominant trend. A number of researchers have looked at educators' attitudes towards inclusion of students with disabilities and found that teachers reported greater peer acceptance of children with disabilities in inclusive settings (Wood, 1998; Bunch et al., 1999). Research has also been conducted on parents' perceptions of inclusive practice (Palmer et al., 1998). Results suggest a general acceptance of the concept of inclusive education; however, there are frequent reports that the necessary supports are not being made available. For example, Bunch et al. found that regular educators were assumed to have the primary responsibility for inclusive practice. Few educators, however, felt they were adequately prepared in terms of professional preparation, special educator support and expertise and resources. Teachers have consistently reported positive attitudes towards inclusion in recent Canadian studies but express apprehension about their ability to cope with the diverse learning needs presented in their classrooms. They are seeking knowledge, additional staff, smaller class sizes, and any other supports that would assist them in doing a good job.

The positive results of inclusive practice are beginning to emerge in the literature. Buysee, Wesley, Bryant and Gardner (1999) studied 180 community based, licensed child care centres, and found that inclusive early childhood programmes were of higher global quality than non-inclusive programmes, (p. 311), as assessed by caregiver responsiveness, appropriateness of learning activities, strategies for promoting peer acceptance and family participation. Similarly, Devore and Maxwell (2000) found that children with disabilities can be successfully served in inclusive community based childcare settings. In addition, a number of authors have noted that inclusive practices for adolescents are important for the development of satisfying friendships and positive peer relationships, which in turn are critical for successful and satisfying school experiences (see e.g. Martin, 1996; Levesque, 1996).

There are some dissenting voices on the Canadian educational scene. Many studies have found that inclusion affects all students in the class (Bauer, 1994; Bunch, 1994; Daniel and King, 1997). The position paper of the Quality of Education Network of Ontario (1992) stated that students with severe disabilities could not be fully integrated into a classroom without seriously encroaching on the educational rights of the majority of students. Crawford (1994) argued that by supporting full inclusion all the time, advocates make it impossible to provide direct instruction any more. Such positions fail to engage with the issue of the human rights of all children to attend their local school, and rest on unreconstructed assumptions about the role and culture of schools and the need for deep transformation.

Ontario is the largest province in Canada and has been slow to adopt inclusive education principles. Some school districts have been more progressive than others, but the largest school district (Toronto) still operates segregated schools. Bunch (1994) discussed how one group of advocates for the continuance of segregated special education feared that widening diversity within regular classes would dilute achievement and place Canada in a weakened competitive position internationally. In her research study, Horne (2001) found that teachers in her province were positive towards the inclusion of all children in the regular classrooms and had very specific requirements for support.

> Teachers of Prince Edward Island are positive about including all students in regular elementary classrooms. Supports such as smaller class size, planning time, teacher assistants, and training must be provided in all schools. When the complexities of providing inclusive education for all students are more fully understood, the more likely all students will be more effectively served. All partners – teachers, parents, school boards, Department of Education, and universities – need to work together to understand and improve education for all students (p. 140).

Along with school districts, teacher education programmes in the country have a varied approach to preparing teachers for diverse classrooms. Some universities do not require their students to take courses on teaching children with diverse needs in the regular classrooms, while other programmes have this area as core curriculum. With appropriate preparation, new teachers can be advocates for inclusive practice. They can benefit from studying areas such as principles of inclusive education, how to work with para-profes-sionals, differentiation of curriculum, and individualized instruction. In my work with student teachers, I have found that they are open to developing a philosophy of educa-tion which is inclusive. They are part of a generation which has embraced social justice as a core value, and they carry these beliefs into their classrooms.

Teacher education programmes which are interested in developing an inclusive education approach to teacher education need to consider including courses which intro-duce the students to an inclusive education philosophy and teaching practices. Ideally, other courses the students take should be infused with inclusive education principles. For example, when they study math methodologies, they need to explore how to differ-entiate math curriculum, how to challenge the student who demonstrated a talent for mathematics, and how to motivate the child who is not confident about his/her math abilities. Inclusive education practices are practical approaches to teaching all children successfully in a classroom with their peers.

The literature regarding achievement and social development notes the benefits emerging when children with special needs are included in regular classrooms. Bunch and Finnegan (2000) identified definite social and academic benefits for students with disabilities when placed in inclusive classrooms. These benefits included greater strength in social situations, understanding of social roles, perception of appropriate and inappro-priate social behaviour, the development of social relationships between individuals, and increased academic motivation.

These benefits are not widely recognized by teachers. Those who support inclusive education often do so from a human rights or social justice perspective. Advocates for inclusive education need to promote inclusive education on the grounds that it benefits all children. When a teacher adopts inclusive education principles in his/her classroom she/he has to introduce differentiated instructions, interactive learning, varied assess-ment practices and strong social interaction. Once teachers understand that inclusive education principles are founded on excellent pedagogical principles, they will be more inclined to adopt this approach to education of all children.

ABORIGINAL EDUCATION ISSUES

The notable exception to the provincial authority over education is Aboriginal education, an area offering many insights on inclusive education. Aboriginal education is overseen by a federal department called Indian and Northern Affairs Canada, which provides fund-ing to local communities for education of Aboriginal children. The history of education of Aboriginal children followed a different pattern from those of other Canadian children. Prior to the 1800s, no formal education was available for children of Aboriginal descent. From the late 1800s until the mid-1900s, both Anglican and Roman Catholic missionary schools were established to educate Aboriginal children (O'Donoghue, 2001). These schools were residential schools often located away from the child's community. According to O'Donoghue:

> in residential schools, children were subjected to a variety of abuses and active
> assimilation, the purpose of which to 'civilize' them and teach them the English

language. Children were indoctrinated with religious beliefs that differed from those taught by Aboriginal families, and Aboriginal languages and cultures were generally banned and negatively labeled. Children were usually separated from their siblings and very harshly punished for infractions of any rules (p. 9).

After the closure of residential schools in the 1950s and 1960s, the federal government opened day schools in some Aboriginal communities or bussed the Aboriginal students to public schools in many adjacent communities. Children of the residential school survivors have little knowledge of their history and culture, as their parents were prevented from learning it.

Recently we are seeing Aboriginal communities work to assume control over the education of their children. These communities are struggling to develop an education system which serves their children well. LaFranco (2000) reports:

numerous studies and commissions that examine 'Indian Education' have been conducted over the past two centuries. However, the larger society has continually failed to recognize that schooling involves cultural negotiation. People of colour worldwide have always recognized the need for education – that is not the debate. The divergence occurs around the concept of education (p. 101).

The community leaders are working on developing a curriculum which reflects their cultures language and histories This is a significant challenge in light of the diverse languages and cultures among Aboriginal communities, as noted by Battiste (1995). Many communities are attempting to deal with this challenge and often resources, loss of language and culture and few Aboriginal people in the community with the educational expertise compounds the situation.

Clearly, education in Aboriginal communities is as distinctive as are those communities and their languages. As Battiste (1999) comments, with over fifty-two Aboriginal languages in Canada in over 300 Aboriginal reserve communities, and with large numbers of off-reserve Aboriginals in all major cities, the diversity of Aboriginal cultures and communities is immense. Provinces have controlled education and curricula for the last century, and it is difficult, if not impossible, for Aboriginal peoples to achieve complete change in twenty years. The questions about Aboriginal education continue, the debate and doubts linger, and the funds and resources to achieve new ends continue to dwindle.

The leaders in Aboriginal communities recognize that education is critical to see their children achieve and break the cycle of poverty and unemployment they have faced over the last few decades. As noted by Castellano *et al.*, (2000):

like their parents and grandparents, today's parents want their children to succeed in school. However, to succeed should not mean that children have to forsake the truth taught to them in the home. Aboriginal control of Aboriginal education has sought to reverse the experience of cultural denial that has been lived by generations of Aboriginal people in assimilative education institutions (p. 253).

There is a significant movement in Canada to support Aboriginal controlled education and to work with communities to ensure children's success in school. The lives of

Aboriginal children and their families are filled with stories of social and economic marginalisation (Timmons, 1999). Canada still has far to go to achieve an inclusive society which embraces all cultures and races, in particular, our Aboriginal communities.

Research in Aboriginal and minority educational contexts globally has demonstrated that the following four factors significantly contribute to academic and personal success: (a) incorporation of culturally and linguistically relevant programmes into schools; (b) participation of the community (particularly parents) in the education of their children; (c) use of transformative pedagogy (interactive, relevant, meaningful, cooperative); and (d) advocacy based assessment (Nieto, 1992; May, 1994; Leavitt, 1995; Ladson Billings, 1995; Cummins, 1996; Corson, 1998; Lipka and Mohatt, 1998; O'Donoghue, 1998).

These factors are critical to success for all students, not just students of Aboriginal descent. Willms (2002) identified family involvement in children's learning as one of the critical factors in ensuring children's school success. In a research project looking at family literacy in rural Atlantic Canada, Timmons (2003) found that families with multi-generational literacy challenges were able to work with researchers to develop curriculum which was culturally and contextually appropriate. This curriculum was meaningful to the children and families and allowed the families' strengths to emerge through the research.

The work on developing a curriculum that met the needs of these families developed their self esteem and provided an opportunity for them to advocate for themselves and their families. The importance of self advocacy can not be underestimated. Advocacy, especially from parents, can promote educational change.

SELF-ADVOCACY

Families of children with 'mental handicaps' are strong advocates for inclusive education in Canada. Recently the national parent advocacy organization, the Canadian Association for Community Living, has identified the promotion of inclusive education as one of its primary foci for the next year.

Other organizations such as advocacy groups for deaf, learning disabled and gifted people are hesitant to embrace inclusive education. They see the potential of losing significant gains they have made in securing specialized resources for their children. They fear that through inclusive education, schools could remove important supports which they have advocated for their children, and specialized instruction may be lost. These are legitimate concerns, and advocates for inclusive education need to be vigilant that all students' unique learning needs are well served in schools that adopt inclusive education principles.

Although in Canada inclusive education is a topic teachers are familiar with and many schools have adopted it, it is the voice of the advocates which are heard rather than the voices of children and adults with disabilities. Wehmeyer and Schwartz (1998) suggested that self-determination contributed to a more positive quality of life for people with disabilities. Timmons and Brown (1997) found that there has been little research on the quality of life of children with disabilities from a personal perspective.

Nevertheless, these children's stories can offer insights into programmes and services. When Timmons (1993) spent time asking disabled teenagers about their life experiences, they were able to clearly articulate the times when they felt part of a social network and times when they were isolated. It was the first time that many of these children had been asked about their experiences and opinions. Goode (1999) stated that research about children with disabilities continues to be more informed by biomedical and behavioural approaches of disability than by the experiences of children themselves (p. 121). He describes current research with children:

> Contemporary studies of children, particularly in educational, psychological, and sociological research, increasingly employ qualitative methods of research such as participant observation, ethnography and ethno methodology, these being particularly suited to capturing a subjective views of actors. Such studies have demonstrated that all children, even those with no formal language, have ways to communicate their views about life (p. 123).

Unless we provide an opportunity to hear the voices of people with disabilities, we will not know the impact of policy and practices on inclusive education on their lives, or what their demands are. Brown (1999) stated, 'Listening to and valuing the views of people with disabilities, and treating them as unique but authentic people is a methodological practice that is probably quite helpful to enhancing self-worth' (p. 105). Timmons (1999a) suggested, 'Research in the new millennium should focus on the development of strategies that assist people with disabilities to become full, contributing citizens in society (p. 76)'. It is rare that we canvas children regarding ways to improve educational practices and even rarer that we solicit the views of children with disabilities.

Mittler (2000) stated, 'the most important challenge for the future is to enable children and young people to speak for themselves, even if they challenge the system and the views of their families and the professionals who work with them (p. 188)'. We need to provide an opportunity to hear the voices of adults and children with disabilities, to value their opinions and views, and to learn from their experiences.

In Canada, we are finally acknowledging the voices of Aboriginal people, and have seen that including them in decision making leads to better decisions which are owned by the people they serve. We need to truly include children and adults with disabilities which affect their lives. By including their voices, we will be able to better assess the impact of inclusive education and the ongoing challenges that exist.

In the field of inclusive education we have made significant strides in educating our teachers about the benefits of inclusive education; however, we have left them feeling under prepared and ill equipped to assume the task of educating all children in the regular classroom. They need to feel confident that inclusive education will benefit all children.

AREAS FOR FURTHER RESEARCH

Despite the progress that has been made on inclusive education, pressing needs exist for research in many areas. Foremost among those, in my opinion, is the need for research into the education needs, wishes, experiences, and insights of children themselves. Development and refinement of pedagogical tools and skills represents another priority, addressing the concerns of teachers about their preparedness to meet the diverse needs of all children in inclusive classrooms. Models and approaches of effectively working with marginalised families have the potential to maximize any school based initiatives. Allowing families to participate in solution building has potential to make a difference for children.

CONCLUSION

Over the past decade, Canada has moved from segregation of persons with disabilities to increasing inclusion in every walk of life. The public school system in many areas has been among the leaders in this evolution, fostering awareness and openness to inclusion in other domains such as post-secondary education and the labour market. The size and diversity of Canada, and the decentralized system of jurisdictional responsibility to the provinces, has meant that this evolution has progressed at different speeds and to different degrees across Canada. While this decentralized model has precluded a national approach to inclusion, it has also enabled policy innovation and leadership and the development of diverse approaches and practices to inform and enhance the quality of inclusive education.

Looking ahead, Canada has the potential to be a leader in the inclusion movement. We are a nation of diversity and have a strong publicly funded educational system. The majority of children are educated in the public system and there is little variety in quality from province to province. In international educational assessments Canada performs well. We have a strong educational foundation and the provinces that have adopted inclusive education philosophies are working hard to support this approach to education.

Teachers in Canada teach classes filled with students from different cultures and religions. They approach this task with the attitude that these diverse classes are a reflection of what Canada is and what we as Canadians hold dear. We pride ourselves on the multi-cultural nature of our society. Aboriginal education is a case in point, offering many insights on the importance of a holistic approach to education which values and integrates diversity, includes communities and families, and demonstrates the value of advocacy.

When it comes to diversity of ability, not all teachers have the same convictions. Many believe in principle that children with disabilities should be included, but they believe this on grounds of social justice, rather than a conviction that such an approach provides the best possible education for children without disabilities as well as those with disabilities. Moreover, teachers are not confident about the adequacy of their professional preparation, special educator support, expertise, and resources. Teachers require targeted training, classroom supports and a school system that embraces inclusive education as excellent Education for ALL. We still have a long way to go before most teachers approach diversity in terms of perceived ability as confidently as they approach cultural diversity. I am optimistic, however, that the next generation of teachers will be raised in a much more inclusive society and will view the schools as a microcosm of the inclusive world in which they live.

REFERENCES

Battiste, M. and Barman, J. (1995) (eds) *First Nations Education in Canada: The Circle Unfolds*, Seattle, Washington: University of Washington Press.

Bauer, N. (1994, April) 'The politics of inclusion: a dissenting perspective' paper presented at the annual spring conference of New York State Association of Teacher Educators, Syracuse, New York.

Brown, I. (1999, May) 'Social processes and integration: synthesis paper', in *Conference Proceedings, Research to Action: Working Together for the Integration of Canadians with Disabilities*, Halifax, NS: Saint Mary's University.

Bunch, G. (1994) 'Canadian perspectives on inclusive education', *Exceptionality Education Canada*, 4, 3 and 4, 23–35.

Bunch, G. and Finnegan, K. (2000) 'Values teachers find in inclusive education' Proceedings, Fifth International Special Education Conference, University of Manchester, Manchester, UK.

Bunch, G. Lupart, J. and Brown, M. (1999) 'Resistance and acceptance: educator attitudes to inclusion of students with disabilities' in *Conference Proceedings, Research to Action: Working Together for the Integration of Canadians with Disabilities*, Halifax NS: Saint Mary's University.

Buysee, V., Wesley, P.W., Bryant, D. and Gardner, D. (1999) 'Quality of early childhood programmes in inclusive and non-inclusive settings', *Exceptional Children*, 65, 3, 301–314.

Castellano, M.B., Davis, L. and Lahache, L. (eds) (2000) *Aboriginal Education: Fulfilling the promise*, Vancouver: University of British Columbia Press.

Corson, D. (1998). *Changing Education for Diversity*, Buckingham, England: Open University Press.

Crawford, D. (1994). Full inclusion: One reason for opposition. [On-line]. Available: http://my.execpc.com/~presswis/inclus.html

Cummins, J. (1996) *Negotiating identities: Education for empowerment in a diverse society*, Ontario, California: California Association for Bilingual Education.

Daniel, L. and King, D. (1997) 'Impact of inclusion education on academic achievement, student behaviour and self-esteem, and parental attitudes', *The Journal of Educational Research*, 91, 2, 67–81.

Devore, S. and Hanley Maxwell, C. (2000) 'I wanted to see if we could make it work: Perspectives on inclusive childcare' *Exceptional Children*, 66, 2, 241–255.

Goode, D. (1999) 'On quality of life for children (with disabilities)', *Exceptionality Education Canada*, 9, 1 and 2, 111–128.

Horne, P. (2001) Making it work: Teachers' perspectives on inclusion. Unpublished master's thesis. Charlottetown: University of Prince Edward Island.

Ladson-Billings, G. (1995) 'Toward a theory of culturally relevant pedagogy' *American Educational Research Journal*, 32, 3, 465–491.

LaFrance, 2000 *Aboriginal Education: Fulfilling the Promise*, Vancouver: University of British Columbia Press.

Leavitt, R. (1995) 'Language and cultural content in native education' M. Battiste and J. Barman, (eds) *First Nations Education in Canada: The Circle Unfolds*. Vancouver: University of British Columbia Press.

Levesque, N. (1996) 'Peer relations of adolescents with learning disabilities: a review of the literature', *Exceptionality Education Canada*, 6, 3 and 4, 87–103.

Lipka, J. and Mohatt, G. (1998) *Transforming the Culture of Schools: Yup'ik Eskimo Examples* Mahwah NJ: Lawrence Erlbaum Associates.

Lupart, J. and Webber, C. (2003) 'Canadian schools in transition: Moving from dual education systems to inclusive schools' *Exceptionality Education Canada*, 12, 2 and 3, 7–52.

Lupart, J. and Snart, F. (1994). 'Creating instructional environments that promote inclusive education', *Exceptionality Education Canada*, 4, 3 and 4, 1–17.

Martin, A.K. (1996) Issues in the education of exceptional adolescents: inclusion, pedagogy, and social competence. *Exceptionality, Education Canada*, 6, 3 and 4, 524.

May, S. (1994) *Making Multicultural Education Work*, Clevedon, England: Multilingual Matters.

Mittler, P. (2000) *Working Towards Inclusive Education: Social Contexts*, London, England: David Fulton Publishers.

Nieto, S. (1992) *Affirming Diversity: The Socio-Political Context of Multicultural Education*, New York: Longman.

O'Donoghue, F. (2001, April) 'Arctic cotton in a southern wind: facilitating inuit leadership in Nunavut', paper presented at the annual meeting of the American Educational Research Association, Seattle, WA.

O'Donoghue, F. (1998) 'The hunger for learning in Nunavut schools' unpublished doctoral dissertation. Toronto, Ontario: University of Toronto/Ontario Institute for Studies in Education.

Palmer, D.S., Borthwick Duffy, S.A. and Widaman, K. (1998) 'Parent perception of inclusive practices for their children with significant cognitive disabilities' *Exceptional Children*, 64, 2, 271–282.

Quality Education Network of Ontario (1992) 'Position paper: overview of the ontario educational systems', Toronto, Ontario.

Timmons, V. (1993) 'Quality of life of teenagers with disabilities' Unpublished doctoral dissertation, Calgary, Alberta: University of Calgary.

Timmons, V. (1999) 'Children and youth: a synthesis' paper presented in Proceedings, Research to Action: Working Together for the Integration of Canadians with Disabilities. Halifax, NS: Saint Mary's University.

Timmons, V. (1999) 'Quality of life of teenagers from Mi'kmaq descent' *Exceptionality Education Canada*, 9, 1 and 2, 514.

Timmons, V. (2003) Family literacy through family history: a case study. [On-line] Available: http://www.abccanada.org/

Timmons, V. and Brown, R.I. (1997) Quality of life: issues for children with handicaps in R.I. Brown (ed.) *Quality of Life for People with Disabilities*, London: Stanley Thorne Ltd.

Wehmeyer, M.L. and Schwartz, M. (1998) 'The relationship between self-determination, quality of life, and life satisfaction for adults with mental retardation', *Education and Training in Mental Retardation and Developmental Disabilities*, 33, 3–12.

Willms, J. (2002) *Vulnerable Children*, Edmonton, Alberta: The University of Alberta Press.

Winzer, M. (1989) *Closing the Gap: Special Learners in Regular Classrooms*, Mississauga, ON: Copp Clark Pitman.

Winzer, M. (1999) *Children with Exceptionalities in Canadian Schools*, 5th edn., Toronto, Canada: Prentice Hall Allyn and Bacon.

Winzer, M. (2001) *Children with Exceptionalities in Canadian Schools*, 6th edn., Toronto, Canada: Prentice Hall Allyn and Bacon.

Wood, M. (1998) 'Whose job is it anyway? Educational roles in inclusion' *Exceptional Children*, 64, 2, 181–195.

HELEN PHTIAKA

10.   EDUCATING THE OTHER: A JOURNEY IN
CYPRUS TIME AND SPACE

INTRODUCTION

In the last 25 years, against a background of the immense social, economic and educational consequences of the Turkish invasion of 1974, the face of Special Education in
Cyprus has drastically altered. We have had enormous changes in philosophy, legislation,
terminology, policy and practice relating to special education. We have also witnessed
important developments in Cypriot teacher education. There have also been major changes
in the administrative structure of the Ministry of Education and Culture as far as Education
in general and Special Education in particular are concerned. Yet, the mode of thinking in
the area of special education has remained unaltered for 75 years – it is that of charity.

At this point in time we need to celebrate these developments (which are mostly
positive), but also to stop and think, examine the models used and plan our future actions.
To this end this chapter offers a brief critical account of the historical development of
Special Education in Cyprus so far, the influences which have shaped it and the policies
and practices which have been developed, focusing in particular on the integration movement. It notes the legislative and philosophical changes over the course of the years, identifies the difficulties apprehended in the implementation of the new legislation and
explores some ideas about the underlying sources of such difficulties. It concludes that
the specific historical and political developments in Cyprus have encouraged and maintained a notable separatist educational ethos in relation to any form of 'otherness'.
Therefore the notion of charity is still dominant in Cyprus as if it were the only notion
which can accommodate the demands of disabled children and adults. This mode of
thinking, exemplified by activities such as the Radiomarathon (Phtiaka, 1999), needs to
be altered if integration and indeed inclusion are to have a future on the island.

THE RADIOMARATHON MODEL – A CHARITY MODEL

A quotation from the Radiomarathon radio programme which exemplifies the charity
model on Cyprus National Radio can ease us into this conversation. It is apparent in this

L. Barton and F. Armstrong (eds.), Policy, Experience and Change, 147–162.

quotation that the organizers of the event, as well as the media people, are quite contented with the appeal the event has on young people and the 'social change' it brings about:

> The children who were eight years old when the Radiomarathon started, are now 21 years old. These children are the change required. They are building the new social conscience we need.
>
> Monday November 4th 2002 8:30 A.M.
>
> (Extract from a conversation at the Radiomarathon radio programme on Cyprus National Radio).

As I have argued elsewhere (Phtiaka, 1999) and I have repeatedly written in the local press (Phtiaka, 2000, 2001, 2001a) the Radiomarathon, the yearly fair which presents itself as the sole defender of the Cyprus children with special needs, and internationally at that, is a very damaging enterprise which for the benefit of an unnecessary fund raising event (Laiki Bank could easily offer 1,000,000 CYP as tax-exempt money with no fuss at all) has securely established the charity model in the area of special needs and disability in Cyprus. The enterprise is all the more damaging as it systematically excludes year after year, despite the questions raised by their organizations, disabled people[1], and becomes increasingly sophisticated in its rhetoric, in response to the limited criticism it receives. This is to say that at a time when the charity model is internationally being replaced by a human rights discourse, Cyprus under the leadership of a ruthless profit making body – such as a bank – and under the cover of a multitude of well meaning volunteers, has 'discovered' charity for children with special needs. This is particularly unfortunate as under this influence the charity approach has come to determine every aspect of our exchange with children with special needs and their parents. This includes the implementation of their integration in the ordinary school under law 113(I) of 1999. Notions of 'them and us', 'fortunate citizens and unfortunate fellow humans' are yearly promoted with an almost unstoppable force through radio and television programmes, through posters, leaflets, balloons, tee-shirts, sweat-shirts and hats (which swallow a fair amount of the budget).

The official state either does not realise how her educational and social policy work is undermined by this fiesta, or is pleased that someone else appears to be sharing the responsibility and the financial burden of the education and training of children with special needs. It was after all a state governed for 10 years, prior to the last election, by a government which embraced wholeheartedly the neo-liberal notion of private initiative in welfare areas such as education. The state therefore joins in the fiesta through the participation of its most senior representatives (Laiki Bank support may well have been useful in presidential or other elections). This is then the current state of affairs in Cyprus:

- a dominant charity model exemplarily represented by the Radiomarathon;
- state support for such notions and events through its elected representatives;
- a bewildered public which, apart from paying local, state, consumer and other taxes, has to constantly fork out the money to support activities such as these which make up for state inefficiencies.

How have we come to this? A critical examination of the development of the special needs area in Cyprus, projected onto the background of the island's political and educational history is necessary in order to answer such questions and provide suggestions for the future. It will then become apparent from the claim of the organisers that the Radiomarathon has brought about the development of a beneficial new social conscience is not substantiated. On the contrary, such a model endangers all the achievements of the state and the organized parents so far concerning the educational and social integration of children with special needs.

For purposes of clarity we need to define how the term 'Special Education' is used in the context of this chapter. Special education refers here to the education and social welfare system which, contrary to the dominant or mainstream education system, has traditionally dealt with the care, the culture, the education and the professional rehabilitation of individuals who have been considered as deviating from the norm in a physical, mental, psychological or some other way.

SPECIAL EDUCATION IN CYPRUS: A CRITICAL HISTORICAL ACCOUNT

Looking back from the 'wisdom' and the 'safety' of the early twenty first century at the history of special education in Cyprus, we are able to note a series of parallel developments and influences which have shaped it into what it is today. It dates back to 1929 with the establishment of separate, independent and charity run special schools, like many other countries before it (Phtiaka, 1997). By 1999 it reached the stage where a number of internal and external pressure factors forced the state to establish new legislation supporting the integration of children with special needs in the mainstream school system. The main factors involved in this period are outlined in Table 1.

Table 1   Factors Influencing Changes in Philosophy, Legislation and Practice

I. International Declarations		
	1959	UN Declaration of the Rights of the Child
	1978	Rights of the Mentally Handicapped
	1981	UN Rights of the Disabled Declaration
	1994	Salamanca Statement
II. Foreign Reports and Legislation		
	1975	Education Act – USA
	1978	Warnock Report – UK
	1981	Education Act – UK
	1981	Education Act – Greece
	1985	Education Act – Greece
III. National Reports		
	1980	UNESCO Report (J. Benevento)
	1990	Markides Report
	1992	Constandinides Report

Table 1   (*continued*)

1993	UNESCO Report (J. Hansen)
1997	Barnard Report
1997	UNESCO Report
1997	Paschalis Report
IV. Other Factors	
1981	Organisations of the Disabled
1992	P.O.SY.GO.P.E.A. (Federation of Parental Organisations)
1992	University of Cyprus

This 75 year old history can be divided into four stages for ease of reference, as follows.

Table 2   Special Education in Cyprus – Four Basic Stages

A. 1929–1979:	Gradual Establishment of Special Schools
B. 1979–1988:	Unified Legislation – Special Schools – Separatism
C. 1988–1999:	Informal Integration Practices
D. 1999:	Legislative Enforcement of Integration

The First Stage can be outlined in the following way:

Table 3   A. 1929–1979 Gradual Establishment of Special Schools

Philosophy
Lack of a Clear Unified Philosophy
Legislation
Lack of Unified Legislation
Practice
Gradual Establishment of Special Schools Starting with
the School for the Blind 1929 and the School for the Deaf 1953

This First Stage officially began in 1929 with the establishment of the School for the Blind by the wife of the English governor of the island at the time, Lady Storrs. This is probably the last major 'act of good will' on behalf of the colonial rulers. In the early thirties (1931) the first serious troubles, known as 'Octovriana', broke out between the English and 'the locals' and relationships between them would never be quite the same again, an event which had serious effects on education (Maratheutis and

Ioannidou-Koutselini, 2000; Persianis, 2002). Like many of the schools which followed, the School for the Blind in its early days was run as a charitable institution offering primarily care and training to our 'less fortunate fellow human beings'. Educational concerns came much later. The Greek Council of Education, which became the Ministry of Education after Independence, assumed responsibility for it in 1957, but even then the School retained a part of its autonomy as it was run by a Board of Directors (School for the Blind, 1989), until the passing of the new law 113(I)/99.

It is important to note that charity was the driving force behind the initial establishment and running of almost all special schools and institutions in Cyprus in the absence of a strong state. To mention but a few, the School for the Deaf was established by the Rotary Club in 1953, the Home for Sick Children in Limassol by the Red Cross in 1957, the special school Evagelismos for Mentally Retarded children by the Association of Greek Ladies 'Enosis' in 1965, the institution Theotokos by a volunteer non profit making group in 1969, the institution Nea Eleousa by the UN Refugee Division in 1977. Even schools which were initially established by the state were occasionally 'taken over' by charitable funds, such as the Training Centre for Children with Mental Retardation established by Archbishop Makarios in 1977, which was renamed as the Christou Steliou Ioannou Foundation in 1981 after a large initial donation by the Ioannou family. In such cases it is interesting to note that although the State still contributed a large amount of money annually (around 1,000,000 CYP in the case of the Christou Steliou Ioannou Foundation) it was almost invisible in the running and the public face of such institutions.

This first stage of development, which lasted until 1979, saw the gradual establishment of special schools. Special institutions and schools were established all over the country, in response to a multitude of disabilities and needs. Each one was run by a Board of Governors, following its own set of rules and regulations, and working in competition with other special schools and institutions. There was no uniform philosophy, policy or legislation, and practice was piecemeal and haphazard. Given this diversity, independence and competition, it is hardly surprising that years later, when the coming together of the mainstream and the special school sector was decreed by law, both areas had great difficulties implementing this policy.

This diverse activity came to an end in 1979 when the Cyprus Parliament passed the 1979 Special Education Law. The year 1979 can therefore be considered as the start of a new era, a new stage for our analysis, which lasted until 1988.

Table 4   B. 1979–1988 Unified Legislation – Specials Schools – Separatism

Philosophy
Special Education Information Bulletin
Legislation
Law 47/79
The Special Education Law of 1979
Practice

This diverse activity came to an end in 1979 when the Cyprus Parliament passed the 1979 Special Education Law. This was the stage of the Unified Legislation. The special schools established during the previous 50 years were now under the same legislation and it was therefore expected that they would flourish. The 1979 legislation was brought about in order to put an end to the multitude of practices used as far as that was possible, and it reflects the conditions of its time. It was separatist in its philosophy and it eulogised the special school as the most appropriate place for the education of children who deviate from the norm. Such children were divided into four categories: maladjusted, trainable mentally retarded, physically disabled and slow learners (Ministry of Education and Culture, 1996). These four categories [far fewer and much more comprehensive than those included in similar British legislation of the 40s (Phtiaka, 1997)] attempted to cover needs across a wide spectrum. During the first few years of this stage the special schools established in the previous period had an opportunity to flourish protected by a national law which unified to an extent policy and practice. This did not last long however. In 1980 (and before the legislation had been implemented in schools) the new law came under criticism from the 1980 'Benevento' UNESCO Report on Special Education in Cyprus, which advocated the 'least restrictive environment' approach (UNESCO, 1980).

After that, and possibly partly because of that, the Ministry of Education and Culture *philosophy* began to change. Instances of integrational *practice* began to appear, with relevant Ministry documents dating back to 1984, and a press conference supporting social and educational integration was given by the Ministry of Education and Culture representatives on May 14th 1985 (Koupannou and Phtiaka, 2004). All this was an *informal practice* in conflict with the legislation 47/79 which officially supported special schools and special classes.

This change of heart on behalf of the Ministry was important enough to bring us into a new era and introduced the third stage of our historical development (1988–1999) as presented in Table 5.

Table 5   C. 1988–1999 Informal Integration Practices

Philosophy
1996 Special Education Information Bulletin
Legislation
Law 47/79
The Special Education Law of 1979
Practice
Parallel Practices
Special Units
Partial Integration

Changes in practice took the form of isolated instances of integration of children with special needs, mainly deaf, into the mainstream school (Koupannou and Phtiaka, 2004). Such instances, as I have already stated, came into direct conflict with the legislation. The conflict between legislation, philosophy and practice which started right in the middle of the second stage (around 1984–1985), finally materialised in the Special Education Bulletin published by the Ministry of Education and Culture in 1988 (Ministry of Education and Culture, 1988). The term integration appears then for the first time *in official documentation*, while the use of integration practices was always in contradiction with existing legislation. The third stage of development in the history of the Cypriot special education is therefore riddled with integration practices which we shall still call informal as they are not backed up by legislation.

The conflict between legislation and practice during this stage can be explained as a product of the simultaneous concurrence of a number of social and historical phenomena (Koupannou and Phtiaka, 2004). Personal ambitions and goals appeared to be fuelled by international circumstances and influences as the integration movement in the eighties swept across Europe (Barton 1989, Visser and Upton, 1993). Cypriot parents developed into a force to be reckoned with, as they came in contact with developments outside Cyprus and appreciated that children just like theirs enjoy many educational opportunities in other contexts. Unwilling to accept segregatory practices for their children, they became the driving force behind integration (Kouppanou and Phtiaka, 2004).

The conflict came to an end in 1999 when the new special education law replaced the outdated and underused 1979 legislation. Joint efforts of the organisations of disabled people, parental groups and some forward-looking education officials, supported by international agreements, international legislation and national reports, came to fruition with the passing of the law 113(I)/99. With the new legislation we have at last achieved, at least on paper, a harmony between the philosophy, the legislation and the practice of special education in Cyprus and they all point in the direction of integration. This most recent period is presented in Table 6.

This legislation has given children with special needs the right to be educated alongside their peers in the neighbourhood school for the first time. The University of Cyprus, which has been present in this debate for the past nine years, has contributed significantly

Table 6   D. 1999 Legislative Enforcement of Integration

Philosophy
Integration
Legislation
Law 113(I)/1999 The Special Education Law of 1999
Practice
Integration

to this achievement. The Rules and Regulations associated with the Law 113(I)/99 were passed on May 4th 2001, and September 2001 ushered in the first school year in which the new legislation was implemented.

What must have become clear through this account is the *separatist nature* of special education in Cyprus by virtue of its historical development. Another important point is the *charitable nature* of the institutions which were first established to 'train' children with special needs, rather than educate them. These are key notions to help us understand the difficulties encountered later in the application of integration, not to mention the development of inclusion.

All evidence so far indicates that a large number of problems are being faced by pupils, teachers, parents and administrators trying to implement the new law. Although the problems reported are mostly practical (Makris, 2002) a careful examination of both the problems arising and the solutions provided indicates that the causes are deeply rooted in the very essence of the philosophy of integration in Cyprus. We need to carefully explore our history and our culture in order to understand these causes (Phtiaka, 2003). An initial brief attempt to do this is provided in the third part of this chapter.

Difficulties Encountered in the Introduction of an Inclusive Ethos in Cypriot Educational Policy and Practice

What we have been discussing so far is the development of what has been called 'special education' in Cyprus. It must be apparent from our story that *integration*, the move of children with special needs from the special to the mainstream school, is as far as discourse has reached in this area. Yet, we know from the international literature (Vlachou, 1997) that integration as an idea was questioned by some in the nineties, because it failed to produce the required effect of offering children with and without special needs equal educational opportunities. The idea of *inclusion* was taken up instead. The terminological and conceptual struggle between integration and inclusion still holds strong, but let me define these terms here as I understand them.

Integration is a move from the special to the mainstream school where, although we may have prepared the ground somehow, we usually neglect the general *milieu*, the broader culture within which we are operating. We may for example still be discussing the pros and the cons of this move for a particular child and we may conclude that integration into the mainstream school is not a policy appropriate for each and every child.

By contrast if we talk about *inclusion*, there is no question of *if* and *but* and *pros* and *cons*. Every child's place is where his or her peers are. The question here is *how* we support the learning of all children most effectively in their neighbourhood school and how we need to transform the school in order to support all children with their varied biographies, diverse skills and learning needs. When we talk about inclusion therefore, we talk about *nothing less* than a new type of school in a new type of world.

If education reflects local culture, and if there is a link between inclusive education and a broad democratic tradition, as I have argued elsewhere (Phtiaka, 2003), the problems we seem to be faced with in our effort to implement the new legislation and promote an integrational ethos in Cyprus can be summarized as follows:

The impact of a heavy cultural reliance on notions of ancient Greek philosophy such as 'a healthy mind inhabits a healthy body':

- The dominance of the Greek Orthodox tradition of charity towards the disabled in body and mind;
- The lack of a strong democratic tradition due to a long history of invasions, occupations and lack of political self-determination;
- The lack, for much the same reason, of a strong civil rights tradition and discourse;
- The dominance of models of elitism copied from western rulers such as the British;
- The prevalence of a capitalist economic system;
- The powerful discourse of meritocracy and antagonism portrayed as an example to be envied and copied – notions imported into education from western notions of economy and market, and which are deemed essential for membership of the European Union (Phtiaka, 2003, pp. 142–143).

In the following sections I shall discuss the historical background to the development of the education system and will draw on some aspects of my own journey in the time and space of Cyprus history and education as a means of illuminating some important points.

My Personal Journey in Cyprus Time and Space

I arrived in Cyprus in the summer of 1992 to be one of the founding members of the Department of Education in the newly established University. The University of Cyprus which opened its gates to its first students in September 1992, having been established on paper in 1989 after long years of acute debate, was seen by many as an act of state compensatory legitimation in Cyprus' European process as Persianis argues quite convincingly for it in the paper I quote (Durrel, 1957).

> The administration was confident that the foreign affiliations of the academic staff
> to be appointed would pave the way for international networks and connect both the
> University and Cyprus to the Community of Europe (Persianis, 1999, p. 59).

In the preceding years, teacher education had never been in the hands of a university, as such an establishment did not exist in the country. Having 'enjoyed' the attention of the British from 1937 till 1958 in the bicommunal, English-speaking teacher training colleges of Morphou and Nicosia, the Greek Cypriot teachers after the independence were accommodated in the brand new purpose built Pedagogical Academy in 1959 (Maratheutis and Koutselini, 2000). This was an interesting change considering the conditions under which it was taking place. The liberation struggle against the British (1955–1959) had just finished. According to the *given* constitution of the London-Zurich agreements Greek Cypriot education was to be kept separate from Turkish Cypriot education. During the liberation struggle, education – especially at secondary level – had operated as the stronghold of resistance against the colonial rule (Durell, 1957; Vlachos, 2003; Persianis, 2004). Naturally therefore, the succession of the departing British chair by the Greek vice chair in the Teacher Training College during a joyful

ceremony in May 1959 was greeted as a national achievement, and as a victory of the
liberation struggle. The feeling of national achievement and the wish to get rid of anything associated with the colonial days led to the closing down of the Teacher Training
College and the establishment of a Pedagogical Academy within a few months. A new
national mission marked the character of the Pedagogical Academy in the years to come
(Maratheutis and Ioannidou-Koutselini, 2000, p. 25). This became apparent in the
speech delivered by the first ever Greek Cypriot Minister of Education on October 5th
1959 in the formal opening ceremony of the Pedagogical Academy. In this speech the
minister announced that he and his team, in cooperation with the professors of the
Academy, have extensively altered the curriculum so that the Academy can fulfill its
high promise to combine theory with praxis. The new curriculum included humanities
and placed emphasis on the religious lessons which had been excluded from the College
curriculum (he meant by the British but does not actually say so). This is seen to be a
very important change, because '*what we call Greek-Christian civilisation must guide
the School from which those who will in the future instruct the youth, will graduate*'
(Maratheutis and Ioannidou-Koutselini, 2000, p. 25). It is important to note that such
ideas had been conspicuously exempt from the Teacher Training College curriculum in
an effort to break the spiritual connections between Cyprus and Greece and strengthen
British rule (Persianis, 2002).

Fifty-five years later, and with hindsight, we can identify in those words and those
decisions the seeds for a disaster to come. But that was not how it was then perceived. It
is clear from the comments of the students interviewed in a study by Maratheutis and
Ioannidou-Koutselini (2000) that such words expressed the general feeling at the time.
This was a time of glory and triumph over the colonial power! Despite the failure of the
national vision to unite with Greece (Mavratsas, 1998), the independence was a time for
Cyprus to taste and enjoy freedom as an independent state for the first time ever in its
millenniums of history. It was a happy time to build a new state and to prepare its teachers to teach its youth something the colonial rulers had denied them for decades: their
links to their roots. This they would do! The bright blue October sky of 1959 and the
vibrant 18-year-old men and women present were not marked by any clouds of doubt.
This new state would materialize the dream of the vast majority of the population by
educating its children in Christian Greek ideals. The option of educating them to live
with the 'other' was not one of their preoccupations at the time. Somewhere, in Nicosia
perhaps, the Turkish Cypriots were possibly participating in a similar ceremony around
the same time, but Greek Cypriot educational research literature has no data on this.
Nor, it seems, has any world power learnt anything from this terrible example to stop
imposing unpopular solutions serving foreign interests on unwilling populations against
their own vision (Hitchens, 2001).

So, it was in glory that the Pedagogical Academy started its life in a beautiful, new,
cloistered, colonial-type building, in a Greek-Christian spirit, a triumph of the local over
the colonial. It was to end it in bitter disappointment and disarray 33 years later in the
old buildings of the Pancyprian Gymnasium, in a Cyprus torn and divided by a long and
hated foreign military occupation. It had to make room for the rising star of the
University of Cyprus in a change of policy which looked to a European future.

The University was to replace the Pedagogical Academy as the most important institution of Higher Education in official records, but possibly not, not yet anyway, in the hearts and minds of those who had kept the Academy alive for thirty odd years. The academic year 1992–1993 saw the functioning of two parallel traditions, one on its death bed, and the other in its birth cradle, and those of us who were lucky enough to be here as educational history was being written will remember the feeling of the unwilling victor being invited to the funeral of their victim at the Pedagogical Academy's last graduation ceremony. It was the end of an era, and the beginning of a new one. And I, at 33, ironically born the same year as the Pedagogical Academy, was to attempt with my colleagues to formulate and teach, within University coordinates now, a new type of Cypriot teacher: a teacher confident of her Greek-Christian identity, a teacher who would develop to become a reflective practitioner, a critical thinker, an active citizen, a tolerant human being, a European member, a globetrotter. A teacher who would be willing and able to live, and teach the young people to live, with 'the other' (Phtiaka, 2002). Obviously, twelve years were not enough for this vision to take a firm hold. At the referendum on the Annan plan for reunification of the island on April 24th 2004, it became apparent. Twenty two years of resistance to an unwelcome British imposed teacher training regime and 33 years of systematic cultivation of a nationalist Greek Christian spirit *despite* the failure of the great vision for Union with Greece and the establishment of a bi-communal independent state (Mavratsas, 1998), had built a powerful national sub-conscience which voiced its fears in no uncertain terms at the referendum. Seventy six per cent of Greek Cypriots voted 'NO' to the Annan plan.[2] So, on writing this chapter shortly after the referendum, my children still need to show a form of identification in order to cross the green line and visit their father's home, which is in any case inhabited by a settler in the occupied Cyprus north following the Turkish invasion of 1974.

And What of Special Education?

The first mention of special education as a topic taught in the Academy is as a specialism in the teacher's curriculum of 1981 (Maratheutis and Ioannidou-Koutselini, 2000). It refers specifically to the teaching of children with special needs in special schools and special classes, according to the letter and the spirit of the Law 47/1979 which began to be implemented in 1981 when the psycho-educational committees who were responsible for the children's assessment were put in place. Its description indicates a clear reference to a medical model of special education (Fulcher, 1989) with explicit reference to different categories of disability and a process of diagnosis, causes, characteristics, types and extent of disability. Indeed on closer examination the reference is to 'mental retardation' alone, as this is the only category to which there is explicit reference. It is interesting to note here that in a piece of research carried out last year in Cypriot schools it became apparent that pupils in primary and secondary education systematically confuse the notion of special needs with the notion of mental retardation and often identify one with the other (Phtiaka *et al.*, 2004). In his introductory note to the teacher curriculum of 1981 Michalakis Maratheutis, the head of the Academy at the time (and for most of its life (1967–1986)) stated that the authors of the curriculum had based their work on the curriculum of the Greek Pedagogical Academies, making the necessary adjustments to fit local needs.

Maratheutis and Ioannidou-Koutselini (2000) very usefully place the graduation oath of the Cyprus Academy graduates next to the oath of the graduates of Greek Pedagogical Academies around the same time. The Cypriot oath appears to be more royalist than the king, shaped in very formal, almost medieval, Greek language, making a direct reference to the Greek-Christian tradition, the great teachers of the nation and the 'beloved country'. A significant reason for this is hopefully apparent from our analysis so far. Small places often look up to a motherland for their national and cultural identity, especially when they fear it is in danger of extinction (Mavratsas, 1998; Persianis, 2002). Their institutions too are torn between local needs and broader national aspirations (Persianis, 2002a). The Cyprus Pedagogical Academy is no exception.

The preparation of teachers to teach children with special needs thus took place within these developments. The last mention of special education in the Academy curriculum was made in 1993. It is briefer but broader in its definition of special needs and appears open to contemporary developments outside Cyprus, mainly in Greece. There also is a reference to integration as follows: '*The application of the principle of integration in Cyprus* (Maratheutis and Ioannidou-Koutselini, 2000, p. 536)'. Nevertheless, the description of the course continues to be firmly located within a medical model and a segregative framework.

It is therefore clear that for complex political and historical reasons education in Cyprus in the beginning of the sixties directed itself towards a model based on the education system of the Greek mainland. This was an attempt to formulate a primarily Greek and secondarily Cypriot identity (Mavratsas, 1998, 2003). With the use of the Greek Orthodox Church and the education system as its basic mechanisms of national formulation, this political process was very similar to that followed in many Balkan and South-Eastern countries in their own process of nation state formulations (Kitromilides quoted in Mavratsas, 1998). However, this way of thinking, which was simultaneously mirrored on the other side, created tension between the majority rule (Greek Cypriots) and the largest minority of the island (Turkish Cypriots). In a climate of constant foreign involvement in Cypriot affairs, this tension was skillfully manipulated to cultivate two contrasting nationalisms and bring about direct conflict between the two communities (Mavratsas, 1998).

What is more to the point for our main thesis, here however, is the fact that this national and political philosophy cultivated a *par excellence* exclusive educational system. An educational system which excludes any notion of deviation or difference in its effort to be true to its final goal, the creation of the ultimate Greek Cypriot. What is apparent to us now, the need for teacher education to prepare the young people to live with 'the other' was not so a few decades ago. Indeed it is still not so in much contemporary Cypriot educational thinking. Paradoxically, the tragic climax of the summer of 1974 confirmed in most people's view the fact that *you cannot trust the other*, rather than causing them to question the historical, political and educational processes which had preceded this military outcome.

Papastephanou quoted in Phtiaka (2002) argues that education should promote the student's encounter with the other in society and in this process heighten their ability for constructive self-critique and self-reflection. And this is exactly what Cypriot education has failed to do with every form of otherness. School children's responses to questions relating to 'the other' in their school a few days before the referendum (Evagelou *et al.*, 2004) indicated that (a) the other had been identified with the Turk (although there were no Turkish Cypriot children in that school but there were children from other ethic origins), (b) the portrait of this other had been constructed in strikingly negative terms, almost as a caricature in a fairy tale, and in contrast with a strikingly positive portrait of the national self, both presented in their stereotypical mode, for example wearing national costume and (c) this stereotypical negative portrait included features which conflicted with any sense of common knowledge and logic. Mavratsas (1998) speaks of the lack of logic in nationalism, for example, 'a Turk is no good in football' a statement which has proved inaccurate by Turkey's performance in the last football World Cup in Japan.

It is, I would argue, in this context of exclusive educational ethos that we have to project the development of special education in Cyprus, and   of course – of the struggling attempts to introduce integration of children with special needs in the ordinary school. It is because of this ethos of lack of empathy to 'the other' as well as other reasons of course (Phtiaka, 2003) that 5 years after passing through parliament and three years after its official implementation, the Law 113(I)/99 for the training and education of children with special needs is struggling so hard.

In the current situation, charity is in fact the only notion which can accommodate children with special needs in people's conscience as deserving of welfare, education and employment. Charity is, I wish to argue, a very dangerous notion indeed, not only because of the impact it has on disabled children and adults themselves, but also because it isolates their case from any other difference, thereby wasting an opportunity for broader educational and social changes which will, in a circular fashion, create the climate we need for an inclusive society, which will provide an inclusive education, promote and sustain inclusive social ideals as a matter of fact.

CONCLUSION

A history of separatism and charity has shaped the way of thinking in Cypriot mainstream and special education. There are very good historical and cultural reasons for that. To transform the education system into inclusive education is a massive task. We have the means to accomplish it however. Once we understand the deeper reasons for the current triumph of a phenomenon such as the Radiomarathon and the ideals it promotes, we can publicly 'call its bluff' and deconstruct it. We can then replace the separatist charity ideal with an informed human rights discourse. This is the best way to serve the cause of special/inclusive education in Cyprus in the future, though we may have failed to do so in the past and fail to do so in the present.

NOTES

[1] By the time this chapter will appear in print, it will be almost a year from the loss of Andros Prokopiou, an important journalist, a visionary activist and a dear friend. I wish to dedicate it to his memory, for without

his insight and his personality I would never have understood what it means to be disabled in Cyprus. Rest
in peace Andro! There are many left to continue the struggle.

2   It would be naive to argue that education rules politics. The opposite is rather more accurate. However our
purpose here is to examine the role of education in a very complex political setting.

REFERENCES

* denotes that the document is in Greek

Barton, L. (1989) (ed.) *Disability and Dependency*, London: Falmer Press.

Durrel, L. (1957) *Bitter Lemons of Cyprus*, London: Penguin.

Evagelou, E., Kourousii, E., Constantinou, F., Rivera, M. and Chrysostomou, A. (2004) 'Minority children in
the Cyprus school, a project submitted for the needs of course EPA311' *Introduction to Special Education,
Spring Semester* 2004, University of Cyprus.*

Fulcher, G. (1989) *Disabling Policies? A comparative approach to education policy and disability*, Lewes:
The Falmer Press.

Hitchens, H. (2001) *The trial of Henry Kissinger*, London: Verso.

Kouppanou, A. and Phtiaka, H. (2004) *Deaf Education: Factors of Configuration on Educational Policy for
the deaf in Cyprus between 1980 and 2003*, Paper presented at the European Conference on Educational
Research, University of Crete, Rethymnon, 22–25 September 2004.

Makris, P. (2002) 'The culture and education of children with special needs law of 1999: implementation in
primary education,' in A. Gagatsis, L. Kyriakides, N. Tsaggaridou, H. Phtiaka, and M. Koutsoulis, (eds)
*Educational Research in the Era of Globalisation, Proceedings of the 7th Pancypriot Conference of the
Cyprus Educational Research Association*, 26–27 April 2002, University of Cyprus, Nicosia, Cyprus.*

Maratheutis, M. and Koutselini, M. (2000) *The function and the curriculum of the Pedagogical Academy of
Cyprus* (1959–1993), Nicosia: the authors.*

Mavratsas, C. (1998) *Perspectives of Greek Nationalism in Cyprus*, Athens: Katarti.*

Mavratsas, C. (2003) *National Unanimity and Political Agreement*, Athens: Katarti.*

Ministry of Education and Culture (1988) *Special Education Bulletin*, Nicosia: Ministry of Education and
Culture.*

Ministry of Education and Culture (1996) *Special Education Bulletin*, Nicosia: Ministry of Education and
Culture.*

Ministry of Education and Culture (1999) *The Training and Education of Children with Special Needs Law*
113(I)/99, Nicosia: Government Printing Office.*

Persianis, P. (1994) *Aspects of Cypriot Education at the End of the 19th and the Beginning of the 20th century*,
Nicosia: Paidagogiko Instituto Kyprou.*

Persianis, P. (1999) 'Higher education and state legitimation in Cyprus' *Mediterranean Journal of Educational
Studies*, 4, 2, 51–68.

Persianis, P. (2002) 'The British attempts to impose cultural hegemony in Cyprus and the role of cultural
resistance', *Journal of Postcolonial Education*, 1, 2, 47–67.

Persianis, P. (2002a) 'Conflict between the International aspiration and localism and its effects on the construction and legitimation of knowledge in Universities of the periphery: the case of the University of
Cyprus', in *Challenges and Problems for the University of Cyprus*, Nicosia: the author.*

Phtiaka, H. (1997a) *Special Kids for Special Treatment? How special do you need to be to find yourself in a
Special School?*, London: Falmer Press.

Phtiaka, H. (1999) 'Disability, human rights and education in cyprus', in L. Barton, and F. Armstrong, (eds)
(1999) *Disability, Human Rights and Education: Cross Cultural Perspectives*, Milton Keynes: Open
University Press.

Phtiaka, H. (2000) Cyprus state and special education, in Kypriotakis, A. (2000) *Proceedings of Special
Education Conference*, University of Crete, Rethymno, Crete 12–14 May 2000.*

Phtiaka, H. (2000a) *We Cannot Wash Off with a Yearly Contribution*, Student Battlement, March 2000, 13,
24–26.*

Phtiaka, H. (2001) 'Radiomarathon 2001: rights and wrongs', *Philelephtheros*, Sunday November 11th 2001, Academic Affairs, 5.*

Phtiaka, H. (2001a) 'Once upon a time there was the fool of the village' ... or *Literature and Mental Retardation*, Aneu, 1, Summer 2001, 64–68.*

Phtiaka, H. (2001b) *Cyprus: 70 Years of Special Education*, Open University at Skali Aglantzias, Lectures, First Year September 1998–February 1999, Nicosia: University of Cyprus.*

Phtiaka, H. (2002) *Teacher Education for a New World, International Studies in Sociology of Education*, 12, 3, 353–374.

Phtiaka, H. (2003) 'The Power to exclude: facing the challenge of inclusive education in cyprus' *International Journal of Contemporary Sociology*, 40, 1, 139–152.

Phtiaka, H., Palmyri, N., Constantinides, G., Dorati, M., Katsamba, P. and Nikodemou, T. (2004) 'Children with special needs and us: attitudes of pupils without special needs towards their peers with special needs' in A. Gagatsis, A. Evaggelidou, H. Phtiaka, L. Kyriakides, N. Tsaggaridou and Koutsoulis, M. (eds) *Current Trends in Educational Research and Practice, Proceedings of the 8th Pancypriot Conference of the Cyprus Educational Research Association, May 2004*, University of Cyprus, Nicosia, Cyprus.*

School for the Blind (1989) *Information Leaflet*, Nicosia: School for the Blind.*

UNESCO Report (1980) Cyprus. *Special Education*, by J. Benevento, Serial No: FMR/ED/SCM/80/150, Paris: UNESCO.

Visser, J. and Upton, G. (eds) (1993) *Special Education in Britain after Warnock*, London: David Fulton Publishers.

Vlachos, A. (2003) *Ten years of Cyprus Problem*, Athens: Estia.*

Vlachou, A. D. (1997) *Struggles for Inclusive Education*, Buckingham: Open University Press.

TINA LOWE AND PATRICK MCDONNELL

11. TO BE OR NOT TO BE INCLUDED – THAT IS THE QUESTION: DISABLED STUDENTS IN THIRD LEVEL EDUCATION IN IRELAND

INTRODUCTION

In personal and professional terms this chapter provides us with an opportunity to address some of our shared concerns about research, policy making and inclusion in relation to disability and education in Ireland. It also enables us as researchers to bring different kinds of experience and knowledge to this undertaking and to work co-operatively in doing so. The impetus to carry out the research outlined here came about as a result of Tina's college experiences:

> As a student I have often found myself placed in a marginalised environment which included practical barriers, such as the lack of accessible reading materials and scanning equipment, limited access to adaptive technology and a limited reading service. Restrictions of this kind lead to unequal participation in classroom activities … In my experience, general awareness about disability has not been one of the characteristics of university life nor has it been subject to any sustained debate … (Lowe, 2002, pp. 3–4).

Patrick's involvement stemmed from his interest in inclusive education (McDonnell, 2000, 2003) and through teaching and research work in disability and equality (Equality Studies Centre, 2000) and in Deaf studies (McDonnell, 2004).

Our aim, however, is not just to replace the passive voices of 'objective' and 'disembodied' researchers with our own active voices and autobiographies. While acknowledging that all research in the human sciences is fundamentally subjective and value laden, we recognise that there is also a place for positivist perspectives (Lynch, 1999, p. 5). To foreground the voices of researchers will not of itself guarantee an emancipatory research undertaking. There is, moreover, the difficulty of attempting to produce a collectivist account of a collective experience (Oliver, 2002, p. 16). We believe, however, that social groups who are affected by policy-making and decision-taking must have space and opportunity to participate in and, if necessary, contest policies and decisions, and that research plays a crucial role in these processes. The study reported here represents our efforts to engage in this work.

L. Barton and F. Armstrong (eds.), Policy, Experience and Change, 163–176.

Our main focus of attention is first, on disabled students' accounts of their academic and social experiences in a large Irish university. Second, we discuss these accounts in relation to the experiences of disabled students in further and higher education in other European countries. Finally, we identify a number of key issues that our analysis supports in terms of further research and policy development in third level education in Ireland. But before going on to these topics, we wish to outline some general features of educational policy in relation to disability.

In a western European context, we can identify three broad phases of policy making with regard to disability and education. The first phase, based on a model of segregated provision, lasted from the end of the eighteenth century until well into the post-World War II period. During this period special schooling constituted one element in a more general process involving the regulation and institutionalisation of 'anomalous' populations in society, especially populations of the poor (see, e.g. Scull, 1993; Foucault, 2002). The second phase was associated with new orientations in general social policy, particularly in movements towards 'normalisation' and de-institutionalisation, most typically associated with developments in the social services in Scandinavia (Reinach, 1987) and with the work of Wolfensberger (1972) in North America.

In special education these movements were articulated in what came to be known as integration or mainstreaming and date roughly from the 1960s (Rispens, 1994). The most recent phase, inclusive education, has developed out of a critique of policies and practices in integration and in continuing segregation. It increasingly reflects the political struggles of disabled people to contest the representation of disability in terms of individual 'conditions' and of responses to disability in terms of 'care' and 'need', and to base this challenge on demands for human rights, social justice and equality in an inclusive society (Dyson and Millward, 1997; Armstrong et al., 2000; McDonnell, 2000; Riddell, 2000).

There are considerable difficulties involved in undertaking any analysis of inclusion in Higher and Further Education (Hurst, 1998, pp. 3–6). By far the greatest degree of attention has been given to policies and practices in sectors that relate to compulsory schooling. Over the past decade, for example, a series of international studies carried out by the Organisation for European Co-operation and Development (1994, 1995, 1997a, 1999, 2000) has tracked, in some detail, educational developments with regard to disability at primary level. The prevailing international pattern is that opportunities for disabled pupils to receive education in inclusive or integrated settings become much more limited or are non-existent after primary level (Ireland, 1993, Section 2.3.2; see also Buzzi, 1995; Randoll, 1995; Tetler, 1995; OECD, 1997b; and Armstrong, Belmont and Verillon, 2000, for brief cross-national perspectives). Thus, issues of policy and practice in Further and Higher Education are only now beginning to be addressed (Corbett, 1993; Reindal, 1995; Ash et al., 1997; OECD, 1997b; Hurst, 1998; Riddell, 1998). Attempts to make cross-national comparisons are problematic because of the distinctive political, economic and social conditions under which national systems of education have developed, because of how they are currently structured, and because of the particular ways in which those systems have responded to disability. Among the countries of the OECD, for example, 'the educational experiences of similar [disabled] students would be vastly different in different countries (OECD, 2000, p. 73)'. However, a number of recent comparative studies of disability in higher education, relevant to the Irish context, have been carried out which examine the legislative, access and equity issues involved (Callaghan *et al.*, 1995; Hurst, 1998; Skilbeck and Connell, 2000).

Currently, disabled students in Ireland may access the third level sector via two different routes. They may qualify for 'standard entry' by obtaining the necessary number of points in their Leaving Certificate examination and by meeting other course requirements where these apply. Disabled students may also gain admission to a third level college through so-called 'non-standard entry', that is, as mature students or through special access schemes (Callaghan, 2001, pp. 10–16; Lowe, 2003). Applying for a place in college through these alternative routes can be complicated and frustrating since application procedures vary from college to college and because the demand for places far exceeds the number of places available. Moreover, while some institutions reserve a limited number of places on particular programmes for disabled students who do not meet the standard entry requirements, in almost all cases 'non-standard' admissions are at the discretion of the institution or the faculty concerned.

A considerable amount of policy making and legislation governs – often indirectly – the relationship between disability and education at third level in Ireland. A series of documents in the 1990s drew attention to educational inequalities experienced by disabled students (Coolahan, 1994; Ireland, 1992a, 1995). The Regional Technical Colleges Act (Ireland, 1992b) and the Universities Act (Ireland, 1997) required their respective institutions to encourage access by social groups who were traditionally excluded from this sector. The remit of the Higher Education Authority – the funding, advisory and monitoring body of the third level sector – includes an obligation to promote equality of opportunity and during the 1990s it provided funding to develop special access schemes for prospective third level students (Osborne and Leith, 2000, p. 5). The main target groups of these schemes were students from lower socio-economic backgrounds, disabled people and mature entrants (ibid.).

Legislation in education and more generally brought about a new equality landscape in Ireland. The Education Act (Ireland, 1998a, p. 10) sets out:

> to give practical effect to the constitutional rights of children, including children who have a disability or who have other special educational needs, as they relate to education ... [and] to promote equality of access and participation in education and to promote the means whereby students may benefit from education ...

The Employment Equality Act (Ireland, 1998b) and the Equal Status Act (Ireland, 2000a) include disability as one of the grounds for non-discrimination. The remit of the Equality Authority and the Office of Director of Equality Investigations, first established under the Employment Equality Act, was extended to include equal status matters in 2000. The establishment of a National Disability Authority (Ireland, 1999) and a Human Rights Commission (Ireland, 2000b) further broadened the rights-based institutional infrastructure.

In spite of these legislative and institutional developments and the fact that numbers have increased somewhat in recent years (Callaghan, 2001, p. 9), the proportion of disabled students in Higher Education remains low. In the academic year 1993–1994, the total number of disabled students in this sector was estimated at 431, or 0.54 per cent of the total (undergraduate and postgraduate) student population (AHEAD, 1994, p. 13). In 1999 the proportion of undergraduate disabled students had risen to 0.8 per cent (AHEAD, 2002, p. 4). Compared with rates of 2 per cent in the UK and Germany (Skilbeck and Connell 2000, pp. 42–43), however, this remains a disturbingly small proportion. Thus, basic access to Higher Education remains a fundamental problem for disabled students in Ireland. Targeted programmes designed to increase access too often remain at the level of rhetoric, lack coherence and determination, and are treated as marginal activities (Osborne and Leith, 2000). At official levels it is increasingly recognised that social barriers rather than individual deficits lie at the root of low participation rates among disabled students (Ireland, 2001).

Two specific institutional initiatives at third level deserve to be mentioned because they interpret disability as a rights issue rather than a medical 'condition'. In 1991, a new Equality Studies Centre at University College Dublin incorporated a Disability Studies module into its teaching and research programme (Equality Studies Centre, 2000, p. 11). Because its philosophy is grounded in principles of equality the Centre is committed to a social model of disability and to the notion of emancipatory research. The Centre has proactively recruited disabled students for its courses and its graduates have produced a significant body of disability/equality related research. A second development has been the establishment of a Centre for Deaf Studies at Trinity College Dublin. The Centre is founded on a cultural and linguistic rather than a medical model of deafness and operates on a bilingual basis, recognising both Irish Sign Language and English as working languages in its educational and training programmes (Centre for Deaf Studies, 2003).

Each of these developments reflects a concern to understand and respond to disability as an equality issue and demonstrates new perspectives and practices in inclusion at third level. In terms of their size and average student intake, however, the Equality Studies Centre and the Centre for Deaf Studies constitute only a very small part of the third level sector. For us, the philosophy and practice of inclusion must be premised on the degree to which disabled students can access, participate in, and successfully complete courses across the whole range of higher and further education programmes. However, the extent to which inclusive structures, relations and practices have been incorporated into the Irish educational system remains very much an open question (McDonnell, 2000, 2003). Furthermore, inclusion must be more than an updated form of sponsored mobility. Crucially, it entails negotiation in which the voices of disabled people are both recognised and represented (Lynch et al., 2001). An important stage in this process involves listening to those voices.

EXPERIENCES OF DISABLED STUDENTS AT THIRD LEVEL

In a study of the experiences of disabled students in further education in the UK, Ash et al., (1997) observe that over the past 20 years there has been growing support for inclusion. Their study identified a number of core issues. First, non-disabled students displayed a lack of knowledge about the circumstances of disabled students' lives and about disabled people generally. Second, social contact between disabled and non-disabled students was not extensive. At the same time the respondents, 96 per cent of whom said they had no impairment, supported the view that early social and educational contact would encourage more understanding and help to overcome barriers. Third, the idea of legislative action to secure the rights of disabled students was strongly supported and while inclusion as a general principle was also supported, respondents were less convinced that inclusion was feasible for all students, especially those with learning difficulties.

A recent Irish study (Collins and O'Mahony, 2001) found significant differences between disabled students and staff with regard to their perceptions of what constituted the main factors hindering disabled students' performance in higher education. For the students the most critical factor was lack of awareness among staff about disability and 'knowing what to do' while staff rated the lack of physical access as the most significant hindering factor (pp. 17–18). Another significant difference was that while students understood disability to be a matter of rights and fairness, staff tended to interpret disability as an individual 'condition'. This divergence of understanding in turn influenced how staff and student respondents rated hindering factors in terms of their seriousness.

Riddell's (1998) analysis of the experiences of disabled students in higher education in Scotland and Reindal's (1995) report on the experiences of disabled students at the University of Oslo reached broadly similar conclusions. In all of these studies, the dominance of medicalised and individualised interpretations of disability was apparent as was the lack of awareness among staff regarding appropriate responses to particular problems. As Riddell (1998, p. 219) puts it: 'Indeed, some schools appear to have made more progress than higher education institutions in thinking through the meaning of inclusive education.' Clearly, this is a significant matter not only in relation to daily practice but also in the context of planning and policy implementation.

It was 'the lack of awareness surrounding disabled students and their learning environment' in the largest Irish university, University College Dublin, that prompted the research described in the following section (Lowe, 2002, p. 3). The research began with a focus group meeting which disabled students were invited to attend. At the meeting, disability as a general issue in third level education was discussed. The idea of disability awareness training[1] was also discussed and our initial sense that this was an important matter was confirmed. Following the focus group meeting, seven students volunteered to participate in a more detailed exploration of their experiences of college life.

Five main concerns had been identified at the initial meeting. Along with disability awareness training, the educational background of the students, their academic careers in higher education, their social life on the campus and the role of the disability support services in the college emerged as important. Each interview lasted approximately one hour and was recorded on cassette tape. The venues chosen for the interviews were decided on by the interviewees in order to suitably accommodate them. The research also incorporated a questionnaire for heads of academic departments as well as for senior officers in administration, services and maintenance sections of the college. However, within the limits of this chapter, we can only discuss the findings of the student interviews.

EXPERIENCES OF DISABLED STUDENTS AT
UNIVERSITY COLLEGE DUBLIN

Whether disabled students at the university had attended special or mainstream schools doesn't appear to have had a direct bearing on their academic and social experiences in higher education. In fact, two students who had attended special schools at first and second levels had contrasting expectations and experiences. One expected the mainstream educational environment to offer better opportunities to develop his academic potential and he felt that this expectation had in fact been met in college. On the other hand, the second student believed that her expectations of third level education had not been met and she felt that she had been 'swallowed up':

> **Mary:** I found it really difficult, got no real help, failed a number of exams in first year … but because I went to a special school I had done well and thought that I would do as well in [college] but it was a culture shock. I couldn't understand the lecturers.

The academic experiences of the students were mixed and much depended on the responses of individual lecturers or particular departments.

> **Mary:** Newer lecturers were more aware of my needs but older staff didn't have a clue and they didn't want to have much to do with disabilities … Some of the tutors didn't help because they didn't know how to …

Some lecturers were 'quite patronising' (Jackie); the gist of their comments could be summed up as, 'Sure, aren't you a good girl … to be doing things like this!' (Mary). Several students noted that lecturers were not particularly *au fait* with the specific needs of disabled students:

> **Kim:** Staff would be much more aware of my needs if they understood my disability better.

Students felt they had to make an extra effort – had to be particularly assertive – to ensure that they could access and participate on equal terms in academic life: 'If you don't shout, you won't be heard' (Jackie). They had reservations about having 'to spell out [their] needs' (Robert) or were nervous about being 'singled out' (Mary). Students wanted to be known for who they were, not for their impairments. Whether students had positive or negative academic experiences also depended on more general departmental responses:

> **Kim:** Although the general attitude was fair enough … one department was very ignorant [with regard] to my situation and I felt that they didn't give a damn.

Students observed that lecturers and departments were in positions of relative power and consequently they felt they were not in a strong position to challenge or negotiate changes in teaching methodologies or departmental attitudes. To deal with this, interviewees suggested a mediating role for the Disability Support Services Unit in situations where students were experiencing difficulties.

> **Kim:** There should be a system in place whereby disabled students and the Disability Support Services Unit [could] communicate problems in access needs to lecturers and tutors.

Access, in a variety of modes, remains an ongoing difficulty for disabled students and was an issue raised by most of the interviewees:

> **Jackie:** I think that physical access is quite bad here at the college; the lifts were not designed with wheelchair-users in mind; the ramps were originally designed for bikes and are too steep for wheelchairs. For me, going to the restaurant nearly brings on a coronary … I can't use lifts on my own because the buttons are too high.

Entry to and exit from classroom and theatre areas was also a concern. The main theatres in the Arts Building contain a 'wheelchair accessible area' situated at the rear of the theatre. This particular location made students feel isolated and excluded from debates and general discussions.

> **Jackie:** I have to use the theatre box, so I am separated from my peers. Notes are not always passed up to the wheelchair boxes, so I am excluded from debates and conversations due to being in a cordoned-off area for wheelchairs.

Jackie also made the point that the Arts Building had been designed at a time when access into buildings was not on the educational agenda for disabled people. However, in order to change this situation, several of the interviewees stated that it would be very useful if physical access to some of the college buildings could be investigated with a view to improvement.

With regard to academic achievement, students felt that they had to make a much greater effort in order to compete with their fellow non-disabled students:

> **Robert:** I have to work harder, double the workload because of my impairment. I have to spell out my needs and this shouldn't be the case.

In general, comments by the interviewees indicated that the difficulties they encountered were due more to a lack of awareness and knowledge about specific needs in relation to disability than to negative attitudes on the part of staff. In spite of negative experiences, the general perception among the interviewees was that of goodwill towards them among college staff. However, students expressed the view that there were difficulties in translating this goodwill into actual practice and suggested that the Disability Support Services Unit could play a more proactive and direct role in enabling this transfer to take place.

> **Kim:** The Access Office [i.e. Disability Support Services Unit] was very good but very slow to act. It could have a much higher profile.

Most of the students stated that the Disability Support Services Unit had been helpful although for one student this took some time.

> **Helen:** I had a lot of problems at the start with the Disability Support Services Unit, but now they are very helpful with regard to my needs and the service has been recently expanded.

During the interviews, the issue of disability awareness was a recurring theme. The majority of the interviewees believed that the Disability Support Services Unit should be involved in instigating an awareness programme throughout the college and that it should be involved in the provision of training in such a programme.

> **Kim:** As far as Disability Awareness Training is concerned the Access Office or Disability Support Services should be the main instigator ... It is up to the student to inform a department about their needs but I believe that there needs to be a backup system from the Disability Support Services Unit ... in place.

> **Robert:** I think that the Access Office should be the main force behind ... awareness training. But they also need support from the relevant departments including lecturers and tutors as they are directly involved with our lives here at the college.

Interviewees emphasised that there should be greater communication between the Disability Support Services Unit, the disabled students and college staff:

> **Mary:** I don't think the tutors know what the Access Office represents or what they do.

Several students expressed the view that disabled people, including the students themselves, should have a primary role in delivering awareness training:

> **Mary:** Students should have a role in the delivery of disability awareness training. The idea of non-disabled people carrying out awareness training is ridiculous. They wouldn't have inside information, wouldn't have lived it.

> **Robert:** Unless you have experienced [disability] yourself it is hard to teach others what to do.

With regard to social life in the college the majority of interviewees felt that participation in social activities was an important and necessary aspect of their overall college experience. For the most part, their experiences were positive:

> **Helen:** I believe that it is important to have the support of a network of friends. It is very important to me here at the college.

> **Mary:** Socially, I can't cope with large groups because of my ... impairment. But I started to give [extra curricular] classes and this generated a lot of interest. I did this outside class time and so it was quite a sociable activity ... The attitudes of my fellow students are good; they treat me as an equal.

> **Robert:** I have a very good rapport with my classmates; they treat me as an equal.

> **Anne:** I am an active member of the students union so my disability never gets in the way of my social life here at the college.

> **Jackie:** I go to the student bar but not to nightclubs due to problems of access. If I can't get in then I can't participate.

> **Kim:** As far as my social life is concerned, I have never encountered problems. My disability is not an issue with my friends.

Differing perceptions of disability among the students reveal some of the complexities of disability as a political, social and cultural issue in western society. Media responses,

for example, have depoliticised the struggles of disabled people by taking an individualised perspective and by focusing on disability as personal misfortune (Shakespeare,
1994, p. 294). Thus, it is not surprising that interviewees frequently interpreted their
difficulties as barriers they experienced as individuals rather than as members of an
excluded social group. Most interviewees did not wish to publicly identify with other
disabled students in the college. Instead, associating with other disabled students was
something to be avoided and disability itself minimised:

> **Jackie:** My disability would be highlighted if I was seen hanging around other
> disabled students. If I were to hang around four or five other disabled stu-
> dents ... then I would be regarded solely for my disability.

> **Anne:** I wasn't comfortable about having to disclose my impairment.

That disabled students did not readily make common cause with one another is understandable given the extent to which the dominant cultural response to disability is
steeped in negative imagery, stereotyping and dependency. As Shakespeare (1994,
p. 284) hypothesises, 'Prejudice in the context of everyday interaction, media and charity imagery, popular assumptions, etc., plays a ... role in reinforcing a subordinate position for disabled people who enter mainstream society'. This prejudice is not just
interpersonal, it is institutionalised in cultural representation, in language and in social
systems (Barnes, 1991). One student referred to the background presence of a cultural
context of discrimination, observing that 'through awareness people begin to realise that
you are not so different' (Anne). Another student observed that she did not 'hang around
with disabled people ... because of people's attitudes and just because they are not
aware' (Jackie). For two of the interviewees, however, identification with other disabled
students was a source of pride, a demonstration of political solidarity and an opportunity
to participate in a supportive network of friends who have shared similar kinds of experiences. Mary recognised that 'Deaf people consider themselves to be a [linguistic and
cultural] minority group' and are 'proud to be Deaf'. Disability can also constitute a
basis for identifying with others who share the same problems:

> **Lorraine:** You have your disabled friends ... and in particular when you come
> across problems you realise that you are all in the same boat ... [It's] very impor-
> tant for a disabled person that they feel that they have the support network of
> other disabled people ... You share a common cultural identity and experience
> with those disabled friends that you make.

DISCUSSION

The themes that emerge in the accounts of disabled students at University College
Dublin are similar to those present in the accounts of students in Higher Education elsewhere. In common with disabled students in other institutions (Reindal, 1995, p. 227;
Riddell, 1998, p. 213; Collins and Mahony, 2001, p. 17), students at University College
Dublin reported considerable variation in levels of awareness about, and attitudes
towards, disability within and between departments. In addition, even where positive
attitudes were present, these were not always reflected in effective responses (Baggett,

1993; Borland and James, 1999, p. 99; Collins and Mahony, 2001, p. 18; Poussu-Olli, 1999, p. 109; Riddell, 1998, pp. 215–216). Related to these difficulties is the larger question of differences between students and staff with regard to how disability is understood. In terms of *institutional* structures and relations, disabled students interpret disability as a matter of fairness, rights and entitlements; staff in Higher Education, for the most part, understand disability as an individual 'condition' or 'problem' (Reindal, 1995, p. 240; Riddell, 1998, p. 213; Collins and Mahony, 2001, p. 18).

Prevailing practices regarding disability in institutions of Higher Education are entrenched in a medical rather than a social framework (Reindal, 1993; Riddell, 1998; Borland and James, 1999; Collins and O'Mahony, 2001) and consequently problems and solutions are seen in individualised rather than structural terms. Such individualised perspectives can be expressed in a number of ways. First, there is the tendency for staff or departments to home in on the impairment or the 'need' (Riddell, 1998, p. 213). As a result, students may feel 'singled out' and if they 'have to spell out' their needs they run the risk of being known, not for who they are, but for their 'problem'. Second, disabled students are often expected to negotiate access to courses and materials with individual staff members on an individual basis (Reindal, 1995, p. 239) and feel they have 'to shout to be heard'. Although some disabled students in our study believed this was in fact the responsibility of the individual concerned, they were also aware of their dependence on the goodwill and co-operation of the staff. Students felt that there was room for a more direct mediating agency, such as the Disability Support Services Unit, in negotiating staff-student and department-student relations. Third, students expressed concern about on-going isolating and segregative practices. Being located in 'the cordoned off area for wheelchairs', for example, meant that students were excluded from debates and conversations. Finally, the very considerable influence of the medical model is evident in that the students themselves have internalised, to some extent, the individualised understanding of disability articulated in that model.

Although considerable changes have taken place in Higher Education in Ireland (O'Sullivan, 1998) the lack of access to buildings, services and facilities creates on-going problems for disabled students: course materials are not accessible, for example, or copies of overheads are not made available. Similar access barriers exist for students in other institutions of higher education (Reindal, 1995, p. 239; Riddell, 1998, p. 212; Collins and O'Mahoney, 2001, p. 18). Connected with the access issue is the perception among disabled students that they have a relatively 'tougher', more physically demanding day (Reindal, 1995, p. 239; Riddell, 1998, p. 212); as Robert put it: 'I have ... double the workload.' Another recurring theme in the accounts of disabled students is their perception that support services are not co-ordinated and that there are poor channels of communication between support services and academic staff (Borland and James, 1999, p. 89; Reindal, 1995, p. 238; Riddell, 1998, p. 217; Collins and O'Mahony, 2001, p. 17).

CONCLUSION

It is evident from their accounts that disabled students experience significant barriers to inclusion. Although the barriers to inclusion experienced by the students in University

College Dublin were broadly similar to those found in institutions of Higher Education elsewhere, we were surprised by their elementary nature. Among the more significant were the wide variations among staff in terms of attitudes, the lack of awareness and information about disability and, even where attitudes are positive, the inability to respond in effective ways to the needs of students. Equally surprising was the extent to which perspectives based on medical interpretations of disability continue to set the agendas in higher education, in spite of equality legislation and a more publicly active disability movement. This perspective is usually articulated in an understanding of disability as an individual 'condition', and is responded to in individual, and often simplistic terms (Riddell, 1998, p. 213). A medical model of disability often involves the assumption, for example, that difficulties experienced by students can be remedied by a particular piece of equipment (ibid. 217). Although students, too, may interpret their difficulties in individualised terms, strong concerns for equality of access and participation run through their accounts.

Recent comparative research on access and equity in higher education in Ireland supports these concerns. Skilbeck and Connell, (2000, pp. 44–45) outline the major responsibilities and challenges facing higher education institutions in relation to disabled students. They must provide accessible physical as well as inclusive pedagogic and social environments; they must develop positive attitudes towards disabled students among staff and the broader student body; and they must promote knowledge and understanding of the needs of disabled students in addition to strategies for responding appropriately and effectively. Skilbeck and Connell (p. 45) go on to remark that 'ignorance and prejudice regarding disabilities are reportedly still rife in many institutions' and in this context recommend the need for 'institution-wide staff training and continuing professional development'.

Our own analysis supports these recommendations and indicates the need for research and programme development in specific areas. First, we believe it is essential to find ways of identifying and resolving contradictions between declarations of policies at a formal level in the institutions, and actual practice on the ground. Second, we stress the importance of establishing feedback channels to assist in the dissemination of good practices and in the identification of problem areas (Borland and James, 1999, p. 99). Third, our study demonstrates the desirability of disabled students having a voice in these processes (Chard and Couch, 1998). In terms of inclusion, the criterion of recognition requires that disabled students are 'seen' and 'listened to' and the criterion of representation requires their presence at the decision-making table to promote or contest particular policies and practices (Phillips, 1995; Fraser, 2000; Lynch et al., 2001).

What form might such programme development take? In our study, students support the idea of disability training as a means of fostering a more inclusive environment. Drawing on the accounts of students, Lowe (2002) argues for a form of disability equality training such as that outlined by the National Disability Authority (2002) in its draft Guidelines for Purchasers of Training. Disability equality training is based on the premise that disability is a consequence of structural and relational barriers found in society rather than in individual 'conditions'. The training incorporates an analysis of disability as an equality issue, an exploration of appropriate and effective ways of interacting with disabled people, and a review of requirements under equality legislation. It highlights the role of an organisation in the removal of structural and relational barriers and focuses on the development of strategies to change attitudes and practices with regard to disabled people. Significantly, disability equality training allocates a central role to disabled people in the delivery of training. As the students themselves put it: 'Everyone needs training' (Kim), 'the lecturers need it most' (Mary), and 'at the end of the day it is a disabled person who can best deliver [it]' (Anne).

NOTES

[1] Conceptual and practical distinctions between disability awareness and disability equality training had not been clearly established at this early stage of the research and issues that properly belonged to disability equality were discussed under the general heading of disability awareness training.

REFERENCES

AHEAD (Association for Higher Education Access and Disability) (1994) *Committee on Access and Participation of Students with Disabilities in Higher Education, Report to the Higher Education Authority.* Dublin: AHEAD.

AHEAD (2003) Survey on *Provision for Students with Disabilities in Third Level for the Academic Year 1998/99,* Initial Findings. Dublin: AHEAD.

Armstrong, F., Armstrong, D. and Barton, L. (2000) (eds) *Inclusive Education: Policy, Contexts and Comparative Perspectives.* London: David Fulton.

Armstrong, F., Belmont, B. and Verillon, A. (2000) 'Vive le différence?' Exploring context, policy and change in special education in France: developing cross-cultural collaboration. In F. Armstrong, D. Armstrong, and L. Barton (eds), *Inclusive Perspectives Education: Policy, Contexts and Comparative.* London: David Fulton.

Ash, A., Bellew, J., Davies, M., Newman, T. and Richardson, L. (1997) 'Everybody in: the experience of disabled students in further education.' *Disability and Society,* 12, 4, 605–621.

Borland, J. and James, S. (1999) 'The learning experience of students with disabilities in higher education: a case study of a UK university.' *Disability and Society,* 14, 1, 85–101.

Buzzi, I. (1995) 'A critical view of integration in Italy,' In C. O'Hanlon (ed.), *Inclusive Education in Europe.* London: David Fulton.

Callaghan, P. (2001) (4th ed) *Accessing Third Level Education in Ireland: A Handbook for Students with Disabilities and Learning Difficulties.* Dublin: AHEAD Education Press.

Callaghan, P., Cooney, T. and Farrell, S. (1995) *Legislation, Disability and Higher Education, A Comparative Study: Europe and the USA.* Dublin: AHEAD Education Press.

Centre for Deaf Studies (2003) *Student Handbook, 2003–2004.* Centre for Deaf Studies, Trinity College Dublin.

Chard, G. and Couch, R. (1998) 'Access to higher education for the disabled student: a building survey at the University of Liverpool.' *Disability and Society,* 13, 4, 603–623.

Collins, B. and O'Mahony, P. (2001) 'Perceiving success? An investigation of disabled students' and academic staff's perception of the factors that hinder disabled students' occupational performance in Trinity College Dublin.' *Irish Journal of Occupational Therapy,* December, 15–19.

Coolahan, J. (ed.) (1994) *Report on the National Education Convention.* Dublin: The National Education Secretariat.

Corbett, J. (1993) 'Hanging on by a thread: integration in further education in Britain,' in R. Slee (ed.), *Is There a Desk with My Name on It? The Politics of Integration.* London: The Falmer Press.

Dyson, A. and Millward, A. (1997) 'The reform of special education or the transformation of mainstream schools.' In S. Pijl, C. Meijer and S. Hegarty (eds), *Inclusive Education: A Global Agenda.* London: Routledge.

Equality Studies Centre (2002) *Equality Studies: Education for Transformation*. Equality Studies Centre, University College Dublin.

Foucault, M. (2002) *Power: Essential Works of Foucault*, vol. 3, J. D. Faubion (ed.) London: Penguin.

Fraser, N. (2000) 'Rethinking recognition.' *New Left Review*, 2/3, 107–120.

Hurst, A. (1998) (ed.) *Higher Education and Disabilities: International Approaches*. Aldershot, Hants: Ashgate.

Ireland (1992a) *Education for a Changing World, Green Paper on Education*. Dublin: The Stationery Office.

Ireland (1992b) *Regional Technical Colleges Act*. Dublin: The Stationery Office.

Ireland (1993) *Report of the Special Education Review Committee*. Dublin: The Stationery Office.

Ireland (1995) *Charting Our Education Future, White Paper on Education*. Dublin: The Stationery Office.

Ireland (1997) *Universities Act*. Dublin: The Stationery Office.

Ireland (1998a) *Education Act*. Dublin: The Stationery Office.

Ireland (1998b) *Employment Equality Act*. Dublin: The Stationery Office.

Ireland (1999) *National Disability Authority Act*. Dublin: The Stationery Office.

Ireland (2000a) *Equal Status Act*. Dublin: The Stationery Office.

Ireland (2000b) *The Human Rights Commission Act*. Dublin: The Stationery Office.

Ireland (2001) *Report of the Action Group on Access to Higher Education*. Dublin: Stationery Office.

Lowe, T. (2002) *Disability Awareness/Equality Training in Third Level Education*. Unpublished thesis, Master of Equality Studies, Equality Studies Centre, University College Dublin.

Lowe, T. (2003) *Access Success: A Guide to Third Level Education for Students with a Disability*. Dublin: AHEAD.

Lynch, K. (1999) 'Equality studies, the academy and the role of research in emancipatory social change.' *The Economic and Social Review*, 30, 1, 41–69.

Lynch, K., Cantillon, S. and Baker, J. (2001) 'Frameworks for Change,' *Revised Draft of a Paper Presented to the National economic and Social Forum*, Equality Studies Centre, University College Dublin.

McDonnell, P. (2000) 'Integration in education in Ireland: rhetoric and reality' in F. Armstrong, D. Armstrong and L. Barton (eds), *Inclusive Education: Policy, Contexts and Comparative Perspectives*. London: David Fulton.

McDonnell, P. (2003) 'Education policy and disability' in S. Quin and B. Redmond (eds) *Disability and Social Policy in Ireland*. Dublin: University College Dublin Press.

McDonnell, P. (2004) (ed.) *Deaf Studies in Ireland: An Introduction*. Coleford, Glos.: Forest Books.

National Disability Authority (2002) *Guidelines for Purchasers of Disability Equality and Disability Awareness Training*. Dublin: National Disability Authority.

Organisation for European Co-operation and Development (OECD) (1994) *The Integration of Disabled Children into Mainstream Education: Ambitions, Theories and Practices*, OECD: Paris.

OECD (1995) *Integrating Students with Special Needs into Mainstream Schools*. Paris: OECD.

OECD (1997a) *Implementing Inclusive Education*. Paris: OECD.

OECD (1997b) *Post Compulsory Education for Disabled People*. Paris: OECD.

OECD (1999) *Inclusive Education at Work: Students with Disabilities in Mainstream Schools*. Paris: OECD.

OECD (2000) *Special Needs Education: Statistics and Indicators*. Paris: OECD.

Oliver, M. (2002) Emancipatory research: a vehicle for social transformation or Policy Development? In Conference Proceedings, Using Emancipatory Methodologies in Disability Research, Inaugural NDA Disability Research Conference, 3rd December. Dublin: National Disability Authority.

Osborne, R. and Leith, H. (2000) *Evaluation of the Targeted Initiative on Widening Access for Young People from Socio-Economically Disadvantaged Backgrounds, Report to the Higher Education Authority*. Dublin: The Higher Education Authority.

Phillips, A. (1995) *The Politics of Presence*. Oxford: Oxford University Press.

Poussu-Olli, H.-S. (1999) 'To be a disabled student in Finland,' *Disability and Society*, 14, 1, 103–113.

Randoll, D. (1995) 'A view of integration in Germany' in C. O' Hanlon (ed.) *Inclusive Education in Europe*. London: David Fulton.

Reindal, S.M. (1995) 'Some problems encountered by disabled students at the University of Oslo – whose responsibility'. *European Journal of Special Needds Education*, 10, 3, 227–241.

Riddell, S. (1998) 'Chipping away at the mountain: disabled students' experience of higher education,' *International Studies in Sociology of Education*, 8, 2, 203–222.

Riddell, S. (2000) 'Inclusion and choice: mutually exclusive principles in special educational needs?' In F. Armstrong, D. Armstrong and L. Barton (eds), *Inclusive Education: Policy, Contexts and Comparative Perspectives*. London: David Fulton.

Rispens, J. (1994) 'Rethinking integration: what can we learn from the past?' in C.J. Meijer, S. Pijl and S. Hegarty (eds), *New Perspectives in Special Education: A Six-Country Study of Integration*. London: Routledge.

Reinach, E. (1987) (ed.) *Normalisation*. Aberdeen: University of Aberdeen, Department of Social Work.

Scull, A. (1993) *The Most Solitary of Afflictions: Madness and Society in Britain 1700–1900*. New Haven, Conn.: Yale University Press.

Skilbeck, M. with the assistance of Helen Connell (2000). *Access and Equity in Higher Education: An International Perspective on Issues and Strategies*. Dublin: The Higher Education Authority.

Tetler, S. (1995) 'Danish efforts in integration' in C. O'Hanlon (ed.), *Inclusive Education in Europe*. London: David Fulton.

Wolfensberger, W. (1972) *The Principle of Normalisation in Human Services*. Toronto: National Institute on Mental Retardation.

ROGER SLEE

12.   IT'S A FIT-UP! INCLUSIVE EDUCATION, HIGHER EDUCATION, POLICY AND THE DISCORDANT VOICE

INTRODUCTION

In Australia, and I suspect elsewhere, 'inclusive education' is at a crossroads. For many this would seem to be too dramatic a claim at a time when inclusive education is surging as an area of academic and education policy interest. For others (Slee, 2004; Allan, 2006; Ware, 2004), perhaps it is not alarming enough? Recently I (Slee, 2004) enlisted Edward Said (Said, 2000) to register a foreboding that the popularizing of inclusive education represented a 'shedding of its insurrectionary force'. In Traveling Theory Reconsidered he argues that:

> ... the first time a human experience is recorded and then given a theoretical formulation, its force comes from being directly connected to and organically provoked by real historical circumstances. Later versions of the theory cannot replicate its original power; because the situation has quieted down and changed, the theory is degraded and subdued, made into a relatively tame academic substitute for the real thing, whose purpose ... was political change. (Said, 2000, p. 436)

Edward Said illustrated his point by contrasting the original work of Lukacs on reification with later adoptions of it by Lucien Goldmann in Paris and Raymond Williams in Cambridge.

> ... the ideas of this theory had shed their insurrectionary force, had been tamed and domesticated somewhat, and became considerably less dramatic in their application and gist. What seemed almost inevitable was that when theories traveled and were used elsewhere they ironically acquired the prestige and authority of age, perhaps even becoming a kind of orthodoxy. (Said, 2000, p. 437)

Once a call to action, a means for analyzing and more importantly changing unequal power relations in Budapest, Lukacs' theory of reification was rendered into little more than 'an interpretive device' (Said, 2000, p. 437).

More than two decades ago a number of British education researchers and activists offered ground breaking accounts of the deleterious impacts of educational psychology and special education on disabled pupils. This body of work (Booth, 1978; Ford, 1982;

L. Barton and F. Armstrong (eds.), Policy, Experience and Change, 177–188.

Tomlinson, 1982; Oliver, 1983; Galloway, 1985; Barton, 1987; Castells, 1996) stands in opposition to the normalizing assumptions and discourse of individual defectiveness at the heart of traditional special education and establishes segregated special education as a project for the social control of difference. For many disabled people special education is a key element in the ensemble of institutions and technologies of subjugation that lead to their immiseration.

At a conference in Rochester, Barton returned to this theme and considered the relationship between special education and the global confluence of neo-conservative education policy and economic forces.

> Within this period of conservative restoration the impact of market ideologies has profoundly influenced how we think and talk about education. We view education through the lens of a form of economic rationality in which cost effectiveness, efficiency, and value for money has entailed the generation of a more competitive, selective, and socially divisive series of policies and practices. (Barton, 2004, p. 64).

In a powerful exposition of the relationship between segregated special education and mainstream schooling he cites five ideological assumptions informing the project of special education. Accordingly, special education is claimed to be necessary because:

> Such schooling is essential in order to provide the type of education and curriculum these children need.
>
> Disabled children and young people need protection from the harsh and cruel realities of the world, including those to be found in mainstream schools – their size, the attitudes of staff and pupils, and verbal and physical abuse.
>
> Normal pupils need to be protected from the damaging influences that disabled pupils will have on their development, especially their academic achievements.
>
> Special schools are staffed by teachers who have those special qualities of patience, dedication, and love. Such schools provide good interpersonal relationships with staff and the necessary staff-pupil ratios.
>
> Special schools are necessary on administrative efficiency grounds. Thus specialist teachers, equipment, and support services are most effectively deployed. (Barton, 2004, p. 68).

Such assumptions reflect a comfortable alliance of professional interest (Tomlinson, 1993) and popular misconception. A recent literature review commissioned by the New Zealand Ministry of Education (MacArthur *et al.*, 2004) designed to examine Building Capability in Education for Students with Moderate and High Needs comprehensively reviewed international research and provides a strong evidence base to negate claims for segregated educational provision on the basis of students' academic and social progress. Segregated education for disabled, different and difficult children, for Barton is at its heart a historical artifact retained as an elaborate administrative expedience for the 'smooth running of mainstream schooling' (Barton, 2004, p. 68).

By the beginning of the 1980s researchers such as Sally Tomlinson had amassed compelling data to demonstrate the 'racialization' of special educational needs in the UK where Caribbean children were disproportionately referred to special educational services (Tomlinson, 1981) – a trend that continues globally (Tomlinson, 1997). The over-representation of indigenous peoples in international data on special education referral rates points to the cultural foundations of diagnosis. Moreover, autobiographical accounts from disabled people (Campling, 1981; Potts, 1991; Humphries, 1992; Oliver, 1996; Moore, 2000) introduced tensions to the 'in your best interest' claim for special education (Walsh, 1993; Lingard, 1998).

Responding to parental challenges in the courts to segregation, predominantly in North America (Minow, 1990), traditional special education advanced conceptually flawed compromises through so-called cascade models, resource rooms and reverse integration. A conditional language of accommodation (Slee, 1996) emerged as individual education plans were mobilized to seek out the least restrictive environment or most appropriate setting for disabled pupils. Professional interpretive latitude maintains the systemic upper hand as parents and their advocates struggled against expert forums (Armstrong, 1995). Thereby special education continued to reconcile the epistemological and structural needs of education departments not intent on fundamental changes to the fabric of schooling. Special education, advancing itself through a sometimes partially modernized lexicon, retained its project notwithstanding a complex mix of convictions across its workforce, of enrolment control for the educational main-game. Special education was able to accommodate a threatening social movement by relocating itself to the mainstream and describing itself in contemporary discourse. Shortcomings in authenticity, idiomatic slips, show through the cracks in the linguistic veneers. For example the Department of Education in Queensland Australia administered integration and later inclusive education through the *Low Incidence Unit*, and McGill University's Education and Counseling Psychology Department offers inclusive education for *special popula tions*. While these observations of discursive tension may seem trivial to some they point to irreconcilable epistemological foundations that policy-makers rarely acknowledge. Moreover, special education was able to simultaneously expand its interests across the education mainstream as teachers struggling against an influx of youthful refugees from a collapsed unskilled labor market pushed for greater levels of calibration, classification and exclusion of difficult students. Special educators and psychologists equipped with powerful knowledge were equal to the task of reconstructing student identities to necessitate different handling procedures in the educational baggage hall. The Australian Disability Discrimination Act (1992), proceeding from profoundly different epistemological foundations presented the Australian special education fraternity, and regular education community for that matter, with a problem of repositioning their craft rather than with a chore of educational reconstruction (Cook, 1999).

In opposition to this response to the changing conditions of schooling critical educators and disability advocacy groups rejected inherently conservative incrementalism, arguing for the reconstruction of schooling through *Inclusive Education*. Inclusive Education, building upon the theoretical foundations of disability studies and parent activism rejected the assimilation imperative of neo-special educational rhetoric and practice. Inclusive Education characterized itself as a cultural project intent on exposing the politics of identity and difference and establishing representation for those marginalized and excluded by the power relations exerted through the dominant culture and constitutive power relations of schooling. As such Inclusive Education is an educational reform movement that is simultaneously about all students, a movement that has drawn its epistemological and tactical lessons from the analysis of educational disadvantage as it relates to class, gender, ethnicity, sexuality and disability. As Tony Booth has argued Inclusive Education is more precisely understood through more rigorous analyses of exclusion (Booth, 1995).

I return to Edward Said. Despite the analytic power and the political intent of Inclusive Education as a counterpoint to special education, its appropriation is imminent if not complete. Across the academy, in the offices of education bureaucracies, in segregated and regular classrooms alike Inclusive Education is offered as a description for all kinds of conceptual frameworks, policy proposals and schooling practices. Some advance the inclusion of marginal and excluded identities, others refract scrutiny from the maintenance of old patterns of exclusion. For many inclusive education has become as self evident in the education lexicon as 'evidence-based research', 'school effectiveness' and 'raising standards'. These are indeed dangerous times for those engaged in educational reform to embrace inclusion through curriculum, pedagogy, assessment and school organization because for some the generalization of inclusive education unfortunately provides a reassuring default vocabulary for 'business as usual'. In this paper I want to argue that just as we are becoming more comfortable with the discourse of inclusive education it is time to expose the unacknowledged tensions that exist. In this way we may recover the insurrectionary project to ensure that schools exercise inclusive practices to complement a now almost universally inclusive rhetoric.

EDUCATION POLICY, THE ACADEMY AND THE POLITICS OF SILENCE

Education Policies and the Curse of Reductionism

The machinations and deleterious impacts of the creation of an education marketplace on public education has been thoroughly described and analyzed in recent education policy sociology (Ball, 1994; Ball, 1998; Lauder, 1999; Apple, 2001; Ball, 2003; Gillborn, 2000). A number of key themes emerge that are central to this discussion. I will consider two.

First, large-scale school reform is being pursued in a climate of shrinking Treasury expenditure on public or government schooling (Levin, 1998). Australian governments at state and federal level encourage, if not openly, a drift to the so-called private or independent schools sector through greater levels of subsidization for private education. Expenditure by the Federal government on so-called private or independent schooling exceeds its financial commitment to Higher Education. It is believed by some that this encouragement to the market will effectively relieve increasing fiscal obligation to public schooling on Treasury and encourage greater levels of competition between state schools to drive up standards. My recent experience in the Education Queensland bureaucracy was that notwithstanding the State's rhetorical commitment to a New Deal on Equity (Queensland, 1999; Taylor, 2003) its expenditure on programme areas that addressed questions of educational disadvantage and inclusion was systematically reduced in favour of other commitments.

Inclusive Education is perceived by Treasury to be an alarmingly escalating call on public funds. It is not regarded as the redress of a neglected public responsibility. The establishment of 'Disability Standards' required by disability discrimination legislation in Australia have been a source of considerable struggle and are generally regarded as compliance instruments rather than a resource for educational improvement. The funding of education is a complex area requiring extended discussion in another forum. At one level Treasury is correct. The measure of the quality of inclusive education is not simply a question of increasing levels of public funding. The formulaic categorical system of diagnosis and resource matching produces 'inclusion students' and disregards capacity building across schools. You have the exponential growth of demand from schools becoming less tolerant of range and diversity in their student cohorts, students becoming bargaining chips for extraction of additional funds. This often has little to do with establishing an inclusive curriculum, pedagogic practices or classroom organization to reconstruct schools. More typically it is a systematic approach to acquiring human resources to mind the disabled student. Herein we have created a significant issue whereby some students in classrooms are taught by less qualified people while the teacher deals with the legitimate inhabitants of the classroom.

Authentic inclusive school reform is costly as it does imply the need for reforms to workforce preparation, pedagogic practice, curriculum orientations and materials, evaluative frameworks and the physical design of many existing school structures. The redeployment of existing structures and incremental increases to special educational resources is regarded as an easier option for government and is industrially more palatable. Such conditions place different students at continuing risk of exclusion in and out of regular schools.

Second, markets press schools to emulate an ideal type of institution based upon a narrow definition of the traditional academic curriculum and a limited and limiting pedagogical repertoire (Gewirtz, 1995). Such schools are incapable, despite rhetorical flourishes, of dealing with diverse student populations or responding in elaborated ways to educational disadvantage (Education Queensland, 2002). While neo-liberal governments advance a discourse of choice and diversity the pressure of the market is to reinforce dominant cultural forms in the curriculum and pedagogy and increase risk for vulnerable students (Slee *et al.*, 1998). As Stephen Ball (1994) has observed, the narrowing of the notion of worthwhile knowledge reinforces old curriculum models where it becomes a 'curriculum for the dead' or 'curriculum as museum'. Schools compete to demonstrate their grip on higher positions on school league tables through the sustained improvement of students on a narrow range of standardized national or statewide tests. Under these conditions schools become increasingly apprehensive about some students who may undermine performance (Slee, 1998). Perversions appear in the form of schools 'inviting' students to absent themselves from school on test days, declining 'risky' students' enrolment or the emergence of niche providers appearing to cleanse school populations through a de facto range of schools dealing with the behaviour disordered, the dyslexic and the spectrum of disorders. Hence we create a legitimate school system for the deserving and a residualised system for the others. In England a thriving system of pupil referral units (PRUs) provides this service. Some years ago now

Denis Mongon (1988) declared that since behaviour units do not generally generate successful paths for those who attend them, one may conclude that they exist for those who never go to them. In other words they exist to guarantee the smooth operation, as we noted from Barton earlier, of mainstream schools.

Education policy is a field for the observation of disconnection and reductionism. We can see this operating in a number of ways. First is the frequent incapacity of or neglect by education to join the dots. Here I refer to the development of contradictory sets of policy initiatives. Hence it is possible for whole sections of an education bureau-cracy to be engaged in the development of policy texts and programmes which demon-strate the organization's commitment to the principles of inclusion. Behind another cubicle officers are engaged in the development of new technologies of exclusion. In large measure this phenomenon reflects a very poorly theorized and or communicated conception of either exclusion or inclusion. It also reflects policy disconnections. Disconnection may itself be symptomatic of the size of the bureaucracy and its constituencies, or it may reflect the complex struggles for discursive supremacy and power that inevitably operate within such organizations (Ball, 1994). As a senior civil servant I was pursuing a programme of education reform that was undermined in other parts of the bureaucracy. This is not uncommon as the struggles in bureaucracy that threaten policy objectives in one direction are generated by differing perceptions of pri-ority, by ideological difference as was very much the case for inclusive education, by positional struggle and by changing political priorities through the electoral cycle.

Reductionism is a condition of our time. Ministers frequently demand stories stripped of complexity and digestible by a popular media dedicated to the news-grab for what they perceive to be an 'unsophisticated' audience. *Fixes* have to be *quick* and are tied to electoral cycles. Windows for reforms that may unsettle electoral equilibrium are very narrow. Governments, according to Watson (2003), a former Prime Ministerial speech writer, are blighted and corroded by the 'death sentence'. There has been a steady constriction of public debate through the atrophy of public language. Buzzwords and clichés leave us with impenetrable death sentences from which meaning is wrung. These are then mobilized to dull the civic imagination. Keywords are deployed as self-evident to stifle the necessity for clarification or debate. Standards, back to basics, school effectiveness, evidence-based, and, dare I say it, Inclusive Education are indica-tive of supposedly self-evident statements that close down discussion of underlying policy assumptions.

Moral panics that create and reinforce a 'common-sense' (Apple, 2001) that standards are falling and that the teaching profession is in crisis have aided the greater regulation of curriculum and pedagogy through the production of high stakes national tests aimed to secure minimum standards. In recent times we have seen the dismantling of programmes to redress educational disadvantage conflated with and reduced to bridg-ing the gap through literacy programmes (Lingard, 1998). In November 2004, in Washington the Annual Meeting of AAU Education Deans listened to an address from Dr. Duane Alexander, Director of the National Institute of Child Health and Human Development (NICHHD). It was for this listener a North American rendition of David Hargreaves's 1996 TTA Lecture on education research. The Deans were told that for education research to have any impact on the field it must be evidence-based and adopt the medical research design of clinical trial and scaling up. Inferentially, the direct instruction of phonics to improve students' performance on national standardized tests would advance scientific knowledge in the future and generate economic recovery. Regard was not afforded to research that has repeatedly demonstrated that the most reliable indicators of education failure in Australia are Aboriginality and poverty. The only evidence that counts is the test score. And as recent analyses (Gipps, 1994; McNeil, 2000; Meier, 2000; Hargreaves, 2003) of the blunt instrument of high stakes tests demonstrate the tests produced drive down the standard of curriculum development and pedagogic practice across our schools.

My fear is that inclusion suffers from the same fate of reductionism. Inclusion can mean the placement of a student in a sealed unit in a school away from their age peers. Equally segregated special school principals in the Australian State of Queensland argue that the introduction of a new curriculum in their schools advances inclusive practice. It can mean the placement of students for set times in a regular classroom or it can mean the unsupported placement of a child in a classroom in which they are bound to fail. It is time to stipulate the language of policy in order to apprehend programme perversions that abound internationally.

The Unreconstructed Academy

Australian universities have been enlisted by education jurisdictions to train a new breed of teachers equipped to work in so-called inclusive schools. They have also been called upon to respond to the on-going professional development of established teachers as they struggle with, and against, student diversity. This is of course a most reasonable request and faculties of education should be in a position to respond in ways that generate new pedagogies for New Times (Lankshear, 2003). That said I am inclined to believe that too few faculties are firstly equipped for this challenge, and secondly too few believe that this is the challenge of Inclusive Education.

'The development of inclusive thinking and practice on the part of student teachers is of fundamental importance' as Barton (2003, p. 21) forcefully reminds us. Teaching remains a deeply political activity (Barton, 2003, pp. 17–18) that must recognize Inclusive Education as a project of identity politics aspiring to the establishment of just social relations in schools and beyond. To engage in teacher education the academy cannot replicate the practices of old that share responsibility for the construction of educational exclusion.

What has generally occurred has been the replication of traditional special education curriculum to equip teachers to understand individual 'defects' and build their knowledge of the etiologies of a range of syndromes and disorders and in turn build a repertoire of remedial interventions. This traditional or neo-special educational orientation tends to be silent on the pathology of schooling that places some students at risk and privileges others. I will return to the politics of silence. Such courses are built upon the revised special educational texts that now carry chapters on 'Inclusive Education' that look at processes for assisting the disabled child in the regular school. The remainder of these texts are largely unchanged save for reflection of the additions to diagnostic schedules such as those carried in DSM IV.

Faculties of Education need to seriously engage with questions of ontology and epistemology to interrogate how traditional notions of special and regular schooling generate the subaltern of schooling. Professional partnerships with 'inclusive practitioners' to interrogate new forms of thinking and practice ought to inform the construction of curriculum. Moreover, Inclusive Education is not an add-on in a crowded Initial Teacher Education curriculum. Inclusive Education is simultaneously a goal and a strategic device for the achievement of democratic schooling.

Previously I proposed (Slee, 2003) that an education for inclusive schooling is simultaneously an education in school reform consistent with the demands of changing times. It establishes schooling as a democratic apprenticeship (Pearl, 1999; Touraine, 2000; Young, 2000) in which diversity becomes a resource rather than an impediment and curriculum and pedagogy connect with the world of the student and the world for which they are bound. Too often schools reflect the world from which educators came. The challenge of multi-literacies (Lankshear, 2003) to existing classroom practice is a resource for achieving inclusive classrooms. The New Basics Research Report (Queensland Government, 2004) demonstrates the centrality of a comprehensive approach to school reform that addresses curriculum, pedagogy and assessment, and teacher professional knowledge in generating different outcomes for diverse student populations. Put simply, my contention is that the challenge for Higher Education in responding to the call for inclusive classrooms invites Faculties of Education to reconstruct teacher education rather than repackage special education.

One can point to individual academics working closely with schools and their communities to reconceptualize education for the changing needs of diverse communities (Tuettemann, 2000; Moss, 2002; Carrington, 2004; Forlin, 2004). However there has not been a genuine development of teacher education as an inclusive educational pursuit. Rather it tends to be a subsidiary requirement within a general teaching qualification. As the Principal of the Staff College of Inclusive Education, Suzanne Carrington was able with her colleagues to have considerable impact upon the culture and programmes across schools in Queensland. The Staff College of Inclusive Education simultaneously worked on a number of fronts to educate the workforce, education decision-makers and the community that inclusive education was about all students, that inclusive education was dedicated to the project of identifying barriers to educational access, participation and success with a view to dismantling those impediments to the inclusive society. First I worked with the Staff College to introduce to Education Queensland different voices who would establish disability and education as a rights issue consistent with other equity concerns affirmed by the organization in the areas of gender, ethnicity and culture. The local Queensland chapter of the Australian Association of Special Education, an organizing forum for many of the senior 'special needs' administrators, was still inviting traditional special education luminaries to speak to teachers about inclusion. It was in this context that I introduced researchers and advocates such as Tom Shakespeare, Julie Allan, Keith Ballard, Mark Vaughan and Mel Ainscow.

The Staff College also dedicated a great deal of energy to the identification of exemplary initiatives in the field that promoted inclusive educational thinking and practice. Conferences were convened where schools applied to present their work and were awarded development grants. Added to this was the work done with local schools to introduce the Index for Inclusion (Booth, 2000; Carrington, 2004). This included some level of work with the universities to look at continuing professional development.

The footnote for this work is extremely disappointing. Sadly, Education Queensland has scaled back this operation, and while its rhetorical commitment to inclusion is high, its practices remain suspect. I await the impact of the recently released Ateleir Report in Tasmania, Essential Learnings for All. Report of the Review of Services for Students with Special or Additional Educational Needs (Tasmania, 2004). It is reassuring to note that recommendation 16, the last of the report, urges the Department 'to liaise with the University of Tasmania to ensure that teacher education programmes address policy and practice in relation to the inclusion of students with special and or additional educational needs'. To that end an Institute for Inclusive Practice is to be established at the University of Tasmania.

The Politics of Silence

There is an intensification of pressure on education workers globally to conform to the requirements of new educational managerialism exerted through centralized fast curriculum and pedagogy development and production, high stakes testing and teacher inspection (Apple, 2001; Hargreaves, 2003; Slee, 2003). The impacts of these technologies of control upon minority students including disabled students, is well documented (Gewirtz, 1995; Slee, 1998). The requirement for alternative voices based upon more sophisticated research-based evidence, and here I infer a range of research methodologies that need to be employed, cannot be overstated. Education has always been intensely political and continues to be so. Coalitions for reform should 'shuffle forward'. Here I am mindful of the poignant line in the Roger McGough poem, The Lesson (The Case for Capital Punishment in Schools), where a teacher brutally establishes order.

> And silence shuffled forward with its hands up in the air. (McGough, 1989)

The silencing of the dissenting voice/s, or for that matter a significant counterpoint to dominant discourses, is achieved in a number of ways. First is the implied or actual negative impact upon one's tenure in an organization or opportunities for advancement. One sees people dig in quietly and become peripheral players in the bureaucracy, or alternatively they second guess the Minister or CEO's disposition and adjust, some do this and then attempt to 'manage upwards', still others become the sidelined critical voice and are cast into bit-parts in the theatre of bureaucracy. The technologies for achieving this are layered and complex. Budget is often used as an instrument of control. Positional power may be used, but power does not always flow consistent with the organizational charts.

Silence is also generated through enlistment. The establishment of a Ministerial advisory body may tactically bring people to the table and thereby take away the more effective forums from participating groups. I believe that notwithstanding altogether different intentions this happened in Queensland. Once again parents and disabled people found themselves to be the minority voice at the table of professional interest. The power of the traditional special educational lobby is pervasive. This is because the most powerful ally is the regular classroom teacher who continues to believe that disability is a threat to rather than a resource for education.

CONCLUSION – THE POLITICS OF THE PERSONAL

The editors have asked that contributors record a sense of how what they describe has affected them personally. This is a very difficult request. It is not that there have been no personal impact and effect. The opposite is the case. It is more a case of how one deals with and responds to the personal impact that is difficult.

An invitation to occupy the second most senior position of the Queensland education bureaucracy in the time of a reforming Labor government offered great promise for the project of inclusive education. I soon learned that reform has its limits and that inclusive education was not a shared aspiration. The Queensland Teachers' Union is given to particularly conservative stances on education reform. Arguments are quickly distilled to resources conundrums to ensure that members' conditions are not under attack. Such a response conjoins with the interest of the segregated sector. Disability and education remains a technical set of problems separable from questions of rights and discrimination within this perspective.

At parent meetings I would receive an avalanche of the most distressing scenarios where children were held hostage in bureaucratic stand-offs. The sense of the size of the task was overwhelming. Among the team with whom I worked I believe there was a will to strike out differently and create the conditions for more enabling schooling. The irreconcilability of policy programmes became untenable. Under the rubric of Education and Training Reforms for the Future the department was establishing complex apparatus for more residualised 'pathways' while preserving the main game and diminishing the promise of New Basics. Inclusive Education rang hollow as numerical thinking occluded conceptual realignment. Early feelings of progress were replaced by a feeling of co-option in a deeply conservative educational agenda with respect to disablement and schooling. The rhetoric of inclusion served to mask this politics. The personal effect was indeed profound and I feel far more effective in pursuing change through reconstructing the Academy.

A major aspect of my work in the education bureaucracy became that of assemblage. Trying to make the elements of the reform jigsaw fit together was the assigned task. Opening the jigsaw puzzle box revealed that they had been incorrectly assigned to their boxes in the policy factory. There were pieces that fitted some puzzles that served traditional exclusionary educational practices in the box. To describe what is going on as inclusive education, though an advance in some respects remains for many families and their children, as they say in the classics, 'a fit-up!'

REFERENCES

Allan, 2006 The repetition of exclusion, International Journal of Inclusive Education 10, 2/3, 121–133.

Apple, M. 2001 *Educating the 'Right' Way: Markets, Standards, God and Inequality*, New York: Routledge Falmer.

Armstrong, D. 1995 'Power and partnership in education'. *Parents, Children and Special Educational Needs*, London: Routledge.

Ball, S. J. 1994 *Education Reform. A Critical and Post-Structural Approach*, Buckingham: Open University Press.

———. 1998 'Educational studies, policy entrepreneurship and social theory' in R. Slee, G. Weiner, S. Tomlinson (eds) *School Effectiveness for Whom?*, London: Falmer Press.

———. 2003 *Class Strategies and the Education Market. The Middle Classes and Social Advantage*, London: Routledge.

Barton, L. 2003 *Inclusive Education and Teacher Education. A Basis for Hope or a Discourse of Delusion*. Professorial Lecture, Institute of Education, London.

Barton, L. (ed.) 1987 *The Politics of Special Educational Needs*, Lewes: Falmer Press.

———. 2004 'The politics of special education: a necessary or irrelevant approach?' in L. Ware (eds) *Ideology and the Politics of (In)Exclusion*, New York: Peter Lang.

Booth, T. 1978 'From normal baby to handicapped child', *Sociology* 12, 2.

———. 1995 'Mapping inclusion and exclusion: concepts for all?' in C. Clark, A. Dyson, and A. Millward, (ed.) *Towards Inclusive Schools?*, London: David Fulton Publishers.

Booth, T., Ainscow, M., Black-Hawkins, K., Vaughan, M. and Shaw, L. 2000 *Index for Inclusion*, Bristol: Centre for Studies on Inclusive Education.

Campling, J. 1981 *Images of Ourselves: Women with Disabilities Talking*, London: Routledge.

Carrington, S. and Robinson, R. 2004 'A case study of inclusive school development: a journey of learning.' *International Journal of Inclusive Education* 8, 2, 141–53.

Castells, M. 1996 *The rise of the network society* (The Information Age) 1, Oxford: Blackwell.

Cook, S. and Slee, R. 1999 'Struggling with the fabric of disablement: picking up the threads of the law and education', In M. B. M. Jones, Lee Ann (ed.), *Disability, Diversability and Legal Change*, The Hague: Martinus Nijhoff Publishers.

Education Queensland 1999 *Queensland State Education – 2010*, Brisbane: Queensland Government Printer.

Ford, J., Mongon, D. and Whelan, J. 1982 *Special Education and Social Control. Invisible Disasters*, London: Routledge and Kegan Paul.

Forlin, C. 2004 'Promoting Inclusivity in Western Australian Schools', *International Journal of Inclusive Education* 8, 2, 185–202.

Galloway, D. 1985 *Schools, Pupils and Special Educational Needs*, London: Croom Helm.

Gewirtz, S., Ball, S. J. and Bowe, R. 1995 *Markets, Choice and Equity in Education*, Buckingham: Open University Press.

Gillborn, D. and Youdell, D. 2000 *Rationing Education: Policy, Practice, Reform and Equity*, Buckingham: Open University Press.

Gipps, C. 1994 *A Fair Test?*, London: Falmer.

Hargreaves, A. 2003 *Teaching in the Knowledge Society. Education in the Age of Insecurity*, New York: Teachers College Press.

Humphries, S. and Gordon, P. 1992 *Out of Sight. The Experience of Disability 1900–1950*, Plymouth: Northcote House.

Lankshear, C. and Knobel, M. 2003 *New Literacies. Changing Knowledge and Classroom Learning*, Buckingham: Open University Press.

Lauder, H. and Hughes, D. 1999 *Trading in Futures: Why Markets in Education Don't Work*, Philadelphia: Open University Press.

Levin, B. 1998 'An epidemic of education policy: (What) can we learn from each other?' *Comparative Education* 34, 2, 131–142.

Lingard, R. 1998 'The disadvantaged schools programme: caught between literacy and local management.' *International Journal of Inclusive Education* 2, 1, 87–107.

McArthur, J., Kelly, B., Higgins, Phillips, H., McDonald, T., Morton, M. and Jackman, S. 2004 *Building Capability in Education for Students, with Moderate and High Needs,* Ministry of Education: Wellington, New Zealand.

McGough, R. 1989 *Blazing Fruit,* London: Penguin Books.

McNeil, L. 2000 *Contradictions of School Reform: Educational Costs of Standardization,* New York: Routledge.

Meier, D., Sizer, T., Nathan, L. and Thernstrom, A. 2000 *Will Standards Save Public Education?,* Boston: Beacon Press.

Minow, M. 1990 *Making all the Difference. Inclusion, Exclusion and American Law,* Ithaca: Cornell University Press.

Moore, M. (ed.) 2000 *Insider Perspectives on Inclusion: Raising Voices, Raising Issues,* Sheffield: Philip Armstrong.

Moss, J. 2002 'Inclusive schooling: representation and textual practice', *International Journal of Inclusive Education* 6, 3, 231–249.

Oliver, M. 1996 *Understanding Disability: From Theory to Practice,* Basingstoke: Macmillan.

Pearl, A. and Knight, T. 1999 *The Democratic Classroom. Theory to Inform Practice,* Cresskill: Hampton Press.

Potts, M. and Fido, R. 1991 *A Fit Person to be Removed,* Plymouth: Northcote House.

Said, E. W. 2000 'Traveling theory reconsidered.' in E. W. Said (ed.), *Reflections on Exile and Other Literary and Cultural Essays,* London: Granta Books.

Slee, R. 1996 'Clauses of Conditionality,' in L. Barton (ed.), *Disability and Society: Emerging Issues and Insights,* London: Longman.

———. 1998 'High reliability organisations and liability students – the politics of recognition', in R. Slee, Weiner, Gaby and Tomlinson, Sally (ed.) *School Effectiveness for Whom?,* London: Falmer.

———. 2003 'Teacher education, government and inclusive schooling: the politics of the Faustian Waltz', in J. Allan (ed.), *Inclusion, Participation and Democracy: What is the Purpose?,* Dordrecht: Kluwer Academic Publishers.

———. 2004 'Education and the Politics of Recognition: Inclusive education, an Australian snapshot.' in D. Mitchell (ed.), *Contextualizing Inclusive Education: Evaluating Old and New International Paradigms,* London: Routledge/Falmer.

Slee, R., Weiner, G. and Tomlinson, S. 1998 *School Effectiveness for Whom?: Challenges to the School Effectiveness and School Improvement Movements,* London; Bristol, PA: Falmer Press.

Tasmanian Department of Education 2004 'Essential Learnings for All. Report of the review of services for students with special and or additional educational needs.' Hobart: Education Department of Tasmania.

Taylor, S. and Henry, M. 2003 'Social justice in a global context: Education Queensland's 2010 strategy.' *International Journal of Inclusive Education* 7, 4, 337–355.

Tomlinson, S. 1981 *Educational Sub-Normality: a Study in Decision-Making,* London: Routledge and Kegan Paul.

———. 1982 *A Sociology of Special Education,* London: Routledge and Kegan Paul.

———. 1993 'Conflicts and dilemmas for professionals in special education', in L. Apelt (ed.), *Social Justice, Equity and Dilemmas of Disability in Education International Working Conference,* Brisbane.

———. 1997 'Diversity, choice and ethnicity: the effects of educational markets on ethnic minorities.' *Oxford Review of Education* 23, 1, 63–76.

Touraine, A. 2000 *Can We Live Together? Equality and Difference,* Cambridge: Polity Press.

Tuettemann, E., Or, L. T., Slee, R. and Punch. K. 2000 'An evaluation of the inclusion programme', Perth: Education Department of Western Australia.

Walsh, B. 1993 'How disabling my handicap is depends on the attitudes and actions of others: a student's perspective.' in R. Slee (ed.) *Is There a Desk With My Name On it?,* London: Falmer Press.

Watson, D. 2003 *Death Sentence. The Decay of Public Language,* Sydney: Knopf.

Young, I. M. 2000 *Inclusion and Democracy,* Oxford: Oxford University Press.

INDEX